10 Secrets to Successful Home Buying and Selling

Using Your Housing Psychology to Make Smarter Decisions

10 Secrets to Successful Home Buying and Selling

Using Your Housing Psychology to Make Smarter Decisions

Lois A. Vitt, Ph.D.

Pearson Education, Inc.

Pearson Education LTD.
Pearson Education Australia PTY, Limited.
Pearson Education Singapore, Pte. Ltd.
Pearson Education North Asia, Ltd.
Pearson Education Canada, Ltd.
Pearson Educatión de Mexico, S.A. de C.V.
Pearson Education—Japan
Pearson Education Malaysia, Pte. Ltd.

Publisher: *Tim Moore*
Executive Editor: *Jim Boyd*
Editorial Assistant: *Richard Winkler*
Development Editor: *Elisa Adams*
Marketing Manager: *Martin Litkowski*
International Marketing Manager: *Tim Galligan*
Cover Designer: *Alan Clements*
Managing Editor: *Gina Kanouse*
Project Editor/Indexer: *Ginny Bess Munroe*
Copy Editor: *David Fender*
Compositor: *Angela Johnson*
Manufacturing Buyer: *Dan Uhrig*

*To Dellabeth, whose restless spirit contributed
to my wanderlust;
to John, Michael, Ginny, Lois, Elle, and Pati who've
gone the distance with me;
and to Noel, whose wit and wisdom helped me
(almost) settle down.*

CONTENTS

Secret 1:
Your housing choices are about all of your life.

Secret 2:
Your housing history influences your housing decisions today.

Secret 3:
You have a housing value system that drives your decisions.

Secret 4:
Your partner's housing value system is as important as yours.

Part 2 Finding Solutions That Work for You..................117

ACKNOWLEDGMENTS

To all those who shared housing experiences with me and with other interviewers, I am grateful. You have given meaning to the ideas presented here by having lived them.

I would like to express my deep gratitude to Jim Boyd at Prentice Hall, who more than anyone else made this book possible—special thanks for your patient encouragement over the bumps. Heartfelt thanks to my friend and colleague, Joyce Thomas, for helping me translate my message from the theoretical to the practical. I am grateful to Jamie Kent for administrative and other assistance and for keeping the office running while I was away. Many thanks to my peer reviewers and to my project editor, Ginny Bess Munroe, for your useful suggestions and comments.

Thank you Fiona Blee, Crystal Collins, Jean Landis, and Louisa Woodville for your timely assistance just when I needed it. Many thanks to Carol and Tom Anderson, Rita and Ron Boothby, Richard Drabik, Craig and Kitty MacBean, Karen McMahon, Karen Murrell, Susan Scolastico, and Jerry Travers for taking the time to read various parts of the text or otherwise give me feedback.

Thanks to Evelyn Reed and Boyd Pauley for your wonderful help on the home front, and to Linda Baker who helped me keep body and mind together during the months I spent in Wintergreen. I am grateful to family, friends, and associates for understanding when I turned down invitations I really wanted to accept. I appreciate the encouragement from family members who followed my progress with interest and enthusiasm. Finally, I am so grateful to Noel, my husband and partner, for your unwavering love and your steadfast confidence in this endeavor.

ABOUT THE AUTHOR

Lois A.Vitt, Ph.D. founded and directs the Institute for Socio-Financial Studies, an organization engaged in evaluation research in personal finance education. She teaches university courses in the social psychology of finance and the finances of aging, and she is Editor-in-Chief of the two-volume *Encyclopedia of Retirement and Finance.* She pioneered the development of financing instruments for home buying and has worked throughout her career to make homeownership more accessible. She is a consultant to organizations on consumer finance and financial literacy education.

Preface

Until recently, the longest time I lived in one place was five years, and my usual limit was two years. I have changed homes, transformed rooms to accommodate new uses, rented, bought, and sold homes, refinanced them, leveraged them, and invested in rental homes.

I've moved to save money, to seek or accept new employment, to find better schools, to move to a different location, or to collapse my commuting time. I moved to change environments—the suburbs, the city, the beach, the country—and for long periods, I shuttled between two homes at a time. My work required me to travel, and sometimes a city became a routine business destination. Whenever that happened, I thought about trading hotel life for local living, and once, I actually did it. Most of my moves, now that I look back on them, were wonderfully happy moves. A few were definitely losers.

Housing was also my business. As a mortgage banker, I financed thousands of houses, apartments, co-ops, and condominiums. As an investor, I rescued, renovated, restored, and remodeled houses. As the Director of Housing for an urban renewal agency, and other non-profit and for-profit organizations, I helped transform and uplift the lives of low-wage, inner-city, middle-income, Caribbean Island, and Native American populations by helping them become homeowners. For my doctoral dissertation, I researched the social and psychological ties we have to housing and I examined the differences homeownership makes to people who are able to achieve it. Not surprisingly, my research results empirically supported the prevailing wisdom surrounding homeownership as a personal and an American ideal.

Since completing my thesis, and increasingly during the past decade, financial research has more frequently crossed the line into the social and behavioral sciences. In turn, the social and behavioral sciences grapple with questions about personal financial literacy and financial management. At the heart of this emerging body of research is *the home*. Perhaps nowhere else can we learn so much about ourselves and one another as when we consider our values, feelings, attitudes, beliefs, and customs in the context of the financial realities, constraints, opportunities, and investment potential of our homes. *Nothing else motivates us to learn how to handle money better than the prospect of owning or investing in our homes.* Yet, partially due to the complexity of the times in which we live, and partially due to credit availability and increasingly creative advertising, we have fallen behind the "personal financial knowledge curve" we need to master. It doesn't have to be this way.

I've learned from my research, teaching, and the people I've helped to house—from college students to older retirees seeking assisted living arrangements—that our decisions about homes can be financially and personally enhancing or exactly the opposite, depending upon the mindset, willingness to learn, and emotional baggage we bring to the transactions. Housing emotions can derail us financially. They can be so powerful in fact that during seminars I offer on home and decision-making, I've seen grown men and women cry over home-connected memories. One man who was about 50 years old, a participant in a half-day workshop, suddenly began weeping uncontrollably and had to leave the room. He later told me he had not allowed himself to grieve over the loss of his wife almost two years earlier. The exercises in the workshop had loosened memories he suppressed "far too long," he said. The experience of home can be so intimate that I've witnessed participants heal childhood trauma by revisiting the homes of their past through exercises designed expressly for this purpose.

My hope is that *10 Secrets to Successful Home Buying and Selling* will simplify what can be a complicated, intimidating, and emotionally draining experience for many. By introducing you to your own "housing psychology," better negotiating and decision skills will be more accessible to you as a homebuyer, seller, renter, and housing investor. *10 Secrets to Successful Home Buying and Selling* is not just a how-to book, but an introduction to a whole new strategy that can transform the way you approach housing decisions—and maybe other financial decisions as well.

Lois A. Vitt
Middleburg, VA
www.RealityStudies.com

Part 1

YOUR HOUSING
PSYCHOLOGY

1

INTRODUCTION TO THE 10 SECRETS

It is our choices...that show what we really are, far more than our abilities.

—J.K. Rowling

A secret is something hidden or known only to insiders. A few behavioral scientists and market researchers might be acquainted with some of the ideas in this book, but these concepts have not been available to consumers prior to now. One of my professional priorities is to change that fact by equipping homeowners, renters, buyers, and sellers with "insider information" that can help them become more comfortable (and savvy) about whatever housing transaction they might contemplate.

Housing decisions are crucial. They can involve the most money you ever spend, the highest debt you ever incur, and the best (or worst) investment you ever make. A moving decision can result in either a frustrating or fulfilling experience that affects not just your life, but the lives of loved ones who move with you. Yet, as one real estate broker observed, buying and selling houses is one of the few businesses in which the principals on both sides are rank amateurs.[1] They get caught up in emotions that rarely benefit the housing negotiations and, on occasion, trap them into making poor housing decisions. Renters also make poor housing choices and some renters' decisions spoil their chances for future home ownership.

Whether you are a buyer, seller, renter, or one who is thinking about remodeling, refinancing, or investing in a second home, you can learn a new way to make housing decisions that go smoothly and enrich your personal life and your relationships while enhancing your enjoyment of the place you call "home." In addition, you can increase your net worth at the same time.

With a little curiosity, inner preparation, and practical guidance about decision making, you can approach your next real estate transaction with new confidence. The discomfort you might have about finances, the markets, or the uncertainty of making the right choice diminishes dramatically when you learn and keep in mind the following 10 secrets of successful home buying and selling:

- Secret 1: Your housing choices are not only about finances. In fact, they are not just about housing. They are about every aspect of your life.

- Secret 2: You have a housing history that influences your housing decisions today and it is key to understanding your housing emotions.

- Secret 3: You have a Housing Value System that consists of your housing history and housing profile. Your Housing Value System drives your housing decisions.

- Secret 4: Your partner (child, mother, or father) has a Housing Value System too, and it is as important as yours when it comes to making housing decisions.

- Secret 5: You can turn your Housing Value System into a decision tool that can help you make your best housing decisions.

- Secret 6: Self-knowledge is personal power in all housing-related transactions. Housing knowledge is financial power that can save you time, money, and grief.

- Secret 7: There is a U.S. Housing System that you must learn to navigate. It includes the agents, organizations, agencies, and regulators with whom you deal with in any housing transaction you undertake.

- Secret 8: Your fears can move with you. To move on, you must pack up your courage and make sound housing choices, even if you do not feel courageous.

- Secret 9: Your mortgage can be the most important financial tool in your investment toolbox. It can be your ticket to future financial security.

- Secret 10: Your Housing Value System lives as long as you do. When it is time to downsize, find a home in retirement, or help to choose housing for an older adult, these secrets will be as valid then as they are today.

The Power of Knowing Your Housing Psychology

As you explore and discover the power of the 10 Housing Secrets, which I discuss in detail throughout the book, you will develop your own personal housing psychology. These secrets allow you to sort through and tame your emotions, understand and deal with the stresses of others, and discuss your feelings openly with less discomfort. Most importantly, these secrets can help you become an all-around better financial decision maker in the process.

My goal is to help skeptics and believers alike learn to access and harness the power of their housing psychology in pending and future housing searches, negotiations, decisions, and transactions.

I specifically want to help you:

- Make you aware of your housing emotions, so that you can interpret them and then use your new understanding to make better housing plans and decisions.

- Enhance your understanding of your partner's and other family members' housing emotions, so that you can minimize conflict during the stages involved in changing where and how you live.

- Learn that the best housing decisions incorporate desire, knowledge, and the ability to successfully navigate your emotions.

- Realize that wise housing choices have the potential to anchor your entire future financial security.

What Is Housing Psychology?

I define housing psychology as "a field of study that synthesizes human-place interactions with finance." It incorporates social psychology, which looks at our behavioral interchanges with others. It borrows from environmental psychology, which examines the roles of "place" in our lives and tries to understand our attachments to home.[2] Almost all of our housing transactions have financial and economic effects, so the dynamics of housing psychology fall within the new and growing field of "behavioral finance."[3]

So how can knowing your housing psychology help you make good housing decisions today and in the future?

Any housing decision—buying, renting, selling, remodeling, or investing in a second home—combines significant financial and personal components and consequences. On average, the cost of renting or carrying mortgage payments sets most of us back each month from about 25 percent to as much as 50 percent of our income. Although finances are definitely a major factor, housing choices are not only about finances. In fact, they are not even just about housing. They involve our ideas, desires, longings, identities, beliefs, attitudes and all the other aspects of our unique personalities, as well as our relationships.

There are two parts to understanding your housing psychology: uncovering your housing history and becoming better acquainted with your housing desires and values. With the combination of this self-knowledge, you can create a personal decision context—call it your Housing Value System—for grappling with even your most difficult housing decisions. It is possible to compare notes and resolve disputes with a partner and/or other family members, so you can make shared housing choices without the emotional flare ups that can make moving so unpleasant.

Understanding your own inner signals and housing preferences, and those of your partner or family members, can help you make decisions you can trust and investment choices you can rely on better. Understanding your housing emotions also positively spills over into other important life areas because you learn how your past history influences your current decisions, especially financial decisions. These are some of the benefits you discover from the *10 Secrets to Successful Home Buying and Selling*.

Learning from the Success and Mistakes of Others

Unlike learning from our own experiences, people are better at learning from the successes and mistakes of others. This book is based on extensive empirical research[4] and on hundreds of case histories from interviews, consulting, seminars, and workshops.[5] The chapters in this book are filled with the housing experiences of real people.

You will quickly learn the winning factors that you can apply to your own circumstances. The housing experiences and problems from actual case histories also illustrate how far-reaching housing decision problems are. Whether or not you are in the same situation as the people whose stories you read in this book, you can become better acquainted with yourself and recognize others you know as well.

You will feel more confident about any type of housing decision you face, even if you must make that decision only once or twice in your lifetime. You will be able to extend the money you have to spend on a house, help an older relative who must solve a housing dilemma, maximize your desirability to a mortgage lender, help a young adult move out of the nest, and deal with every aspect of a housing transaction with less stress and much more self-assurance.

Get the Most from the 10 Secrets to Successful Home Buying and Selling

Use this book in the way that works best for you: either as uninterrupted reading or as a guide for making a pending housing decision.

Part 1, "Your Housing Psychology," acquaints you with your unique housing psychology and the underlying reasons for the sometimes euphoric and sometimes painful housing emotions most of us have experienced in our lives. In my seminars on home and decision-making, I've seen people cry[6] and watched others break through decision paralysis by "revisiting" homes of their past. And anyone who has ever "fallen in love" with a home knows the emotion that can accompany—and sometimes sabotage—their housing negotiations.

Chapters 2–8 show you just how the non-financial areas of your life impact your finances to your benefit or your detriment, depending upon your Housing Value System and your approach to housing decision-making. Each reader must learn for himself or herself the underlying experiences and values that make up his or her own Housing Value System before moving on to compare notes with a loved one or another family member.

Chapter 9, "When Housing Values Differ," is especially helpful to couples and family members who make joint housing decisions. You and your partner should be able to compare and discuss your housing personalities and past experiences when informed by insight and a shared sense of purpose. No longer must you deal silently (or otherwise uncomfortably) with your housing differences. Instead, you can use the framework outlined in chapters 4–8 to better understand and more openly deal with individual issues that might remain unresolved.

Note: Throughout the book, I use "partner" to refer to spouses, significant others, and other housemates because a shared living arrangement in one way or another makes you partners. People who have shared the responsibilities of a home know the pit-of-the-stomach feeling that can accompany an unresolved housing problem with a live-in partner.

Part 2, "Finding Solutions That Work for You," provides a variety of ideas and suggestions for how to use your Housing Value System to make housing choices and decisions. If you skip to your pending housing problem in Part 2, here is a decision tip at the outset: Return to the housing history and housing profile exercises in Chapters 3, "Your Housing History," and 4, "Creating Your Housing Profile," and read through the analyses in Chapters 5–8. The results of these exercises and elaborations form the core of a powerful system that can set you straight on the path to housing and financial security. You will clearly see how your unique housing history and housing profile are programmed right into your present lifestyle, relationships, and housing decisions.

Regardless of how you use this book, if you apply its principles, you will never have to look at housing decisions with fear or anxiety again. Instead, you can take great pleasure in both your future decisions and your future moves. Choosing the right home at the right time can be a mystical experience. A bond can begin to form with the place you call "home," whether you are renting or buying. When you buy your own home or trade up (or down) to that next home of your dreams, you will experience a feeling of well-being that extends far beyond the home itself.[7]

End Notes

1   A New York City real estate broker confided this to Marjorie Garber who recounts the conversation in her book, *Sex and Real Estate*, (Anchor Books, New York: 2000). The broker also refers to clients who experience emotional rawness during real estate transactions, especially when selling a home is exacerbated by another personal crisis, such as a divorce. The broker reveals that he often acts as a counselor as well as a salesman to stressed clients. I have listened to many other brokers with similar stories about their clients.

2   Issues related to housing, the environment, privacy, and place are among major topics of interest to environmental psychologists. (See the "Current Trends in Environmental Psychology" article, by Gary W. Evans, which you can find at http://www.ucm.es/info/Psyap/iaap/evans.htm.) Collaborative projects that cut across cultures study crowding and noise, restorative environments, alternative work and living environments, transportation impacts, women and housing, and childcare facilities.

Conceptual topics of interest in housing psychology include the concepts of place and home. How do places acquire meaning to people, how are they related to their decisions, preferences, and even to emotional reactions and well being? What does the concept of place (or home) mean across generations or across cultures?

3   Behavioral economics is the combination of psychology and economics that investigates what happens in markets in which some of the agents display human limitations and complications. See Sendhil Mul-lainathan's and Richard Thaler's, "Behavioral Economics," which is a working paper (September, 2000) and is located at http://papers.ssrn.com/paper.taf?abstract_id=245828. Because saving to buy a home, obtaining a mortgage to finance a home, and many other activities related to socio-financial interactions about one's home require both complex calculations and social psychological elements, behavioral factors are essential elements of any complete descriptive economic theory.

4   My doctoral dissertation research, "Homeownership, Well-Being, Class, and Politics: Perceptions of American Homeowners and Renters," was completed and published by The Institute for Socio Financial Studies (Middleburg, VA) in 1993. In this paper, I examine the social psychological dimensions of housing and the "get ahead" theories inherent in the American Dream. GSS survey data for the years 1985 through 1991 are used to detect the differences in the perceptions of homeowners and renters using a quality of life (QOL) approach that measures subjective well-being. A subjective social class measure tests for feelings of being "middle class" and various measures are used to determine whether homeowners are more "conservative" than renters. The conceptualization of new housing theory emerges from the research and is presented to provide a reframed and expanded way of looking at the social psychology of housing and homeownership.

5   The case studies in this book are based on interviews I conducted on my analyses of qualitative data collected by other researchers and on the experiences of clients or workshop participants.

6   One man who is about 50 years old and who participated in a half-day workshop suddenly began to weep uncontrollably and had to leave the room. Later, he told me he had not allowed himself to grieve over the loss of his wife who passed away two years earlier. The exercises in the workshop loosened memories he had suppressed "far too long," he said.

7   The conventional wisdom about homeownership and increased well-being is supported by research results reported in "Homeownership, Well-Being, Class, and Politics." Homeowners experience significantly higher feelings of family satisfaction than

renters; they are more satisfied with leisure time activities; and they are more satisfied than renters with their financial condition. Homeowners, in general, feel significantly happier than renters. The belief that homeownership enhances feelings of social status is also supported. Homeowners see themselves as "middle class" people more often than renters do, signifying their feelings of enhanced social status.

Chapter 2
Secret 1

Your housing choices are about all of your life.

2

YOUR HOME AND
YOUR LIFE

Home is the centre and circumference, the start and the finish,
of most of our lives...we cling to it with the tenacity of every...
instinct of our animal natures.

—Charlotte Perkins Gilman

Every second, around the clock, someone makes a housing decision—to move, remain a renter, become a homeowner, trade up, buy a second home, or buy a home for investment. Each of these is a real estate transaction; however, each can also be an affair of the heart, a solution to a difficult life event, a tough financial call, or a personal disaster.

When thinking about changing homes, you must consider many factors before making your decision: the personal side, the home itself and its surroundings, people who are moving with you, and, of course, all the financial details involved. Making a good move requires that you weigh the pros and cons and successfully consider all sides. To get it right, you also need to steer clear of emotional pitfalls, especially while dealing honestly with your finances. Part One, "Your Housing Psychology," examines how to manage your inner motivations and personal relationships—as well as your housing and financial goals—to make a smooth transition to the home you really want. The clues are in your feelings.

You might already be familiar with some of the roller-coaster feelings that accompany housing transactions. Feeling anxious while waiting to learn whether an offer to buy a home has been accepted is more or less a normal state. Having mixed emotions about leaving a home recently sold can be expected.

However, what about your decision paralysis when trying to choose between two homes you love? What's going on when you and your partner fight over whether to remodel or move? Why are you irritable when you are "just out looking to see what homes might be available?" What causes your panic attack while waiting for loan approval? These are all times to navigate your housing decisions in a calm and deliberate manner. Even so, as most of us know all too well, the process of making housing decisions can be fraught with emotional peril.

Buying a home can feel like falling in love—the excitement, the fantasies, driving by to glimpse the object of your affection, and keeping your cell phone charged up and ready.[1] You can expect to fidget and daydream until at long last the phone rings. Your offer to buy has been accepted. Flushed with excitement, you punch in the numbers of relatives and best friends to share the good news. As with all affairs of the heart, however, things can go wrong. Some homes may break our hearts, whether we are trying to buy them or have lived in them for years.

A bid to buy the home of our dreams can be flatly rejected. Poor spending habits can eat into our equity, meaning that when we encounter that inevitable bump in the road, or when the market turns, we are stuck with our excesses, our excuses, and our housing losses. A furious act of nature can force us to leave a destroyed home.[2] The family home might have to be sold as a consequence of divorce, illness, or death. In all likelihood, most of us at some point will have to wrestle with anxiety and grief over the loss of a loved one and a home.

Home Sweet Home for Two

Few things test a relationship more dramatically than a search for your dream home. You get a sinking feeling in the pit of your stomach when your partner rejects a home you believe suits you perfectly. If the attraction is shared, two hearts beat as one. If the attraction is not mutual, a couple can experience a range of painful emotions and conflict with the home as the "other person" in a relationship-threatening love triangle. Remodeling or building a home from scratch can be even worse.

I recently met a woman who was waiting tables who told me her day job was "building her own house." She and her husband broke ground for the project against strong advice from friends, and they indeed divorced before the house was finished. "We were warned not to build a home together," she said, "but we didn't listen, and the house turned out to be our undoing." It is not unusual for couples searching for or making plans to build a home to clash over issues that might have been laying dormant until the housing pressures erupted and damaged the relationship itself. Tugs of war over homes are familiar scenes to realtors, architects, and homebuilders. Unfortunately, they are also well known to therapists, marriage counselors, and divorce lawyers.

The Decision to Change Homes

When considering changing homes, you face some big decisions. Even before you decide to buy or rent, you first must decide to move. Is this a good time to move? How much can I afford? Where should we move? Do we trade up, remodel, or build? Answers to these and many other housing-related questions can be crucial to both your financial and emotional well-being. In fact, a decision to leave one home for another can be a heart wrencher. It is a one-two punch that can leave you and those who move with you feeling exhilarated or exhausted, depending upon the emotional and financial savvy you bring to this big-ticket decision.

Although housing decisions are an essential part of life, many of us are not very good at making consistently good life decisions. We decide according to how we think or feel at the moment. Or we put off making tough decisions while we wait for heaven knows what; then, at almost the last minute, we rush to assess our alternatives and then hope we have made the right choice. We add up all the reasons we can muster to convince ourselves that our last-minute decision was sound so that we can live with it in peace. But how often do we fool ourselves?

An unexamined-decision approach can trap you into making poor housing choices in a number of ways, including the following:

- Acting in haste without thinking through the consequences that affect not just you, but anyone moving with you

- Saying too much and spoiling a negotiation

- Failing to speak up when a critical issue is on the table and regretting it later

- Erupting in ways that mystify your agent, your partner, other family members, and even yourself

- "Falling in love" with a home and overlooking or dismissing the need for contract safeguards

Each of these behaviors can have negative and potentially long-lasting personal and financial consequences. You can rationalize them away or choose instead to become aware of any patterns of behaviors that can spoil the pleasures of your home-related negotiations. You can choose to become a savvy housing decision maker.

Your Haven or Your Trap

Consider this. Your relationship to your home, even if you insist you feel nothing, is so personal and close that no other nonhuman relationship is quite like it. It is the setting for the most intimate aspects of your development and personal relations. Your home is unique—even your idea of home belongs only to you. Your home might look like your neighbor's home; it might even be furnished in a similar way, but it is still not the same. Virtually everyone enjoys a personal relationship with his or her home without quite knowing what makes that relationship special. Like a close family member, sometimes home can push your buttons.

You can love a home or hate it, ignore it or obsess over it, lavish money on it, exploit it, or deprive it of basic care and maintenance. Housing-related behaviors can sabotage your plans and be your financial undoing. Home can exert so much power over you that you refuse to leave it, even for your own good. You can allow it to derail your best intentions, interfere with a career promotion, conflict with ambitions, or trap you in agonies of indecision. Or you can move from home to home at the drop of a hat, always searching for greener pastures, never wanting to put down roots or feel tied down.

Home is something we "provide" for ourselves, our partners, and our families. Home symbolizes our capacity to control a physical setting and to enjoy the leisure and other activities we choose. We seek security at home. It is a place to recharge our batteries to face the next day. Home is the touchstone for our sense of independence. It counters workplace frustrations and provides a sanctuary from many of life's pressures and complexities.[3] But home is not always a sanctuary. On the dark side, memories of home may be about a place where ghostly figures lurk long after the past is over—a place where stillness covers shame and guilt, and safety is elusive. When the door closes on decency and civility, we can feel trapped, desperate for a breath of air, condemned to remembered cruelty. No matter how brutal our recollections, however, we can still dream our dreams and move forward with courage to make them come true. Perhaps the most persistent dream of all is having a peaceful home of our own.

After her divorce, Carolyn returned to school to earn the Foreign Service degree she had always wanted. She knew that a career in her field would eventually mean a move to a different location; for the time being, however, she decided to stay in her own community. She obtained a generous home-equity loan and commuted more than a 100 miles a day to attend classes at the university. Upon graduation, Carolyn was offered her dream job, but to accept the position, she would have to move. She also needed time to fix up and dispose of her home, so she turned it down.

Carolyn attended to her neglected personal affairs and fixed up her home, but she couldn't decide whether to rent or sell it. Agent after agent advised her, and Carolyn sought advice from everyone else she knew. After a while, her equity gone and her finances depleted, Carolyn took a temporary job close to home. Months stretched into years. Her career prospects dried up as Carolyn failed to pursue them. She continues to work at temporary jobs and vacillates over whether to sell her house. For lack of a decision to make any move at all, her career prospects—at least those in her chosen field—seem remote indeed.

Carolyn's early home was not a safe place, and she experienced similar cruelty during her marriage. In the divorce, she won full ownership of her house, and for the first time in her life, her living space came under her own control. She enjoyed her new feelings of safety, peacefulness, and autonomy and soon made her house and gardens a community showplace. But Carolyn became so attached to the house that even when the career of a lifetime was offered to her, she didn't leave home to take it. What Carolyn has yet to learn is that with courage and careful planning, she can bring the same creativity, peace, and love of her particular "place in the world" to entirely new surroundings. In Carolyn's case, she is also missing the boat financially.

Bottom-Line Lessons

Carolyn, age 52, increased her living costs when she borrowed $76,000 from her home to finance her education. She is not earning what she planned from a career in her field and is barely making ends meet. She has no savings, health insurance, or retirement benefits.

- Procrastination sabotages good planning. You may miss the market entirely, whether it involves your home or your career.
- If you're emotionally stuck, get practical. Let your finances be your guide.

The most important lesson to take from Carolyn's home-related decision paralysis is that she needs to decide something because she cannot afford to live in her house without the means to carry it.

A serious or prolonged illness could be Carolyn's financial undoing. Although she does not have to build a Foreign Service career, sell or rent her home, or even move to a different location, her continued failure to address her stagnating home situation risks both her home and future financial security. If she wants to make a conscious decision to remain where she is, she must explore other options including the following:

- Sharing her home with one or more paying housemates to offset her increased living costs

- Finding full-time employment and commuting whatever distance she must

- Telecommuting or starting a home-based business

Housing Is About Everything in Your Life

As Carolyn's story illustrates, a housing decision is about everything in your life: the physical aspects of where and how you live; how and where you earn your living; your physical, emotional, and financial well-being; your safety and security; your intimate and social relationships; your sense of community; your greatest pleasures; and your deepest pain. Although Carolyn's story and those that follow in this chapter might seem very different, they have one noteworthy similarity. All illustrate choices that carry lifestyle, emotional, and financial price tags—as nearly all housing decisions do.

Even financially accomplished people make disastrous housing decisions that can cost many thousands of dollars. People can squander their financial and emotional well-being by bullying a partner or other family member into a housing choice the other person does not want to make, by settling for a location or neighborhood that is too far away from their workplace, by hiring the wrong contractor to build an addition, by listing a house for sale without knowing where they are going, and by making just about every other self-defeating choice you can imagine.

The savviest real estate professional usually lacks the time or skill to help you through your sometimes paralyzing, sometimes precipitous housing decisions. Real estate agents tally up numbers, show you alternatives, and focus on amenities and locations—that is their job. They see houses as the buildings, settings, and locations that can bring you and your loved ones joy and delight when they get it right. But they're not mind readers. They do not see your deepest dreams, fantasies, ambitions, and fears, which might be triggered by your home search. These are for you to detect, understand, and sort through during your housing search and decision making. Your life quality and relationships with your loved ones can depend upon it.

Then there are the times when we ask too much of our housing. We are vulnerable and can fall prey to unscrupulous agents or homebuilders who are ready to take full advantage of our naiveté and unmet needs. I recently read a *New York Times* article that recounted the stories of middle-income renters who left New York City, lured by commercials offering homeownership, fresh air, good schools, and gated communities in the Pocono Mountains of Pennsylvania.[4] The ads hit a responsive note for thousands of teachers and bus drivers, paralegals, and postal workers desperate to have a home and a green yard to call their own.

Later, homebuyers complained that builders pressured them to "buy now and buy fast" or the best deals would be gone. They were also helped with good financing, sometimes given free decks and fireplaces, and even offered counseling and savings plans to clear bad credit and build a down payment.

No matter how fair the deals—and some were clearly not—many could ill afford the cost of commuting, food, taxes, and other expenses. "It seemed like $10 one way or another would make it or break it for them," said one local closing official. Some buyers were in over their heads, and soon enough, their new homes proved far beyond their means and the five-hour daily round-trip commute to New York City jobs. Although others struggled to hang on, all too often the stress of unexpectedly high housing and commuting costs resulted in dashed financial hopes and broken marriages. The painful experiences recounted in this article are about how easily we can fall prey to promises too good to be true. More than one New York City buyer had second thoughts but chose to ignore them. And buying into a deal too good to be true is not the only way we fall victim to homes that seduce us when we are vulnerable.

Be especially wary if you find yourself daydreaming about a move to a five-bedroom house after all the kids have left home for good. Be cautious if you are feeling down and want to escape by moving to a town across the country where "you have always wanted to live." Ask yourself what is going on if you suddenly long for an extra room when you already live in a spacious home. Your restlessness, wanderlust, or other feelings of discomfort with where you live might have more to do with emotional issues than with your actual housing needs. Juliet's story is a case in point.

Juliet sounded so excited on the phone that day. The busiest person I have ever known, Juliet called to describe the mountain cabin she found while visiting friends. "It's a real haven," she told me, "I've found the perfect place to wind down from all the stress in my life." I knew about Juliet's work schedule, not to mention her family and graduate school obligations. How would she find time to make the four-hour drive to the cabin? She could surely use a break now and then, but I doubted she would take one. However, the price was right, and Juliet's husband Paul had okayed the deal by phone from someplace in the Middle East.

Tapped by the United Nations for a special assignment, Paul left for the Middle East soon after retiring from his career in the military. That stymied the settling down Juliet wanted after years of posts around the world, but at least she had been with Paul during most of his recent tours of duty. "Juliet," I asked, "Have you taken time to feel sad about your separation from Paul?" In mid-sentence, she stopped talking. Silence, awful heartrending silence, and then came the tears. Within a day or so, I learned that Juliet had decided not to buy the cabin after all. Her desire for a place to get away to disappeared after she dealt with the real problem in her life—her separation from Paul.

Although most of us happily accept a certain amount of nurturing from the homes we cherish, in a time of crisis, there is no substitute for the human nurturing we must give to another or to ourselves. A restful haven or vacation home is an attractive option when we take the time to plan what our aims and ambitions are for such a venture. However, our pursuits to satisfy other inner needs, as Juliet's case clearly shows, can translate into misguided housing decisions.

Bottom-Line Lessons

Juliet saved nearly $28,000 by withdrawing from the pending negotiation. If she had bought the cabin, she calculates that she might have used it two or three times during that year before selling it. Because it appreciated a little over those 12 months, her net loss after costs would have been close to $20,000.

- If you are motivated out of the blue to invest in a "haven," ask yourself what you might be fleeing in other life areas before you sign on the dotted line.

- Estimate carefully the amount of time as well as money you want to invest in a second home before you commit to buy it.

When we are living through uncertainty or periods of disruption, we may seek homes we believe will redefine us, protect us from unwanted intrusions, provide a haven from painful stresses, or otherwise help us to satisfy unrelated emotional needs.

Transcending Your Housing Emotions

Some of the most serious moving mistakes are preventable when people understand the powerful role their vulnerabilities play in housing decisions. A young man I know asked my advice about listing his home for sale. He said he was thinking of relocating, but I suggested his timing was poor and that he could clear more on the sale if he waited. I felt certain that his home would increase substantially in value in a year or two because of its location in a rapidly expanding suburban corridor. But Scott had an overriding agenda that prevented him from considering my advice.

It turned out that Scott was romantically involved with Allyson, a coworker who was in a rocky marriage and who promised they would be together "someday." Scott was stressed by the uncertainty of the relationship and he was also deeply in debt. He decided to list his townhouse for sale and pay off his debts. He also believed that by moving to a different city, Allyson would break free from her troubled marriage and follow him.

Scott's home sold quickly at the listed price. He found a new job, but there would be no cash left over from the sale to buy a new home. Worse, available rental homes in his destination city cost much more than his former house payments. Scott had few choices left except to move to a less expensive, less desirable home. He had to make an entirely new life start, and to his dismay and eventual regret, he ended up doing this alone.

Bottom-Line Lessons

The home Scott sold appreciated more than $80,000 in the following two years. Had he tightened his belt and taken out a home-equity loan, he could have climbed out of debt, kept his home, and avoided the unfortunate upheaval caused by his ill-conceived decision to move.

- Never, ever make a housing decision based solely on emotions.
- Before you list your present home for sale, carefully research your housing options in the area where you plan to move.

Scott chose moving to a different location as a way to solve both his emotional and financial problems, but neither problem was solved for very long. He tried to repeat the "fixes" he had learned from his parents who moved frequently during his childhood. In every move, they cashed in or lost some or all of their equity, as Scott did, and they wound up significantly poorer as a result.

Although Scott's housing behavior may have been extreme, few of us have the tools to make consistently good life decisions based on solid principles and values rather than on half-baked emotions or circumstances. Obviously our housing decisions would be a lot easier if we acted according to our deepest values instead of reacting to the emotions or circumstances of the moment. What we all need is a little space and time to help us wise up—a shortcut to remind us how to pro-act in our best interests, not react based on feelings or events that can spin us out of control.

When Your Housing Past Is Prologue

I have been struck by the fact that, when explaining their feelings about their current homes, homeowners and renters alike often mention where and how they lived as children. There is wisdom in their spontaneous recollections. Just by knowing yourself better—especially your childhood experiences of home—it is possible to develop the capacity to make easier, quicker, and more effective housing decisions. Your personal and family situation, your present home, your finances, and your decision to move to your next home are influenced by what I call your "housing history."

Your housing history involves how you were brought up, the home life you experienced, and your unique concept of "home" in your conscious and unconscious memories. Your housing past can flare up when least expected in present home-related decisions and transactions, which is why it is important to recognize and let go childhood impressions that no longer serve you. Your housing history might be a set of positive experiences or a hodgepodge of mistaken notions grounded in childhood perceptions. Most likely it is a combination of these, and our task together will be to learn what works best for you in the present, so you can make successful housing decisions based on knowing how you are affected by your housing history.

Few, if any of us, are able to avoid emotional barriers as we contemplate changing homes. For us to change this tendency, however, and move more easily to where we want to go, we have to know first where we are coming from. Using your housing history to help you make good decisions from here on out is the focus of the next chapter.

The American Dream of having one's own home endures because the concept of home is rooted in your emotions as well as in your head. It reflects who you are, who you want to be, and where you want to go. Home has always been a deeply personal resource as well as an actual place or location—even when you are not really sure about your direction in life. That is why your ability to make good housing decisions is so important. What's more, your home can be your ticket to financial security when you manage your housing life as though your financial life depends upon it. For most of us, as discussed in later chapters, it does.

Points to Ponder

- **A housing decision is about everything in your life**. Reflect for a minute on your present home and how it connects you to your lifestyle; your family and friends; your finances; your work life and commuting time and distance; your community interests; your ambitions, hobbies, achievements; and any other life dynamic that you can think of.

- **Remember a time when you bought or sold a home**. What were the factors that led to your decision? How did you handle the details of your move? Was it an emotionally loaded experience as well as a real estate transaction?

- **Housing decisions often follow other upsets in life**. Recall whether an upsetting time in your life was accompanied or followed by a decision to move. As you look back, could you have made a better housing choice under the circumstances?

- **How would you have handled Carolyn's problem**? **Or Juliet's**? **Or Scott's**? What would you have done differently? What would you have advised these people if any of them had been a friend or family member?

End Notes

1 Garber, Marjorie. *Sex and Real Estate.* New York: Random House, Inc., 2000.

2 According to the Federal Emergency Management Agency (FEMA), there were 56 major (natural) disaster declarations in 2003. In the first five months of 2004, a total of 14 major disaster declarations were made by the governors of Iowa, Nebraska, Arkansas, North Dakota, New Mexico, Illinois, Massachusetts, Federated States of

Micronesia, Oregon, South Carolina, Maine, Ohio, American Samoa, and California. Disaster types included tornados, severe storms, flooding, landslides, typhoons, ice storms, heavy rain, high surf, high winds, cyclones, and earthquakes. In all cases, homes were partially or totally destroyed. See http://www.fema.gov/news/disasters. fema?year=2004 for more information.

3 Saunders, Peter. *A Nation of Homeowners.* London: Unwin Hyman, 1990. Although this is a British study of people's attachments to home and to the transformation that homeownership can bring, the principles and human interactions with home are the same as those experienced by people who live in the United States.

4 Moss, Michael and Andrew Jacobs. "Blue Skies and Green Yards, All Lost to Red Ink." Metropolitan Desk, New York: *The New York Times,* April 11, 2004, Sunday.

Chapter 3
Secret 2

**Your housing history influences
your housing decisions today.**

3

YOUR HOUSING HISTORY

As the child matures, he ventures into...the neighborhood, the city, the region, the world...But all the time, the house is home, the place of first conscious thoughts, of security and roots.

—*Clare Cooper*

Dreams and fantasies about house and home begin in childhood and stay with us more or less over the years as we grow and mature. Think of the enduring popularity of the classic 1947 film *Miracle on 34th Street*. Is this just a Santa Claus fable or the story of a child who longs for a home and family? You decide.

In the film, Macy's department store Santa, Kris Kringle, believes he really is Santa Claus.[1] Macy's executive, Dorey, who is a single mom, and her neighbor Bryan, a lawyer, fall in love in a romantic subplot. Dorey, a realist, has taught her 8-year-old daughter Susan that Santa Claus is a myth. However, Susan has a secret longing for a particular house and, unknown to her mother, has challenged Kris Kringle—if he really is Santa—to give her the house for Christmas.

When a Macy's psychologist declares Kris Kringle insane, Bryan comes to his defense. During the sanity hearing, Bryan attempts to prove that Kris is Santa Claus, but Kringle's legal prospects look bleak until the U.S. Postal Service delivers dozens of bags of Santa's mail to him in the courtroom. The relieved judge rules that if Kris Kringle has been recognized by the U.S. government as Santa, he must indeed be the real Santa Claus.

If this were the end of the film, it might long ago have been forgotten. The clever creators, however, tapped into a theme even deeper than our childhood hope that Santa Claus is real. Following Kris Kringle's directions, Dorey, Bryan, and Susan drive to a Long Island suburb on Christmas Day. "Stop, stop," Susan cries as the car approaches the very house—vacant and for sale—she told Kris was the only thing she wanted for Christmas. Susan runs into the vacant house followed by Dorey and Bryan who, once inside, declare their love for one another. Susan's attachment to the house motivates them to decide to buy it. So in the end, Santa doesn't disappoint anyone. The lovers connect, Susan gets the home and family she has secretly been longing for, and people everywhere can enjoy the story of the "real" Santa Claus every Christmas season on TV.

Like Susan, young children often dream of a home where they can live happily ever after. They long for father, mother, prince, princess, or as in Susan's case, a whole family restored in a picture-perfect home of their dreams. The dream of having a secure and happy home is both a symbolic and literal desire for children, and the dream—like the story in the movie—endures for most people throughout adulthood.

Think of the traditions and meanings behind "home sweet home," "homecoming," "homeland," "home for the holidays," "home and hearth," and "home is where the heart is." Whether we know it consciously or not, our childhood development, inner growth, sense of prosperity, and our socialization into an American Dream culture are all linked together in dramatic ways. When we more closely examine the heart-warming story of *Miracle on 34th Street*, we can see how important the subplot is to the strength of the film.

In exactly the same way, your challenge in this chapter is to look for and become aware of the "subplots" in your life. When you examine more closely your unique housing history, including your dreams and fantasies about the homes of your past, you will greatly improve the extent and quality of your housing self-knowledge and your future housing decision-making ability. You will also improve your chances of reaping both the personal and financial rewards the American Dream promises to bestow.

Dreams and Houses

Dream accounts go back thousands of years, and ancient texts give us many explanations of dreams. In religious traditions, angels are sent into dreams with important messages. Dreams have been variously interpreted as prophecies of the future, statements of our truest nature, messages from our soul, and expressions of our desires, wishes, fears, and aggressions.[2] Although many people understand dreams to be intrusions into their sleep that can delight or disturb them, others take a more practical approach that recognizes their usefulness. Dreams about homes, houses, or other forms of dwellings are especially insightful.

Homes play an important role in our individual dream lives as well as in the bigger dreams we all have in common.[3] Every dream comes with a message, or more accurately, more than one message, as can be seen in the following story. After losing his wife to cancer and his home to creditors some years ago, Greg was left to raise two small boys. During a particularly low period, he had this dream:

> *Unmade beds crowded a small room lit by a single window set too high for Greg to see outside. Clothes were strewn about the room and spilled out from open dresser drawers. In the wall above the dresser, Greg saw a trapdoor he had not noticed before. Curious and happy to postpone the disagreeable task of cleaning up the room, he climbed to the dresser top, pulled open the trapdoor, and crawled into a small, dark passageway, feeling his way to the door at the other end. It opened into a large and beautiful house, and Greg jumped down into a large dining room with high ceilings and walls decorated in hues and prints of sage, pale blues, and ivory. A crystal chandelier was suspended over a table surrounded by upholstered armchairs. He was alone in a beautiful house and able to explore other rooms and the gardens just outside. Greg wanted to remain, but "knew" he must return to clean up the messy room at the other end of the passageway before he could come again to stay.*

This classic "house dream" occurred when Greg was struggling to care for his two boys in a cramped rented house. He was trying to make ends meet from his job as a branch bank manager trainee. He saw the contrasting houses as a metaphor for his life, and the dream held the promise that his difficult and disorganized existence would in time become more orderly and financially secure. On a deeper level, which he understood later with help from a therapist, the houses were symbols of Greg's "self." Seen in this way, the dream meant that after returning to "clean up" the emotional debris of his childhood, he would be able to enter the relative calm and inner security that comes with psychological maturity. On both levels, Greg had to remind himself over the years that in his dream, the passageway was small, long, and dark, and that he had crawled through it on his hands and knees.

Today, after many years of hard work and persistent effort, Greg is justifiably proud of his boys, who are now enjoying promising careers and are married with children of their own. Greg is also remarried and likes to say his dream delivered "exactly what was promised." Greg and his wife Susan even live in a house that looks a lot like the one he saw in his dream when life seemed so messy and hopeless.

Home Is an Extension of Yourself

Home has symbolic meaning in your waking life too. It is an "outer skin," a shell that covers and protects you. It reflects "who you really are." You make your apartment, house, or condo into a home, and in turn, it reflects your lifestyle, financial means, patterns of activity, and social experiences.[4] You do not have to be dreaming to test aspects of home as an extension of yourself. Take the case of Noah and Katherine.

They returned home from a night out to discover they had suffered a home invasion. Still laughing about the hilarious play they had just seen, Noah suddenly went cold as he realized the front door was unlocked and standing slightly ajar. The police checked the house and wrote up their report, as the couple took inventory of their missing items—an accounting that would grow in the coming days. Soon enough, they dismissed the importance of their material losses, but the feeling they had been "violated" would not be so easily dismissed.

Noah and Katherine both grew up in the city and lived an active urban lifestyle before the burglary. Now, they became increasingly jumpy and Katherine, in particular, found she could not shake her growing fear of city life. To calm her fears, they sold their recently purchased condo at a loss and abandoned their city lifestyle altogether for a gated community in the suburbs. Their new house—complete with alarm system—is lovely, but Noah and Katherine are anything but happy about their move.

Katherine felt personally violated by the break-in. The burglary felt to her as though she had been "raped," a term she used often to describe her feelings. But instead of treating the cause of her fears—anxieties that were rooted in childhood fantasies of ghosts and invaders—Katherine and Noah made a precipitous set of lifestyle and financial choices that treated the symptoms and not the cause. She says she still feels vulnerable to break-ins even in the safe, new neighborhood. She has recently started seeing a therapist.

Bottom-Line Lessons

Noah and Katherine sold their city home for $35,000 less than they paid for it and abandoned the lifestyle they both prefer. Moving and a new alarm system cost an additional $15,000, and they have discovered they now need a second car. Noah and Katherine would like to return to the city, but they are financially stuck for now.

- If you're financially stuck, be patient. Markets and personal circumstances inevitably change. In the meantime, try to make the best of where you are.

Childhood Memories

Did you grow up in a home your parents owned? Are you attracted to new houses or older homes in established neighborhoods? Do you prefer the suburbs or love city living? Have you felt especially excited when you've seen a house that feels familiar?

Preferences and feelings about home are deeply rooted in childhood, and when we choose how and where to live as adults, we often try to copy, recreate, or escape aspects of our childhood homes.

We learn how to behave and perform tasks by imitating our parents and other adults. We typically do not question the reasons behind what we are learning. Imitation requires no logical understanding or reasoning on our part. We learn by watching and copying. But imitating does not mean we know what we are doing or why. So revisiting what we have learned as children helps us let go of patterns that no longer serve us as adults. By taking time to understand and deal with the circumstances beneath outmoded patterns, you might learn some amazing things about yourself, as Jennifer did.

After they married, Carter moved into the home Jennifer had built a few years earlier but had never quite finished. Although the unframed doorways and empty second bathroom bothered Carter more than Jennifer, he was content to postpone the needed construction because money was tight when they got married. Two years passed and both Carter and Jennifer achieved career successes. To Carter's mounting frustration and dismay, however, the house remained unfinished. Why, he asked her many times, was Jennifer so unconcerned about completing the construction they could now easily afford?

They soon discovered the answer to Carter's question with a little help. When I asked about her childhood home, Jennifer described in detail the Victorian house her father renovated himself. She remembered her toys, her friends, her room, the neighborhood, and the rivers that flow through the beautiful town that is now a popular tourist attraction. Significantly, she remembered too that although Dad worked continuously on the big old house they both loved, he never quite got around to finishing it. No wonder Jennifer felt so completely at home in her own unfinished house.

Jennifer's housing "preferences" in the present, like yours and mine, are often the stuff of childhood. Whether you lived in homes you loved, hated, or just took for granted, the house or lifestyle you seek today is influenced—consciously or unconsciously—by your experiences when you were growing up. You might be seeking the comfort or avoiding the discomfort you felt as a child. When Jennifer learned she was replicating her father's housing behavior, she was ready to give up living in an unfinished house. She and Carter happily called in the contractors to complete their home.

Bottom-Line Lessons

Costs to finish Jennifer and Carter's house nearly doubled from the time she contracted to have it built. Jennifer also failed to take advantage of falling interest rates. The combination of lower interest and construction costs would have allowed her to finish the house years earlier with no increase in monthly payments.

- Stay alert to mortgage and real estate markets where you live by reading local newspapers and checking with "trusted advisors."

- Don't put off making needed repairs and improvements to your home if you can help it. The costs are likely to climb, and a home needing attention is less valuable than one kept in good repair.

When you reminisce about your childhood, new revelations about your housing choices will emerge. Sometimes the source of a present dilemma will stem from an internal clash between the parent in you and the child in you. Even if you insist that you dislike your parents' ways, you may be repeating the very housing behaviors you saw in them when you were growing up. It could be that the childhood you experienced and the parent you have internalized are causing you inner conflict and conflict with others today. Consider the case of Jason.

Jason uncharacteristically complained several times to coworkers during his company's relocation to new space that "he hated to move." At first, no one took him very seriously. After all, moving is not high on anyone's list of favorites. It was just assumed that Jason would pitch in on moving day along with everyone else. But as the date drew closer, Jason took more time away from work than usual and was conveniently "called out of town" over the weekend of the move itself.

When his colleagues taunted him about having to pack and move his stuff, Jason shifted the conversation to his elderly mother's need to move from the family home. He described the house as badly in need of repair, too big to maintain, and located in a neighborhood that for years has been seriously declining. A coworker asked whether Jason had any regrets about selling his childhood home. To her surprise, Jason replied that he "hated" the house and would "rejoice when it is sold."

When he was 11, Jason explained, his dad had wanted to buy property, build a house, and move the family to the country, but his mom was adamantly opposed. Although he and his little brother were game to move too, their mother convinced her husband that a change of schools would not be in their best interests. Nearly 40 years later, Jason's mom remains in the inner-city home she refused to leave. Jason too is convinced that moving is an event to be avoided at all costs. He has continued to rent for many years even though he says that he would like to live and build equity in a home of his own.

If you are willing to revisit and work through childhood patterns still interfering in your housing life, chances are you will be able to kiss them goodbye forever. Some might seem harmless, but others can bring disharmony to close relationships, as in Jennifer's case, or missed opportunity, as Jason is learning.

Bottom-Line Lessons

Jason's biggest regret is financial. If his father had moved to the country, the family would have reaped the rewards of accelerating values. Jason now lives in a country village, and he too has denied himself the rewards of homeownership by continuing to rent at a below-market rental.

- A below-market rental for an extended period is a wise choice when the rental savings are paid into alternative investments.
- Over time, it costs more to rent than to own. Only homeownership offers the wealth-building power of home equity.

Your Childhood Housing

Identifying your childhood relationship to home will help give you insight into what you value in your housing today. In his memoirs, Swiss psychoanalyst Carl Jung offered evidence that understanding our housing psychology can be of great personal benefit.

For 32 years, Jung lived in a home he built on the shores of the upper lake of Zurich. During that time, he continuously modified, extended, and enlarged his home. Beginning with a low, circular dwelling he called "the maternal hearth" to symbolize mother and security, he expanded to two towers linked within a walled courtyard. Years later, following his wife's death, Jung continued building to cope with his grief. "I suddenly realized that the small central section that crouched so low, so hidden, was myself! I could no longer hide myself behind the 'maternal' and the 'spiritual' towers." So Jung built a tall, imposing upper story that dominated the two towers. He transformed his life during this final building process and observed, "I am in the midst of my true life, I am most deeply myself."[5]

Most of us will not continuously modify and extend one home to symbolize our journey to maturity. But we can evolve into homes that fully reflect our adult values rather than the needs that may still be mired in our childhood.

Beyond the Maternal Hearth

Carl Jung is not the only writer who uses the symbolism of mother to describe how we experience home. In *Sex and Real Estate*, Marjorie Garber counts the ways home is like Mother.[6] Here are some of them:

- Home contains you.

- Home will take you "the way you are," without dress-up or pretense.

- Home is comfortable, not challenging or threatening.

- Home makes you feel safe.

- Home nurtures you.

- Home loves you unconditionally.

"Not my home," you might be thinking. Or, "not my mother," Maureen would probably say.

Tim and Maureen bought an old house on a farm near an East Coast city. In its day, the house might have been stately, but now the old place looked unkempt and forlorn. Excited by its potential and "the feel of the place," Tim and Maureen moved in, began the renovations, and hired an architect to design a new addition. When the drawings were presented, Tim and Maureen disagreed over the architect's design. Tim liked the proposed symmetry of the old and new "wings" of the house. Maureen was dismayed that a large window would be destroyed in the construction. She wanted to preserve the window, but this required the new addition to be set back several feet to accommodate it. Neither Tim nor Maureen would give in, and the design process stalled for several weeks.

Tim invited me to help resolve the perplexing stalemate. I led the couple through the exercise you will find in this chapter, and the source of the problem was soon uncovered. The preservation of that window was rooted in a childhood memory brought to light by the exercise. Maureen's mother had reminded her many times as a child that "this is my house, it does not belong to you." Tim had chosen the couple's first house pretty much on his own. Unwittingly, he had made it "his" home in Maureen's mind, but she was ready to claim this home as "hers."

Understanding this for the first time after 20 years of marriage, Tim easily backed off from his earlier position, and the architect redesigned the addition to accommodate Maureen's window.

For Tim, Maureen's rebellion over the window was new housing behavior. Repeating her deference to her mother, Maureen had been content to let Tim select and more or less run their home early in their marriage. When he encountered Maureen's changed behavior, however, Tim had two choices: rethink his position and accommodate the desires of his partner or become withholding and further heighten the hostility. Tim was able to let go of the need to win in this situation and let Maureen take the lead. The result was not only an improved outcome for the couple, but it produced an award-winning design for the architect.

Recalling Your Own Housing History

With the following exercise, you will see your "housing history" emerge, and you will understand more about your housing preferences as a result. The first exercise is designed to help you understand the foundations of your housing history. If you feel uncomfortable with your present home but do not know why, or the process of finding another home is not going well, chances are excellent that you will find at least part of the explanation through this exercise. It is especially important if any tension exists between you and another person with whom you'll be moving.

The payoffs of learning about your housing history can be huge. Ask your partner and your children to take the exercise too because the issues you will uncover can help smooth the way for improved communication and mutual understanding among all of your family members. Better yet, the relationship benefits that can emerge are immediately transferable to other personal and professional choices. So immerse yourself in your past and then come into the present to learn how your unique housing history influences your housing values today. Get out some paper and a pen or pencil to record your results.

Your Housing History

Part One: The following exercise will help you recall your childhood home or homes.

1. Think carefully about what went on in your home(s) and think about how you interacted with the following:

The home(s): _____

_____

_____

The neighborhood: _____

_____

_____

The backyard: _____

_____

_____

The front porch: _____

_____

_____

Your room: _____

_____

_____

Your parents: _____

_____

_____

Sisters and brothers: _____

_____

_____

Other family members: _____

_____

Roommates or housemates: _____

_____

_____

Friends: _____

_____

_____

Neighbors: _____

_____

_____

People in the larger community: _____

_____

_____

Other spaces inside or outside: _____

_____

_____

Other visitors or people: _____

_____

_____

2. List as thoroughly as you can your feelings about each home: your favorite home and your least favorite home. Recall if you can and make notes about the events that caused the following and other feelings that might not be listed here.

Did you experience any of the following feelings?

Loved	Proud	Cozy
Vulnerable	Free	Protected
Independent	Frightened	Well off
Strong	Lonely	Deprived
Sad	Happy	Other feeling(s)

When you reminisce about your childhood, new revelations about your housing choices and preferences will emerge.

3. Continue this exercise by creating two brief written descriptions, one positive and the other negative, of homes you have lived in as an adult.

A. Positive Home Experiences

Go back in time to your favorite adult home. List or make note of the following: _____

_____

_____

The things you enjoyed about this home: _____

_____

_____

Any special features you liked: _____

_____

_____

The location of special features: _____

_____

_____

Roominess: _____

_____

_____

The style: _____

_____

_____

Anything else you want to remember that made the place feel like "home" for you: _____

_____

B. Negative Home Experiences

Go back in time and think of the home you liked least in your adult life. List or make note of the following:

What you disliked when you were in this home: _____

_____

_____

Any features of the home you did not like: _____

_____

_____

Its location: _____

_____

_____

Its size: _____

_____

_____

Its style: _____

_____

_____

Everything about the home you did not like and, perhaps, could not wait to leave: _____

_____

_____

Take as much time as you need, write down not only what you liked and did not like, but why this may have been so, and try to be thorough. If you have lived only in one home, list all the things you like and do not like about that one place.

Now compare your childhood homes with your positive and negative housing experiences as an adult. Can you recognize any childhood patterns you brought with you into adulthood? If so, are these patterns or housing preferences compatible with your adult values and lifestyle today? Or do they cause disharmony in your present life? If so, in what ways might you be continuing a behavior or preference that no longer serves you? Are you able to let it go?

You may notice that you feel uncomfortable, restless, bored, or anxious as you proceed through these exercises, but just notice your feelings and continue with your reflections to the extent you can. Because few of us live through childhood without experiencing some kind of housing anxiety, it is helpful to uncover the source of your discomfort. It can arise from a personal disaster such as the divorce of your parents. As a child, you are not certain of all the causes of divorce, but you know well how awful it feels. Or it can even follow a financial or career success: For example, a parent gets a promotion, but that means you have to move and leave your friends.

It is not easy to separate from your family housing culture. We are deeply invested in the patterns we bring with us into adulthood, no matter how destructive or uncomfortable they might be. Think of Jennifer's refusal to finish her house even though it caused friction in her marriage. Think of Jason's moving avoidance, even though he dislikes the same behavior in his mother. To stop these patterns, along with the accompanying anxiety, you must drop them and look forward to the great rewards that are certain to follow.

Resisting Repetition

Of course we do not always repeat our childhood experiences. Some of us go to great lengths not to repeat hard-won lessons from childhood. But if you are actively resisting a pattern or housing behavior so you will not end up repeating it, take particular note of Martha's story.

Martha grew up in a crowded apartment in New York city. Her parents were from the Old World, and theirs was an open-door policy. Family, friends, and neighbors were invited to visit at any hour of any day, and they often did. There was no privacy, no room, no quiet, and in Martha's experience, no peace.

Martha carried into adulthood her parental bent for entertaining and remains a gracious and welcoming hostess. Guests are regularly invited to her spacious New York co-op apartment for weekends, for dinner, and lavish parties. With open arms and haute cuisine, Martha is the family member of choice for large gatherings or holiday events. Woe to the person who rings her doorbell unannounced, however. She becomes angry, anxious, and anything but gracious. Martha certainly is not repeating the open-door policy of her parents, but she is trapped in a childhood experience anyway.

Just as Martha had no privacy as a child, she feels violated when an unexpected visitor arrives today. She believes she should live up to the ideal way of her parents, so it is difficult for her to level with family and friends about how she feels or to turn them away if they do drop by.

Martha has developed her own adult values, which clearly differ from those of her parents. If you—like Martha—are still having trouble claiming your own adult values, or if your unwanted housing past is still influencing your present behavior and decisions, there are steps you can take, as you will see in a later chapter about decision making for couples and families to help you claim your own adult housing values without ever again having to look back in time.

Points to Ponder

- When making housing decisions, you can unwittingly re-enact your original family culture without being aware of what you're doing or even why you are doing it.

- You may be imitating a parent's housing behavior *even when you do not like the behavior.*

- If your family housing patterns conflict with the family housing patterns of your partner, there can be strong discord in your relationship. Look for the reasons beneath the discord. Explore the reasons. Try to understand why they still influence your current housing behavior, talk them over with your partner, and let go of any patterns that no longer serve you.

End Notes

1 Berardinelli, James. *Miracle on 34th Street.* A Film Review, http://movie-reviews. colossus.net/movies/m/miracle.html, 1994.

2 Sechrist, Elsie. *Dreams, Your Magic Mirror.* New York: Gramercy Books, 1995.

3 Mazza, Joan. *Dreaming Your Real Self: A Personal Approach to Dream Interpretation.* New York: The Berkley Publishing Group, a division of Penguin Putnam Inc., 1998.

4 Csikszentmihalyi, Mihaly, and Eugene Rochberg-Halton. *The Meaning of Things: Domestic Symbols of the Self.* New York: Cambridge University Press, 1991.

5 Jung, Carl. *Memories, Dreams, and Reflections,* The Fontana Library Series. London, England: Collins, 1969.

6 Garber, Marjorie. *Sex and Real Estate.* New York: Random House, Inc., 2000.

Secret 3

You have a housing value system that drives your decisions.

4

CREATING YOUR HOUSING PROFILE

You see, buyers' purchasing decisions are based on emotions, not logic…
After they make their emotional decision, they use logic to justify it.
I have seen it happen hundreds of times.

—Kevin Wood

Companies spend lavishly on research to examine your deeper urges, innermost longings, and lifestyle patterns. Market researchers probe your spending habits and values to try to learn what motivates you to buy all sorts of services and products, including homes.[1] The research is used to target you with savvy advertising that taps right into your dreams and fantasies.

This chapter introduces you to a tool similar to, but even more advanced than those used by big-spending advertisers. You will be able to use a thoroughly researched, proven method that helps you understand your own housing decision patterns and motivations before you make your next move. Here are the three most important questions to ask yourself as you think about making a change in your housing situation:

1. Why do I want to move?

2. How do I make decisions?

3. Does my decision-making approach help or hurt me?

This chapter and those that follow guide you through a process to sharpen your answers to these questions. You will discover how to bring together the four major deciding factors that define your housing value system as you decide whether and when to move, and how and where to live. One of the biggest mistakes almost everyone in the housing industry makes—and many homebuyers as well—is to presume that a housing decision is exclusively, or even predominantly, an objective decision. It usually is not.

Home and Comfort

Home and *comfort* have been paired in the literature for centuries. Comfort is contented enjoyment in physical or mental well-being (living a life of ease and comfort). *Discomfort* is the lack of comfort or feeling uneasy about something.

A decision to move (or as discussed in a later chapter, a decision to invest in a second home) is almost always triggered by a feeling of discomfort, which can range from vague to intense. Sometimes the unease can even be caused by a joyful event.

Miriam and Tony were thrilled to learn they were expecting twins. When the reality sank in, they tried to imagine welcoming two babies instead of one into their already cramped space. They looked at each other in dismay. With three other children under ten years of age in their home, they became increasingly uncomfortable with its adequacy. They soon found and moved into another home with two additional bedrooms, one for the babies, and one for Miriam's mom, who volunteered to help out with the children after the blessed event.

Miriam and Tony had a straightforward housing situation to solve, and the solution was equally straightforward. They knew exactly why they wanted to move. Like this couple, your primary goal as a housing decision maker is to find a solution that will relieve or solve the "discomfort" you may be feeling about your present home. As you will discover in the following chapters, the "urge to move" and the solution can be more complicated than it seems with Miriam and Tony. Contrast their situation with Trish and Bennett's story about a much more severe degree of discomfort and their urge to move.

Trish and Bennett moved into a country home they found after a long search. It was their dream to take long walks and let their two dogs run free. Life in retirement looked bright, and they were jubilant. Their joy turned to grief a month or so later when a neighbor called and told them to claim the dogs he had just shot. "I presume they're yours," he growled, "They were in my chicken coop." With the care of a good local vet, Amy survived, but Duke did not make it. Trish and Bennett felt trapped.

They immediately wanted to move, but moving was not an option. Their financial investment could not be recovered, and their retirement budget would not allow another move in so short a period of time. As Amy healed, Trish and Bennett assessed their uncomfortable situation and decided to solve it by blocking out their neighbor and his chicken coop. With the help of the sympathetic garden center owner, they developed a landscape around limited fencing. New trees and native flowering bushes gave the couple the privacy and security they needed and restored their comfort in their country home.

As different as these situations may seem, they have similarities. Each couple experienced an event that made them uncomfortable with their present home and led to a housing decision. Miriam and Tony moved, Trish and Bennett did not. A smart housing decision requires the following:

- Identifying the cause of the discomfort

- Taking a decision-making approach that will help you avoid costly mistakes

We will revisit the housing changes made by Miriam and Tony in a future chapter to learn whether their housing decision helped them or hurt them.

Creating Your Housing Profile

In the preceding chapter, you addressed your housing history and the foundations of your housing preferences. Now you can relate your past thoughts and feelings to those you still have in the present. Because you have a baseline—a general idea—of your current relationship to home, you can move to the following "housing profile quiz."[2]

By taking this quiz, you will learn which of the four major decision-factor categories best matches your housing priorities. Expect your categories to overlap a lot, and remember that there are no right or wrong answers, just preferences. Remember too that your answers are intensely personal—do not answer what you believe someone else may want or value. Choose only one answer per statement and write the corresponding letter on a separate piece of paper, so that your spouse, partner, and other family members can also take the quiz. Or, you might find it useful to take it again after you read Chapters 5–8, which explain each of the decision-factor categories in more detail.

Be as honest with yourself as you can about your priorities!

Housing Profile Quiz

1. One important priority I have in looking for my next home includes finding

   a. A place where I can make new friends (and/or my children can find friends and playmates.)

   b. A home in a location where I can have more quiet and privacy.

   c. A home in a nice neighborhood that will appreciate in value.

   d. A home that has more space, more interesting amenities, or modern features than where I presently live.

2. Another important objective in my search for my next home is

   a. Having a backyard or patio where I can spend time outdoors.

   b. Being able to fix up the place exactly as I please.

   c. Finding a good school system for my children.

   d. Looking forward to building up equity when I make my monthly payments.

3. When it comes to the price I can pay for my next home

   a. I would go out on a limb to find the right home for my family.

   b. I would sacrifice ease of commuting time and move further out if I have to find a better house that I could afford.

   d. I have set a budget for what I can afford and that's it. I won't exceed my budgeted amount even if I have to give up a place that I find attractive.

   e. I should have enough savings to qualify for the home I really want for myself.

4. It is very important for me to have

   a. A very nice home in a prestigious neighborhood.

   b. A place to live that represents equity buildup and a form of forced savings.

   c. A spacious home that has all the latest comforts.

   d. A home in a familiar community where I already have put down "roots."

5. When it comes to safety

    a. I would settle for smaller space in a safer area rather than a big, gracious home in an area with a higher crime rate.

    b. If the crime rate was a little higher than average but the school system was the best in the area, I would move there anyway and just be more aware and teach my kids to be careful.

    c. If homes were appreciating in a particular area at a very fast rate, even though it was an area with a higher crime rate, I would go for it.

    d. Nothing could make me move to an area where the crime rate is higher than average.

6. I tend to deal with my housing priorities

    a. In terms of lifestyle. I keep reworking my ideas about my next home to figure out what it is that I really want for myself.

    b. On a bottom-line basis. Do I have enough to make a comfortable down payment, and can I handle the monthly payments without worrying all the time about making ends meet?

    c. In terms of physical space. Will the home have enough amenities? Are there enough extra bedrooms for guests? Are there enough closets? Is there a fireplace? Is there enough light?

    d. By regarding home as the center of my family and social life, a place where I can entertain and my children will have room to hang out with their own friends, too.

7. To feel totally satisfied with my housing, I would need

    a. A place where I can live as I please and that reflects the "real me" to the outer world.

    b. To know my family was 100 percent satisfied and comfortable in the home in which we live.

    c. To know that my home represents a good investment as well as a comfortable place to live.

    d. A different location or more physical space to expand into than I have in my present home.

8. To me, homeownership represents the following important financial advantage:

    a. Growing equity that I can tap into whenever and for whatever I choose.

b. An opportunity to preserve or leverage a tax-sheltered, appreciating capital asset.

c. The chance to trade up to a bigger home when I am ready.

d. A source of savings for future educational or family retirement needs.

9. If I "fell in love with" and wanted to buy a particular home, but it is not within my budget

   a. I would figure out how to adjust my budget to be able afford it, if the home, the environment, and the neighborhood were extremely attractive to me,

   b. I would figure out a way to be able to afford a home and environment just like that at some point in the future.

   c. I would decide I do not really want it, or I may buy it on impulse even though it may make me feel very uncomfortable later.

   d. If I thought it was good for my family and could also be near friends, I would sacrifice to buy it. I would scrape together the down payment and work harder—maybe take another job—to make sure I could always make the payments.

10. Most of all, I want any home that I move into

    a. To be my haven, my castle, the place to which I can retreat and re-create myself for whatever lies ahead.

    b. To be completely comfortable, a place where all of my physical needs can be met nicely.

    c. To be a good value and appreciating asset.

    d. To be close to family and friends and to be where I feel like a member of the local community.

11. Where I live now, I have the freedom I need

    a. To be independent, to come and go as I please, and live my life as I see fit.

    b. To share many common interests with friends and family who live close by.

    c. To pay off my mortgage quickly because I would like to own it free and clear as soon as possible.

    d. To make any changes I would like to expand, remodel, or improve the property.

12. I enjoy

    a. Having the physical space to entertain many people, family gatherings, or just a few friends as often as possible.

    b. Entertaining business friends and colleagues on occasion.

    c. Calling up family members or friends and inviting them over to spend time with me, perhaps on the spur of the moment.

    d. Spending quiet, uninterrupted time all alone doing whatever I want to do.

13. On my days off or when I am on vacation, I look forward to

    a. Planning or working on projects that will enhance the value of my home.

    b. Locking up and leaving home without worry as often as the mood strikes me.

    c. Catching up on needed repairs, finishing the basement, or working on other projects to make my home more comfortable.

    d. Watching movies or sports on TV with my partner, spouse, kids, or buddies.

14. When it comes to having pets

    a. I have (or would like to have) a dog or cat.

    b. Cats or dogs (or snakes, turtles, rabbits, guinea pigs, or birds) are a big part of the family.

    c. No pets. They cost half as much to raise as kids these days.

    d. If I had more room, or a fenced-in yard (or my own place where they allowed pets), I would like to have one or more.

15. The particular style of my home is more or less important to me. I tend to like

    a. Traditional, roomy, and welcoming homes that will accommodate family and friends.

    b. Any style as long as it is attractive to look at, is well located, and has something unique about it.

    c. Traditional homes with all the latest upgrades and physical comforts.

    d. Bargains in good locations that can be transformed into great homes with growing value.

16. When it comes to conveniences

    a. I want my commute to work, schools, shopping, houses of worship, and anything else I need accessible within a short distance.

    b. I seek value above all else and assume that the best homes in the best neighborhoods will be located close to the best conveniences.

    c. I do not mind a commute of up to an hour as long as my home is located in an area with a good school system, in a pleasant community, and/or close to anything else that my family is likely to require.

    d. I do not mind giving up some convenience for beauty, for unusual location, for a location that is near water or in the country, or has a lovely view or some other amenity that makes it particularly special.

17. Financing (or lease) terms must not only be available to me, I also need them to be

    a. As hassle-free as possible because I am busy with family and have no time to wory about financial details.

    b. Flexible, so that I can more easily afford the comfort, style, beauty, and location I seek in a home.

    c. As reasonable as possible, so I will not be too tied down to a home.

    d. The best possible deal with the ability to make extra monthly payments as often as I can.

18. When it comes to thinking about my home as a form of personal saving

    a. The equity buildup in my home is my most important family asset.

    b. Even the best lease terms are not an option for me. Only owning my own home can be a form of savings as I build up equity.

    c. The equity buildup in my home allows me to make alterations, repairs, or additions to modernize, beautify, or make it more comfortable.

    d. I choose "safe" and conservative investments and consider my home as a "no-brainer" form of savings.

19. When people see my home

    a. They can learn a lot about who I am.

    b. They know that my family and community take priority in my life.

    c. They have no idea whether or not I am financially successful because that does not necessarily show up in my personal surroundings.

    d. They know that I take great pride in the comfort and beauty of my home and in its surroundings.

20. When I look around my community

    a. I enjoy knowing my neighbors and others in my community and would look for another home nearby if I were to move.

    b. When the time is right to reap whatever profit I can from the sale of my current home, I will move on to my next new address wherever that may be—within reason of course.

    c. I feel somewhat connected to the area I currently live in, but I know I could put down roots if I chose to move somewhere else.

    d. I would move only if I could find another home that would be more beautiful, or if it offered more style and comfort than my present home.

Scoring Your Housing Profile Results

Now that you have completed the quiz, here is the key to determining which combination of deciding factors tend to influence your housing decisions:

- P stands for personal factors.

- S stands for social factors.

- T stands for tangible factors.

- M stands for money factors.

Refer to the following list as you score your answers, keeping count of, how many Ps, Ss, Ts, and Ms you have chosen.

1. a) S	b) P	c) M	d) T
2. a) T	b) P	c) S	d) M
3. a) S	b) T	c) M	d) P
4. a) P	b) M	c) T	d) S
5. a) T	b) S	c) M	d) P
6. a) P	b) M	c) T	d) S
7. a) P	b) S	c) M	d) T
8. a) P	b) M	c) T	d) S
9. a) T	b) M	c) P	d) S
10. a) P	b) T	c) M	d) S
11. a) P	b) S	c) M	d) T
12. a) T	b) M	c) S	d) P
13. a) M	b) P	c) T	d) S
14. a) P	b) S	c) M	d) T
15. a) S	b) P	c) T	d) M
16. a) P	b) M	c) S	d) T
17. a) S	b) T	c) P	d) M
18. a) S	b) P	c) T	d) M
19. a) P	b) S	c) M	d) T
20. a) S	b) M	c) P	d) T

After you count how many Ps, Ss, Ms, and Ts you have chosen, refer to the following to learn briefly what they mean. The higher the score for a particular deciding factor, the more likely it is to drive your value system and your housing choices:

- **Personal factors** refer to subjective personal values about home, such as identity, autonomy, safety, security, and other aspects of the "real you."

- **Social factors** refer to values that concern others, such as your spouse, partner, children, other family members, friends, neighbors, and community members.

- **Tangible factors** relate specifically to the physical comforts and other tangible aspects of the dwelling itself. This category includes the physical environment, convenience, commuting time, views, physical setting, and/or your perceived beauty of the home.

- **Money factors** refer to all things financial or monetary. This is a subjective category—it is what you think or believe about your financial affairs. It represents how you value your money, or other material goods, or investments, not how much you actually have.

Evaluating Your Housing Profile

Congratulations! If you have completed and scored your housing profile quiz, you now have a general idea of which combination of factors tends to drive your housing value system and your housing choices. Remember that everyone scores a mixture of these factors, and it is even possible that in the course of reading this book your scores will vary on a later quiz.

If you are in a couple relationship, there may well be a shift to a different score for one or both of you as you work to understand and accommodate one another's particular housing needs and values. Before you adjust your thinking to match or accommodate a partner's score, however, you need to understand thoroughly the meaning of each of the four deciding factors and how they apply just to you.

Each deciding factor plays a role in your decision making. They provide a convenient inventory to help you discover for yourself how the dimensions of your life impact your housing choices. When you are true to your value system as you make your decisions, the probability of making the right decision is much greater.[3] However, if you attempt to "force fit" your decision criteria to what the world tells you, or to your spouse or partner's wishes or desires, or to some other outside influence, your choices may end up being costly in both money and emotional outcomes.

Encourage your spouse, partner, and others in your household to create a housing profile. Together assess where your points of view are in alignment or where they collide after you read Chapters 5 through 8. Remember that your priorities can and do change over time. You will be able to explore the deciding factors in more depth in coming chapters and how you can balance them for more effective results. In Chapter 9, "When Housing Values Differ," couples will learn ways to help smooth housing differences and the emotions of making joint housing decisions. Then, in Part Two, "Finding Soluions that Work for You," you can put the framework to use on some specific housing decision areas you may be facing.

Primary Reasons Given for Moving

According to the 2003 National Association of Realtors' "Profile of Home Buyers and Sellers," 82 percent of first-time buyers said a desire for homeownership was their primary reason for moving. Just 6 percent said they wanted more living space, and 4 percent moved in connection with a job.

Among repeat buyers, 31 percent wanted more space; 13 percent moved to a job in another area; 10 percent moved to downsize; 9 percent wanted to be closer to a job, school, relatives, or transit; and 6 percent moved to retire.

Why do you want to move? Would this survey capture your primary reason?

The following are the three most important questions to ask as you think about making a change in your housing situation:

1. Why do I want to move?
2. How do I make decisions?
3. Does my decision-making approach help me or hurt me?

End Notes

1   Market research and advertising firms have long known that "consumer values" inform the process of major purchase decisions (e.g., Dittmar, Helga. *The Social Psychology of Material Possessions: To Have is To Be*. Sussex: St. Martin's Press; Pham, Michel Tuan, 1992. "Representativeness, Relevance, and the Use of Feelings in Decision Making," *Journal of Consumer Research*, Vol. 25, 1998; Ray, Paul H. "Using Values to Study Customers," *American Demographics*, Vol. 19:2:34, 1997; Stern, Barbara B. "Escape from the Tyranny of Time: Temporal Themes and Consumer Values in Advertising," *Research in Consumer Behavior*, Vol. 5: 215–232, 1991. Witkowski, Terrence H. "The Early American Style: A History of Marketing and Consumer Values," *Psychology & Marketing*, Vol. 15(2): 125–143, 1998. Recent marketing efforts have targeted ambitious campaigns around studies of the values of older adults in order to sell them products and services (e.g., Seniors Research Group and J. Walter Thompson, 2000). They know too that each of us forms a unique set of personal values that underlie our ties to *home*. We use these values rationally,

if sometimes unconsciously, to guide decisions about our living environments. What we value might differ significantly from other family members, and painful conflicts can transpire when a change of living environment must be considered and, or implemented.

2   The housing profile quiz is based on the author's theoretical model, the LifeValues decision framework. The framework has been used since 1993 in several studies, workshops, and seminars, and in proprietary research conducted for corporate clients. The purpose of the LifeValues framework is to organize human values that are profoundly important to consumers. The author's conceptual approach constitutes a perspective based on research across the social sciences and on the practical urgency of increasing knowledge about consumer financial behaviors and decision making, particularly in housing and in healthcare.

3   Personal values are the standards or principles people use for evaluating the actual or potential consequences of their action and inaction. They are used as guidelines for discerning priorities, for making trade-offs, for forming preferences among available choices, and for taking action or deciding not to act. Discussions about values and how values function at personal levels have occurred over centuries. They can be found in all fields of the social sciences, in law, the physical sciences, education, philosophy, and religion. (See: Feather, Norman T. *Values, Achievement, and Justice: Studies in the Psychology of Deservingness.* New York: Kluwer Academic/ Plenum Publishers, 1999; Keeney, Ralph L. *Value-Focused Thinking: A Path to Creative Decisionmaking.* Cambridge, MA: Harvard University Press, 1992; Rokeach, Milton. *Beliefs, Attitudes and Values: A Theory of Organization and Change.* San Francisco, CA: Jossey-Bass, 1968.)

5

LEARNING ABOUT YOURSELF— THE PERSONAL FACTOR

When making a decision of minor importance, I...consider all the pros and cons. In vital matters, however, the decision should come...from somewhere within ourselves.

—Sigmund Freud

When completing the housing history and profile exercises, you sorted through influences from parents, spouse, partner, children, friends, and the rest of society to pick the deciding factors that matter most to you. To apply this new knowledge to your future housing choices, you need to understand (and be able to name and discuss) the array of needs and values that make up your unique housing value system: your Personal, Social, Tangible, and Money Factors. This chapter elaborates on the Personal Factor; Chapters 6 through 8 tackle the other factors.

Whether you live alone, with a housemate or spouse, or with a bustling family, you have an active "life" that is all your own. Although a lot of people and organizations may still try to influence your housing decisions, you have now ranked your own priorities. If your needs and values happen to be compatible with those who live with you, that is great! If they do not, well that is great too—after all, opposites attract. There are ways of synchronizing personal environments to suit even opposite needs and values, and you will learn some of them in later chapters.

Finding your ideal home requires that you connect with your value system on all four dimensions. The process starts with identifying Personal Factors, and for the time being at least, it involves only you. Although you are likely to be curious about what the critical P factor means in this analysis, if you scored especially low—4 and under—or especially high—9 and over—read this chapter carefully. You could be on the road to making a serious blunder in your next housing decision if you give it a once-over-lightly treatment.

Your Unique Housing Psychology

Housing needs and values are the main components of your unique housing psychology. Everyone's housing needs are driven by basic human requirements, such as shelter from the elements and physical safety. Other housing needs occur for many of us as a result of some conscious or unconscious childhood experience. As we consider making new housing arrangements, fulfilling housing needs is the most urgent part of our decision process, so they lie at one end of the housing-decision spectrum. At the other end lie the housing dreams and values that (also consciously or unconsciously) guide our choices as adults. We typically let go of "childish things" after we actually outgrow them—a condition that may bear little relationship to age or life stage.

In Chapter 2, "Your Home and Life," you saw how childhood experiences at home can still impact our current housing choices. Jennifer and Carter, a young married couple, lived in an unfinished house, which bothered Carter but not Jennifer. When she discovered her reason for feeling so comfortable in an unfinished house, Jennifer let go of this childhood need, and they called in the builder to complete the home. We also learned about Maureen and Tim, who came to an impasse in the design of an addition to their home. As a child, Maureen had been repeatedly told by her mother that she was "only a guest" in her house. When Maureen insisted to the architects and to her husband, Tim, that "the old window must stay," she was claiming her "first real home." She felt a need to experience the home as hers. A new grandmother at the time, Maureen was in no mood to give up what she had waited half a lifetime to experience.

The unique housing needs from your childhood that may be lingering should have surfaced as you reflected on your housing history. Your inner concepts of the following—autonomy and control, security, identity, and spirituality—will also influence your housing decisions more or less. In your pursuit to satisfy an inner longing in your housing, think of the urgency you feel: Needs are felt urgently; values are experienced as ideals, dreams, and desires. If you have discovered, from reviewing your housing history, a need is still at work in your housing psychology, share it, discuss it, let go of it if you can; if you cannot, then like Maureen and Tim, deal with it! As you go through the process of identifying, sharing with significant others, and claiming what you need and value for yourself, remember that only you can decipher and communicate the degree of their importance to you.

Autonomy and Control

Autonomy and control form the essence of the American character and include our self-determination, freedom, independence, and liberty of choice and action. Autonomy, the desire to be independent and to "do for myself," can be so strong that it is the last value many of us are willing to give up, even when we become feeble and unable to care for ourselves. Control is our ability to direct the day-to-day details of our lives and beyond.

Autonomy and control endow you with the freedom to shape your long-range goals and purposes, to determine your life priorities and commitments, and to feel in charge of the content and direction of your personal history. The combination is a powerful personal motivator. Having the ability to act independently and the freedom to control your physical setting are what drive many of us to become homeowners.[1] If you have ever been required to move against your will, Betty's experience may seem familiar to you.

Betty's parents moved to what she calls "the family home" when she was four and her brother and sister were six and seven. The three children had their own rooms, a big yard, lots of friends nearby, and plenty of space to play. When Betty was 16, the family moved to a neighboring town and into a house her parents had dreamed about building for years. Betty's parents were thrilled with their new home, but after the move Betty cried herself to sleep every night for weeks. "They took me out of the place where I'd grown up and away from the friends I'd known since kindergarten. I lost a big part of me in that move." Since college, Betty has been employed by a company in a major East Coast city. She wants a home of her own and sees homeownership as necessary for stability in her life. "I want to be in a house I own and can stay in as long as I want. It doesn't matter if I'm single or married, what matters is having a place to call my own."

Betty's father, an accountant, remains unapologetic for the housing decision that upset her when she was younger. But he is a strong advocate of homeownership, and he has influenced Betty's approach to her finances. Following his guidance, Betty has been saving for a down payment. She also established excellent credit, researched her mortgage options thoroughly, and developed a good relationship with a local bank. She knows exactly what kind of home she wants and in what neighborhood. "My goal is to be into my own home by the end of this year."

Betty's determination to buy her own home is driven both by a need to control her housing environment and by the value she attaches to homeownership. There is little doubt that Betty will realize her desire to buy a home for herself. She is financially practical, knows the downside of paying out money for rent with no equity buildup, and wants the tax advantages that ownership brings. Her strongest motivator, however, is her desire to have control over her life. "For me, the number one thing is to be independent, to control my destiny, to have a house I own—for myself—and then maybe someday for my family-to-come."

Security

Feeling secure in your home is a basic need for everyone, and pursuit of that security—if you feel that you lack it—should take precedence over just about everything else.[2] When you feel secure, you feel safe from perceived harm or loss. You experience freedom from fear of actual physical danger and from anxiety that some calamity—including financial upheaval—could occur at any moment.

Real security is a feeling that you have the wherewithal to survive whatever you encounter. It is having deep-rooted confidence in others, in the social order, in your place in the world, and in your right to be yourself. A sense of security bestows its own rewards like those that awaited Sara when she achieved it. Security is worth pursuing even when the immediate stakes seem high.

After she and her husband divorced, Sara suddenly found herself with nowhere to live and very little income. Despite court-ordered support, the checks did not come. Sara and her two children were in real crisis. They lived in a house owned by her mother-in-law, who wanted to rent it to "paying tenants," so she had them evicted. With the help of her own mother, Sara was able to rent a two-bedroom apartment in the same school district where the kids went to school and where Sara worked. This gave them all some welcomed continuity in the midst of the family upheaval. Sara inherited a little money that first year and was able to supplement the $12,500 from her job as an instructional assistant. "Money for food was tight" she recalls, "but at least we had a safe place to live."

Moving from a five-bedroom home with a finished basement and a backyard into a two-bedroom apartment was difficult for Sara and the kids, but the apartment was "theirs." "My ex-husband and his mother could not come in whenever they felt like it, as they had in the house." The apartment had an alarm system that was backed up by a 24-hour monitoring company. "If we set off the alarm by mistake, the company called. Our little apartment felt like an oasis. Although I signed a six-month lease, we ended up staying there for three years."

Today Sara owns her own home and directs a physical fitness center near a major East Coast city. Her son is a doctoral student in physics, and her daughter has just entered college. Sara's life is full of accomplishment and promise, but she vividly recalls climbing out of crises rung by rung. Her most urgent inner need was to rebuild her sense of security, and Sara chose to do it, first, by creating a secure home environment for herself and her children. However you define security, it is both a need and a value, and it must be satisfied to the extent possible in every housing decision you will ever make.

Identity

Does your home capture the essence of "who you really are?" What does your home communicate about you to the world? Identity is central to everyone's "inner life." It remains more or less stable and integrates three inner perspectives:

1. The "real you" known only to yourself

2. The "you" you allow others to see

3. The "you" you believe others really see

Our identity begins at home and within its surroundings, and eventually incorporates all of our interactions.[3] We classify our interactions and experiences—with people, objects, and events—into categories: sex, age, race, ethnicity, religion, family status, education, communities of interest, and so on. During our lives, we add new classifications according to our jobs, our health, legal or economic status, and our interests. We become lawyers, mechanics, cashiers, artists, data processors, and nurses. We are single, married, widowed, or divorced. We are rich, poor, well-off, or "okay." We are workers, retirees, club members, drivers, patients, investors, and subscribers to the opera. These are all categories to which we "belong," categories that constitute our social identity.

Home captures all three aspects of our personal and social identity. In a personal sense, home is our "outer skin," and somewhere underneath that shield resides the "real me." In a social sense, home is an aspect of the self we allow others to see and believe they "really see." The stronger our belief that homeowner is a desirable social identity, the more we will aspire to own a home of our own.

For most of us, homeownership is a status symbol—a public sign of achievement and success in the world. It is a fulfillment of the American Dream, a sign for all to see that we have "made it." When Megan went house hunting with her husband, Ron, she failed to see or understand that he needed his home to reflect his achievements and new social status appropriately.

Symbols

Something that stands for or suggests something else by reason of relationship, association, convention, or accidental resemblance; *especially* a visible sign of something invisible. (Home is a *symbol* of the self.)

Megan grew up in a rural, midwestern community. Everyone knew everyone else, and a lot about them besides. Ron was from a Brooklyn neighborhood that was fast going downhill. Although most of his friends and their families had moved out long ago, Ron's parents were holdouts who clung to their old ways and to "the old neighborhood." Ron even disliked visiting them and often arranged for them to be picked up and brought to Manhattan, where he would take them on outings.

Megan and Ron were married after they graduated from business school and found work in Boston, where they decided to live permanently. As they grew in their careers, the urge to move from their rented apartment became stronger, and they began to search for a home of their own. Their housing values collided immediately. She set her sights on a modest suburban area. He wanted a luxury urban condo. The last thing Ron wanted to do was put down roots in a "modest" community. He was enjoying his material success as an investment banker, and he wanted the world to know it. Megan's housing values were entirely different. She had taken a position as assistant director of a nonprofit firm that encouraged immigrants to become financially literate. The restraint and moderation she desired in her surroundings matched her past and present identity.

Although they looked at prospective homes for several months, they could never settle on a place that satisfied them both. Prices in the Boston area were high and going higher, which did not bother Ron. He saw the escalation as investment potential and wanted a home that suited his new station in life. Megan was unhappy to think that so much of their income would go toward housing, leaving little for the family she wanted to start. They fought a lot about their divergent visions of home but never really got to the heart of the matter—their different identity needs and values. They gave up trying to find a home that would please them both and wondered how they could ever bridge the gap in their perspectives.

If you found yourself in a similar situation, would you know what to do? Is there enough information here to analyze what course you might take to improve or even to solve this housing dilemma? It is possible, of course, that this couple's differences are too great to be reconciled. Megan's identity is on the line, and so is her desire for financial security. She does not share Ron's free-spending confidence in their financial future. But Ron's identity as a successful investment banker who doesn't want to "go back where he came from" is also on the line. Chapter 8, "The Real Deal about Finances—The Money Factor," continues the story of Megan and Ron, as you learn more about how they fared on the four deciding factors underlying their aborted housing search and their now troubled marriage.

Spirituality

Does home represent an inner connection you feel for the sacred in life? Is it a place of worship, prayer, or meditation? Do you adhere to the symbolism and placement principles of Feng Shui or other wisdom teachings? Throughout history, cultures around the world have believed that the spiritual is present in nature, the weather, and in locations that are considered unique and special, including the home.

Spirituality is subjective, intangible, and multidimensional. It alludes to a search for purpose and meaning in life, principles by which to live, and the need for and capacity to transcend everyday material or sensory experience. It involves a relationship with a higher universal power. Spirituality may or may not be related to one's religion, which can also be seen as multidimensional. Most people experience religion as both a social institution and an organized system of beliefs, practices, prayers, and rituals designed to facilitate a relationship to and understanding of God.

Home is a powerful symbolic representation of spirituality. We may speak of dying as "going home" to God. We think of certain transcendent experiences and "coming home" to ourselves. For centuries, religious and spiritual holidays and rituals have been practiced in the home, and for many, home is the center of spiritual life. Architect Anthony Lawlor's book, *A Home for the Soul*, is a guide for transforming a living environment into a home that will nurture the soul.[4]

Some people, like Jack, feel a spiritual connectedness to place, to home, or at times, to a certain home.

Jack's ideas about home are in transition. After his divorce, he found the rented house he now shares with his 12-year-old son, who lives with him part time. "In the past I often thought that home really meant love, being in love with someone. Sometimes I still think about that, but I was drawn here, and this house has a strong spiritual component for me." Jack would like to be a homeowner again someday, but not yet. Although he understands the financial and other personal advantages of homeownership, he says he is not into "status and achievement right now, but wants to find his real spiritual home."

Jack likes open spaces, quiet and natural places. These images, he believes, are etched deeply in his soul from "a kind of collective unconscious, a longing he was born with." He remembers, as a boy, riding his bike along country roads and taking long hikes. He has thought about pulling up stakes and moving to the Northwest, but he isn't sure he could make the break. "It's hard to tell what's practical. I am seeking the spiritual guidance that will help me to change my life and ultimately to live my dream. I'll know when it is time for me to move on."

Whereas Jack's experience of home and spirituality seems more personal and intangible, people of many cultures enjoy home as a place for regular prayer, ritual, and religious worship. Cheryl's experience of home details a much more explicit spiritual connection.

When she was raising a family, a home with enough space in a decent neighborhood was important to her. Now Cheryl sees the use of her house as her way "to glorify God, and I do not look at it as ownership of the house anymore. I look at it as being God's house, and it is going to be here when I'm gone for somebody else." Her house is open to members of her church for Bible study groups, choir rehearsals, and counseling sessions. "I'm interested in my house reflecting the love of God. I want people to feel when they come in and out that God loves them and that I love them, too."

Many national holidays are occasions for families to gather in remembrance of the sacred. However you conceptualize spirituality, be sure that your housing decisions give adequate attention to your spiritual side. As you have seen so far throughout this book, housing is a multidimensional decision, and people who ignore this may be asking for trouble—financially and otherwise—for just that reason.

Reality Checks for People with Low or High P Scores

A low P score (4 and below) may signal that you are seeing your housing through someone else's eyes or are deferring to someone else's expectations regarding where and how you want to live. Reflect carefully on the inner characteristics covered in this chapter to learn whether you are experiencing a too narrow expression of life in your own home. Take the time to think again about what you need and value in your ideal home. And if you find that your housing profile really reflects the needs and values of someone else, take the quiz again and make sure the answers this time are your own.

A high P score (9 and above) may reflect your commitment to lead an independent or even a solitary life. Or it may signal, as it did in Jack's case, that recent events have been unusually stressful and you need both a place and the time to heal. Jack's rented home suits his temporary identity as a recently divorced single parent and provides a place for him to pursue the inner comfort and guidance he needs on his way to claiming a new life. It is a place where he can safely begin to create his future, and perhaps as he suggests, opt for a different lifestyle altogether in an entirely new location.

Even without a marriage breakup or other forced move, changing homes can contribute to the feeling that we are in charge of our life when something is amiss or seriously shifting in other life domains. Some people move to prove this to themselves symbolically. In practical terms, that means you may be searching for a home as a stand-in for something missing or gone awry in other parts of your recent life. When you are fully aware of this tendency and can financially afford it, a move can be a blessing—a remedy that is restorative and even stimulating. When you are oblivious to the "stand-in effect" that shows itself as vague and growing dissatisfaction with your home, you may make a housing decision you will live to regret. In either case, give yourself the moving-decision reality check you will find at the end of Chapter 10, "Whether to Move and When to Move," to learn what is going wrong in some area of your life that you may be attributing unwittingly to your home.

Points to Ponder

Your Personal Factors include the following:

- Autonomy and control

- Security

- Identity and social identity

- Spirituality

How important to you is each of these dimensions of your "inner life?"
Taking your unique housing history into account, how much do you need/value each dimension when it comes to making your housing choices?

End Notes

1 See, for example, Fitchen, Janet M. "When Toxic Chemicals Pollute Residential Environments: The Cultural Meanings of Home and Homeownership." *Human Organization* 48(4):313–324, 1989; Gans, Herbert J. *Middle American Individualism: The Future of Liberal Democracy*. New York: The Free Press, 1988; Howell, Sandra C. "Home: A Source of Meaning in Elders' Lives," *Generations* 9, no. 3: 58–60, 1985; Kron, Joan. *Home Psych: The Social Psychology of Home and Decoration*. New York: Clarkson N. Potter, Inc./Crown Publishers, 1997.

2 Home symbolizes "security" in its deepest sense. See Beyer, Glenn H. *Housing and Society*. London: Collier-Macmillan, Ltd., 1969; Chapin, F. Stuart.. "New Methods of Sociological Research on Housing Problems," *Sociological Research on Housing Problems*, 1946.

3 Home communicates our identity to others and reflects how people view themselves. See Baumeister, Roy F. *Identity: Cultural Change and the Struggle for Self*. New York: Oxford University Press, 1986.

4 Lawlor, Anthony, with photographs by Rick Donhauser. *A Home for the Soul*. New York: Clarkson Potter Publishers, 1997.

6

FAMILY, FRIENDS, AND COMMUNITIES—THE SOCIAL FACTOR

My home is not a place, it is people.

—Lois McMaster Bujold

People. Your everyday life is bound up with the lives of many other people—family members, friends, neighbors, acquaintances, colleagues, co-workers, service people, and others. As you work, date and mate, care for your health, educate yourself or your kids, get around, help older parents, run errands, shop, volunteer, save and invest, your life is full of social interactions that spice up your day-to-day activities. Some of your encounters with other people—and often a lot of them—happen in and around your home and your neighborhood.

For the sake of simplicity, we have assumed that when it comes to decision-making, there are four basic areas into which everything that matters to you can be categorized and explored. The previous chapter deals with the first of these areas, your inner life or "Personal Factors." Now, we move into the area of social interactions, the "Social Factors" or S Factor, which influences your housing choices. Although known for our independent spirit and "individualism," Americans are social beings with strong family ties and many intertwining networks of friends and acquaintances. Perhaps nothing brings this out more clearly than when we make housing choices.

Your "S Factor" is all about the other people in your life. If you live alone, enjoy your solitude, or seldom if ever entertain family or friends at home, you are likely to have a low "S" score. If you score a high "S," chances are that you live an interactive lifestyle. You like to help others, you enjoy the company of family and friends at home, and you want to put down roots in a neighborhood or community that feels right. In either case, home is where most of us experience not only the intimate aspects of our personal development, but also the most important social interactions that occur during the course of our lives. The "S" Factor intersects with housing decision-making in two important ways:

- It reflects the amount and type of social activity you need and want in your daily life at home.

- It highlights your compatibility with the "S" (social) needs and values of the others with whom you live and interact.

Relationship problems often occur because of a mismatch among roommates, housemates, partners, spouses, and other family members on the critical "S" scale. To learn what this indicator means to you as you attempt to establish an ideal home life, review the historical housing relationships in your life. Then, become familiar with your present social needs and values at home. Be honest. Make sure you understand what works for you, what doesn't, and why. Here are some things to consider:

- **Your living habits:** Are you a night owl or a morning person, are you messy or neat, and do you like the thermostat up or down?

- **Your housing finances:** Do you share costs, pay bills, or provide for others? Are you generous with household expenditures and clear about your joint budgeting? Do you feel anxious, or perhaps resentful, because you pay too much of the share of costs and are too timid to bring it up?

- **Your social plans:** Are you a social planner, or do you drag friends home or invite them over on the spur of the moment?

- **Other personal habits:** Do you share information or keep to yourself, come and go as you please or check in with others, arrive late for dinner, help with the dishes, and take out the garbage?

Your Unique Housing Sociology

In this part of your housing decision analysis, examine only your social needs and values informed by your unique housing history. Later, you can compare them with significant others; however, for now, only those beliefs, attitudes, feelings, and experiences that underlie your own social needs and values should concern you. Consider the following:

- Do you have a strong need for peace and quiet at home?

- Do you love the hustle and bustle of people around you and the sounds of laughter and spontaneous play?

- When the doorbell unexpectedly rings, do you run to hide or are you open and curious about who might be dropping by?

Recall Martha's experience in Chapter 2, "Your Home and Your Life." As a child, her parents had an "open-door policy" at home. Friends, relatives, neighbors, and acquaintances were equally welcome to visit at any time. Martha's childhood provided her no privacy, peace or quiet, and today, she regards home as her private sanctuary. Although she is a generous host and entertains family and friends frequently, Martha is protected from spontaneous intrusion by a doorman, an intercom, and caller ID. Woe to anyone who might slip through this protective system.

Your social life consists of your family (regardless of how you define family), friends, and the members of your "communities of interest[1]." Understanding more about your housing history can be useful in any area in which you interact with family members, friends, and individuals from your affiliated social groups. Whether you live alone, with roommates, housemates, or with one or many family members, your relationship preferences, needs, and values are reflected in your housing choices. Together they make up your lifestyle, or your particular pattern of living.

Evelyn Lewis and Carolyn Turner, authors of *Housing Decisions,*[2] capture the array of living patterns we refer to as our "lifestyle." Each of us has a certain lifestyle. A lifestyle can take many forms and is influenced by our social needs and values, our age and life stage, our experiences, personality, and goals. Most of all, it is influenced—or not—by our relationship to the other people in our lives:

- **Individualistic Lifestyle:** When you prefer to "go your own way and do your own thing," you have an individualistic lifestyle. You are unconcerned about what others think about your choices and simply want to follow your inner desires and feelings.

- **Supportive Lifestyle:** If your cultural preferences or desires are rooted in shared living or you just like helping others, your home could be shared by family members or others. You might take in boarders or value living with another unrelated family.

- **Basic Lifestyle:** If you and your family choose to—or must— live simply without the array of modern conveniences that others may take for granted, you have a basic lifestyle. People who are concerned about the effects of pollution and the depletion of natural resources often try this way of life. Others live simply because of financial constraints or because they prefer to accumulate wealth in investments other than their housing.

- **Community Lifestyle:** You might enjoy group activities or share common goals that bring you together frequently with many others. Community living arrangements are often preferred by people who have similar interests, hobbies, or share certain life stages.

- **Influential Lifestyle:** If you like to entertain, to influence others, are motivated to lead and be active in several social organizations, you have an influential lifestyle. Your housing will allow you to devote your time and energy to the activities that are important to you.

Your housing history, habits, and cultural preferences are rooted in your social relationships. These in turn, are reflected in your housing choices. Whether you choose to live alone or with members of several generations or other family members, you have a distinct lifestyle. It is an extension of who you are and an example of how you choose to express yourself through your home.

Home and Family Life

How interrelated are home and family in your life? When you look at a prospective home, do you picture space for family gatherings? Is the quality of local schools your number one concern? Are you motivated by a strong inner need to "provide" a home for your family members? Is your priority to live closer to your children or grandchildren? Home and family are so intimately and thoroughly interrelated that for many people, this ideal or "supportive lifestyle" is often taken for granted.

Clay, a research assistant in our office, took a few days off last summer to find housing for the coming semester. When he returned, I asked him how he made his decision. "I saw three apartments," he told me, "and I rented the one closest to the university." Clay insisted that his on-the-spot choice had been based solely on its proximity to campus, but I pressed for more details. Had he pictured his girlfriend in each of the apartments for an overnight stay? Was there bunking-in room for family members when they came for a visit? Clay soon became aware of the social aspects of his life that, although only half consciously, he considered when he selected the "right apartment." Although distance to campus was indeed a priority, it turned out that the other two choices were just as convenient in terms of location. Clay chose the apartment because it had the best layout for work and for accommodating company.

Like Clay, many of us take the social aspects of home as a given, even as we unconsciously use them to make decisions. For others, fulfilling family needs and values is our highest priority. In the context of stable and satisfying family relationships, home takes on special significance. Because family love is not easily defined or measured, we might look for something clear and tangible that conveys devotion to family. "Providing a home" does this for some of us. When Sonny recently bought his first house, he was motivated to provide a home that his family would own. He also wanted to fulfill an unmet childhood need in his own life.

Sonny is a go-getter. The owner of a growing computer-based business, he is savvy about the fast-paced world of the Internet, and he knows how to negotiate and close a deal. But his home is not about financial know-how or investment value. Sonny likes to say that "it is all about his family." When he was a child, Sonny's parents did not own their home. Uncertain that they could manage the expense, they kept putting off buying until it was too late for him. Sonny was off to college and to a new phase of his life, but he didn't forget this void in his childhood. "When I looked at my parent's experience, I thought that I should go for it—the sooner, the better for the family."

Sonny and his wife Mimi love their new suburban Chicago location, which is only 20 minutes from Sonny's place of employment. Most of his neighbors are at the same stage of life and several of the women are stay-at-home moms like Mimi. "They all have kids who are about the same age. When we moved here, there were four young babies in seven houses on our cul-de-sac and we had one of them." Mimi also wanted a place where the kids could play and where there were good schools." Now expecting another child, Sonny says he is growing both his business and the family. Sonny and Mimi make extra payments on their mortgage to get the house paid off earlier, so that "my kids will always have a home they can call their own." Sonny and Mimi believe they will live in the house a long time because they haven't used up all the space yet. "The basement is available to expand into. We feel really at home here. It's the best place to be with our family."

Unlike Sonny, some people are not as secure about family ties. Despite images of the family as a warm fuzzy group in which people feel secure, some family relationships are ambiguous, unequal, unsteady, uncertain, and even untrustworthy. Long into adulthood, some question whether their parents truly love them. And parents too may feel unloved because their adult children seem neglectful or indifferent.[3] Because society provides few explicit conventions for dealing with family relationships in the home, people can get stuck in childhood patterns. Some develop lifestyle choices that are similar to (or deliberately opposite of) those experienced as children. Until we develop adult lifestyles that we value, we usually mimic or reject aspects of our own social past without examining the origin of them.

The lack of explicit guidelines and the reluctance of many families to discuss issues of interdependence can lead to expectations for family relationships that surpass what we expect from others—even close friends. When these expectations are disappointed, we can be devastated and turn our back altogether on family members.[4]

Home, Children, and "Family Mergers"

When I was about six, I went with my mother on a warm sunny day to see a house that was under construction. Together, we climbed over foundation walls to the home's future dining room area and pretended to have tea. We also explored other rooms-to-be, and I "saw" my future bedroom. Time passed—it seemed like a lot of time to me—but we didn't move to my dream house. When I finally asked my mother about moving, my question surprised her. Early on, she had decided that the house was unaffordable, but she either forgot or thought it unimportant to share this decision with me.

It's always a good idea to note the impressions and feelings of your children—even very young ones—and to communicate and encourage dialogue with them when making plans to move. Sharing your moving intentions and the decision-making process is especially critical if you plan a "family merger." Shifting gears from single parenting to life as a merged family can be tricky. If your plans also involve a move to a new location, you might find it especially helpful to treat the upcoming move as an interim step on the way to encouraging communication among all family members.

Good family moves require group planning and decision-making strategies that leave no one out. There are many problems to solve, and every problem presents an opportunity for all family members to share the decision process. First, spread the problems among family members, and then support and help children to solve them. Being included in the decision-making process through shared problem-solving teaches kids that they matter to their parents. When the process is supported and creative, it can transcend the move itself and diffuse the tension kids might otherwise keep inside. Following are examples of the concerns most kids who have to move might need to share with you:

"Where will I go to school?"

"Will I have my own room?"

"Who will pack little Jerry's room?"

"How will we be able to pay the movers?"

"What do we do about helping Reggie deal with the pain of leaving his friends?"

"What will we do about meals after the kitchen is all packed up?"

"How will I meet new friends?"

We often underrate the concerns of children. Amber was an army brat and remembers asking if she would ever see her friends again. She was also worried about joining new sports teams because it seemed as though she was always moving in mid-season. Children are concerned about making new friends and being liked wherever they go. This is important to keep in mind, especially when you live an individualistic lifestyle yourself.

A good move doesn't signal that all will be stable and rosy in coming days. It won't. However, the focus must be on creating positive solutions together, so that the family can develop a blueprint for future communication and problem-solving.

Home and Friendships

A photograph hangs above my desk at home. When I need a break, or I'm stuck for a particular way of phrasing a thought, I look at the photo. It is a picture of my friends and me, which was taken on a trip to Asia a few years ago. It reminds me of that trip and the many other good times we have shared since we were teenagers. Those friendships are still a source of support and comfort today. I receive email messages from friends with jokes that make me laugh out loud, welcome words of inspiration, or news of current events I might have otherwise missed. Friends enrich our good times and carry us through difficult periods. Friendship ties can also grow among family members. They strengthen family relationships and outlast life changes, disagreements, competition, and separation.

Bonds between friends often take root at home or in the surrounding neighborhood. They are also formed in homes away from home, such as at boarding school, a college dorm, or a Quonset hut. Although home might be a setting where new friendships are formed and old friendships deepen and grow, friendship needs and values vary. Difficulties can and do arise when couples hold different views about nurturing social ties at home. Consider the case of Chester and Gwen, whose different "S" values clarified the trouble they had finding their ideal home.

Chester and Gwen planned a mid-life wedding and began looking for a home in which to settle. Gwen's life had been socially active. She enjoyed the casual visits of neighbors and co-workers who dropped by, the overnight visits of relatives and friends, spontaneous dinner parties, and two or three large gatherings a year. Chester had an active business life, but he preferred solitude and privacy at home. He maintained a few close friendships, but he rarely saw his friends because they lived in other geographic areas. When they did come to town, Chester usually met his friends at a local restaurant or bar.

Chester and Gwen's whirlwind courtship had included dinners for two, trips abroad, weekends out of town, and a few small gatherings, but the chasm between Gwen and Chester's social values didn't show up until they started the search for a new home. Gwen was attracted to homes that had plenty of room for frequent guests and social gatherings. Chester wanted a home office, a separate library, and spaces outfitted for private living. Until they came to grips with the depth of their differences, as shown by their "S" scores (Chester's was a 2, whereas Gwen scored a 9), the house-hunting trips were not pleasant.

Because their housing decision problem highlighted serious differences in their social support needs and values, Chester and Gwen had to confront their individual visions of their future life together, and they had to compromise. Gwen stopped extending her spontaneous invitations and planned fewer social engagements at home. Chester learned to tolerate and eventually to welcome and cherish Gwen's large circle of friends. As with all such differences between couples who live together, cherished values must be respected and accommodated. They may never be negotiated away.

Home and Community

We tend to think of "neighborhood" when we speak about "community," but the two concepts are not necessarily linked together. Members of communities share interests and have at least one aspect of their lives in common. On occasion they also share geographic proximity. For Sonny and his family, the neighborhood in which they live is also a "community" because families who live there share a life stage and family interests. Other communities—and sometimes the neighborhoods within them—are populated by people who share religious beliefs, hobbies, political concerns, educational interests, or the same recreational pursuits.

If you scored high on the "S Factor," you are likely to enjoy group activities, and you can prefer planned communities, condominium living, or perhaps even a community lifestyle. Communities vary widely. They can be large, small, or they might even consist of one house or another type of dwelling unit. Members can differ in age, sex, and background because their common interests are the glue that holds them together. Some communities are organized around a life stage, such as retirement communities. The success of retirement communities—whether they are formally planned or spring up in areas that attract older adults—reflect the satisfaction we feel with living arrangements that accommodate like-minded people. Many retirees have a great deal of leisure time and enjoy similar interests, hobbies, and other planned leisure activities. People often seek to live in an established community where they can feel more at home.

Cindy grew up in Philadelphia and went to college in Atlanta. After college, she was recruited by a Washington, D.C. firm, so she started to look for a home located near her new job. Cindy intended to put down roots—at least for a while—and she excelled at the public relations position for which she had trained. She loved her job and the frequent travel that it required. However, finding the right home was another matter, although she continued to look in the D.C. area. "I felt I could really stay there, live there, and feel good about my circle of friends and my job. Every Saturday morning I went out with a real estate guy. I met him at the office for several months." Cindy finally found a place and made an offer, but after she signed the contract she said, "I almost freaked out. I got the only migraine I've ever had in my life. I just freaked out and knew I couldn't go through with it."

"It was the permanence of staying there that hit me. I wasn't ready to make Washington, D.C. my home, and I felt trapped." In a short time, Cindy found another job that took her back to her native Philadelphia and to the community where she felt she belonged. "I'm Jewish," she said, "and I ultimately want to meet a Jewish guy, so that was a factor in my return to Philadelphia. I wanted a community where I could increase my opportunities to meet someone of my religion. I also wanted to be closer to my family." Cindy easily chose a townhouse in a Philadelphia suburb where she now says she feels "completely at home."

The concept of community is so important and strong that career members of the military and their families often thrive in their assigned homes for decades. A retired commander told me that in his 30-year Navy career he had lived in 16 homes, not counting temporary lodging. "The style, cost, and location of my housing was not as important as making the best of the situation in which I found myself. As long as my family's needs were met, the house itself made little difference."

For Cindy the emotional pull toward community was very strong, but it took the near-purchase of the wrong house for her to recognize her own social needs and values. Some people are not as lucky as Cindy and never confront the social voids in their life. Others push down the feelings that well up inside them when a housing decision is going wrong. "They'll just make the best of it," they think, or "everything will turn out all right in the end." This is not always the case. People can feel estranged from their homes. They can become disaffected and unfulfilled, and their feelings can grow beyond their housing to include their community, society, and potentially even themselves.

Examine your social needs and values carefully as you look for your next home. Compare them with important other people in your life. Evaluate the all-important "S Factor," and then honor it. You might also find this process useful when interpreting the world around you. It can be useful in your day-to-day contacts with authority figures, colleagues, co-workers, salespeople, service workers, and others to whom you send social messages and from whom you receive them. The competition or cooperation of racial, ethnic, cultural, and political groups almost always involves a struggle for ownership of various forms of property.

End Notes

1   To the extent that individual values are shared, people are able to fit together "in community," meeting the needs of others while fulfilling one's own needs. David M. Chavis, James H. Hogge, David W. McMillan, and Abraham Wandersman's "Sense of Community Through Brunswick's Lens: A First Look" presents an example. You can find this article in the *Journal of Community Psychology,* 1986: 14:24-40.

2   Lewis, Evelyn L. and Carolyn S. Turner. *Housing Decisions.* Tinley Park, Illinois: The Goodheart-Willcox Company, Inc., 2000. These two professors have written the ultimate textbook for understanding the array of decisions people face about home and housing. It is especially useful for anyone thinking of remodeling or redecorating a home.

3   Millman, Marcia, *Warm Hearts and Cold Cash.* New York: The Free Press, 1991.

4   Ibid.

7

FEELING "AT HOME"— THE TANGIBLE FACTOR

Most homebuyers, indeed most people, know when they feel comfortable, but they do not always know or cannot say...why.

—Carolyn Janik

So you have moved through the personal and relationship areas of your housing profile. Now it is time to look at the physical aspects of your potential home. Piece of cake. You want a brick townhouse with three bedrooms, two baths, backyard, garage, and family room with an easy commute. "That's about it," you tell your new agent. What you do not tell the agent is that you have already seen many brick townhouses with three bedrooms, two baths, backyard, garage, and family room in convenient neighborhoods. But you have not seen one that you really liked.

At play here is the third, and most obvious, area that influences your housing decisions, the "Tangible Factors," the heart and soul of your housing transaction.

The T Factor is the physical dwelling and its surroundings—the sights, sounds, smells, and feel of the home you seek. It includes the distance to your work, the quality of nearby learning centers, nature, culture, parks, and transportation. It is the roominess of the place, the landscaping, the corner store, the fabulous kitchen, the bus stop at the corner, the front porch with a view. Your T Factor is all this and more—or less—depending on how strongly you view the physical and environmental aspects of the housing you seek.

Even more than the other dimensions of your housing value system, your T Factor can surprise you—and possibly even become your undoing. You may "know" what type of home you are looking for, but then your ideas keep changing. That picture of your ideal home becomes vague or blurs as you tour one home after another. Or the impact of your T Factor can hit you like love at first sight. Just when you have found your perfect brick townhouse, you are suddenly seduced by a white-frame cottage with one bathroom, no family room, and no garage on three acres in the woods.

High- and Low-Scoring T Factors

If you have scored high on the T Factor, you are aware of your physical surroundings. You like function and comfort, but also style and beauty to the extent you can afford it. When you first move in, home may be your chief occupation until you feel settled. You will obsess if something is "missing," "all wrong," or "out of place." You will fuss, move things around, and then move them around again the next day. When the place feels right, life can begin again, but until it does, feathering your new nest may be your major focus. Oddly, you can have trouble envisioning exactly how to decorate your home after you have it. But that's all right, as long as there are home magazines, "makeover artists," decorators, talented friends, Home Depot, and Loews to help.

A low T score may signal that home is where you bunk in, watch ESPN, store your stuff, unwind briefly and go off again, play with the kids and help out with homework, surf the Internet, or just putter around. Either you have a sixth sense about decorating so everything comes together quickly without much effort, or you care little about décor. It is not that the physical aspects of home are unimportant to you. They are important. It is just that, well, you will get around to fixing up your home when the spirit moves you. There are so many other things to do.

Whether your T Factor is high or low, or somewhere in between, this critical decision dimension springs, consciously or unconsciously, from your housing history, and it acts in concert with your personal and social factors. By awakening your tangible housing preferences, you will be better prepared to collect, analyze, and comprehend all the relevant facts about your next home. You will be more motivated to learn exactly what you are getting in terms of structural soundness, neighborhood, setting, size, age, convenience, and the all-important sensory comfort potential of your new home and its surroundings.

Be forewarned! The more attracted you are to a prospective home, the more "in love" you are with it, the less you will want to pursue these checks and safeguards. You will tend to overlook flaws and clues, leaving them unchallenged in the heat of your contract negotiations. If you have been looking for a brick townhouse in an ideal location and suddenly fall in love with that frame cottage in the woods (or a houseboat, or farm, or a condo in the Bahamas), you owe yourself—and the loved ones who may be looking on—some sort of explanation. Here are three possible reasons for a sudden ardent attraction to a prospective home that seems out of line with your current lifestyle or your up-until-a-moment-ago preferences:

1. The home signals a return to a childhood need that you may or may not decide to indulge after you discover its source and current importance.

2. The home symbolizes some desired change in the way you are living that you may not be aware of. Or, if you are aware of it, you have yet to seriously address and resolve it.

3. The home is an out and out "turn on." You simply love an adventure. But you will need to assess the consequences of any serious change in homestyle—especially if significant others are involved.

As with any physical attraction, you hope it will lead to a great relationship. But keeping your head in the heat of passion can save you anguish later. Here's to passion, but not blind passion.

More Housing Psychology

We already discussed the differences between housing values and housing needs. Now it is time to add the two other components of everyone's housing psychology, our housing wants and housing shoulds, because they most often interject themselves when we are attracted to, or struggling with a decision about, a particular home. Trying to fulfill and balance these twin trouble-makers can sabotage our finest decision-making efforts. At best, they are barometers that enable us to measure our progress (or lack of it) throughout the housing-decision process. At worst, they subvert our best intentions and get in the way of a good housing choice. Here's why.

A housing want is a "must-have" drive to possess something tangible, a sort of lusting after the object of our desire. Like its sexual relative, lusting after a home is an instinct from somewhere primal—an animal-like impulse to act with little or no conscious thought of the consequences. When a housing want is thwarted, watch for tell-tale pouting or a fit of temper to follow, which is unlike the real deprivation that follows an unmet housing need.

Housing Psychology Recap

Housing values—Standards that guide our desires and choices as responsible adults.

Housing needs—Shelter from the elements and physical safety. Needs also result from unresolved childhood experiences.

Housing wants—Impulses to act without regard for the consequences.

Housing shoulds—Someone else's standard imposed upon us as though it were our own.

The ubiquitous housing should is the final component of our housing-decision psychology. Whereas a *housing value* is a principle or standard we embrace as our own, a *housing should* is someone else's standard imposed upon us as though it were our own. When we fail to obtain something we value, we are disappointed and can even feel ashamed; when we fail to live up to what someone else believes we should do or have, we feel guilty. Be aware that we can internalize someone else's value as our own when it really is not. The clue is always that seriously guilty feeling about not living up to a standard someone else is setting for us. Watch out for guilt. It does not belong anywhere in your housing decision making. The truth is that decision making is tricky. If it weren't, there would not be whole academic disciplines devoted to the study of decision making. Nor would whole research departments working in and for multinational corporations be trying to guess how we are likely to decide. The more you can increase your awareness of the housing values, needs, wants, and shoulds in your housing psychology, the more you will increase your actual housing options.

Good decisions are value-driven, and our housing profile is teaching us to recognize exactly what it is we value about the homes we choose. But as you have been learning, values are only one component of our housing-decision psychology. The other three components are our housing needs, wants, and shoulds. Our job as decision makers is to distinguish our values from the other three components of our housing psychology and to learn to favor our values. In other words, we are the executive director of our own decision process—we choose among our values, needs, wants, and shoulds every time we make an important decision. Our job, then, is to go with our values to the extent we possibly can. In Chapters 8, "The Real Deal About Finances—The Money Factor," and 10, "Whether to Move and When to Move," later in Part Two, "Finding Solutions that Work for You," you will learn exactly how to apply your unique housing profile (your housing value system) to the actual decisions that you are most likely to confront.

Meanwhile, if you are mired in love-sick indecision or are having other trouble making a housing choice, ask yourself the following questions:

1. What is my attraction to this home (desire to move, and so on) based upon?

   a. A cherished value

   b. A housing need

   c. A want

   d. A should

2. If I let go of my attraction to this home, (desire to move, and so on), what will happen?

   a. I will feel very disappointed. (If so, you value it.)

   b. I will experience real anxiety and deprivation. (If so, you need it.)

   c. I will feel anger and frustration. (If so, you want it.)

   d. I will feel guilty. (If so, someone else thinks you should want, need, or value it.)

We return to the problem of letting go of inappropriate attractions in later chapters, but for now it is important to pursue the meaning and usefulness of the ever-critical T Factor.

T Factor Dimensions: Physical and Environmental Comfort

Is your picture-perfect home a sprawling ranch, a row house in the city, or a vine-covered cottage? Do you love backyard barbeques and a basketball hoop over the garage door? Do you value a home with lots of space, or is a carefree condo the home of your dreams? Are you aware of your "natural environment," the place—city, suburbs, country, north, south, east or west—you feel most comfortable? Do you long for the health benefits of a certain climate? Have you even thought about the housing features you value most, or do you look at homes in an "I'll-know-it-when-I-see-it" frame of mind?

Your T Factor consists of those physical and environmental aspects of your housing where you are likely to feel most comfortable or to which you are irresistibly drawn, including the following:

- The house itself

- The living room where your easy chair can fit by the fireplace

- The built-in kitchen nook where you can have tea with friends or watch the soaps in the afternoon

- The sun, sand, and sea, or anywhere else you feel most healthy and alive

- The view from an upstairs window

- The great-looking Jacuzzi for two

- The gardens and terraces

- The neighborhood, because your folks live just down the street

Your T Factor, just as all of the deciding factors in your housing profile, concerns only you. You will want to do some hard thinking about the physical and environmental features of homes you have lived in during your lifetime. The task is to identify and explore your unique values and needs when it comes to the tangible housing features you find attractive. Later it will be important to learn whether the features you most care about match those of your significant others. If they do, great. If they do not, you will soon be able to recognize mutually held values and to make trade-offs that can facilitate all of your future shared housing decisions.

The Physical Comforts of Home

A real estate agent was helping a client find a new home. She asked him when he had decided his current home was inadequate. "When my girlfriend told me it was," he said. The client's shift in perceived satisfaction followed the suggestion that his home was somehow lacking. Such seeds of discontent can be planted by a visit to someone else's home, an advertisement, a decorating magazine, an inadvertent comment by a visitor, a housing makeover seen on TV, or a drive through an up-and-coming neighborhood. Every homebuilder and real estate professional knows that the power of suggestion can trigger an itch to start looking for your next home. We tell ourselves that our housing no longer suits us or that we want a change of scenery. We look at our present surroundings and begin to feel discontent.

We will feel uncomfortable over some tangible condition at home: It is too drafty, requires too much maintenance, has too many stairs to climb, lacks enough space, is poorly located, or it has any number of other flaws that cause us actual discomfort. This tantalizing dance of perceived inadequacy and perceived physical discomfort, whichever may come first, affects us all. Sooner or later, these perceptions merge and reinforce each other. They spur us on to relieve our discomfort and to make our next housing decision.

We will decide to find a different home, make needed repairs, remodel, redecorate, buy a second home, or move to keep up with the Joneses. We may even decide to do nothing, because the time is not right, money is tight, or any number of other good reasons. Recall that a smart housing decision requires us to do the following:

1.   Identify the cause or causes of our discomfort.

2.   Approach our decisions so that we avoid costly mistakes.

In light of these guidelines, consider the housing decision made by Miriam and Tony, whom you met in an earlier chapter, and who learned they would be having twins. Space was already tight with three other children under 10-years-old, and they became alarmed over the adequacy of their present home. They purchased a home with two additional bedrooms—one for the twins and one for Miriam's mom, Doris, who volunteered to help out after the babies were born. Although they correctly identified lack of needed space as the source of their discomfort, Miriam and Tony's decision approach turned out to be costly and ineffective.

In their panic over the adequacy of their previous home, Miriam and Tony rushed to purchase another home. Understandably, they wanted to feel settled before the arrival of the twins, but they approached their housing decision with anxiety and little long-range planning. Their new house has larger rooms, but it is drafty and expensive to heat and cool. There are more bedrooms, but no more bathrooms than they had before. The home has no flexible "public space" like the family room in their former home, which results in constant messes in the children's rooms and little privacy for the adults. Their most serious problem, however, is that the new home is located in a different school district. They have been trying to obtain permission for the kids to attend their old schools, but last I knew, that permission had not been granted.

The root of their troubles are the shoulds that Miriam imposed upon Tony. When she first saw the old frame house with a wraparound front porch, she "knew" it was right for the family. It sat on a hill, had the fenced yard she wanted, and it had two, not just one, additional bedrooms. Miriam fell instantly in love with the charm of the place and pressured Tony to "love" it too. In his zeal to get the house for Miriam, Tony failed to check the school district boundary or get a house inspection. They settled in 60 days and moved the family to their new home. Six months later, Doris left her rented apartment and moved in with the family "permanently." Although this gives Miriam and Tony the help they need and appreciate, the family's housing woes are anything but resolved. In addition to the added expense and discomfort, they must now make do with the space they have, deal with the school situation, and hope for the best. "It is unrealistic," Tony told me regretfully, "to think about buying another home in the foreseeable future. I really wish we'd been more patient about moving." What Tony is really saying is "I wish I hadn't bought into Miriam's housing value system and neglected my own values to please her."

A recent article by Rebecca Kahlenberg in the *Washington Post*[1] speculates that a house purchase can turn into a home wrecker. "When it comes to buying, renovating, or decorating a house, many couples young and old have more conflict than common ground," writes Kahlenberg. Contrasting housing values are a major source of upset for many couples. More often than not, one of the two will give in to avoid open warfare, but this is not a lasting solution, as demonstrated in Miriam and Tony's experience. Burying one's feelings, desires, values, and needs is no better than burying the hatchet without resolving the underlying conflict. Regret is likely to set in along with resentment that can build and harm the relationship itself.

Your housing history includes the way you were brought up and your cultural background. "British people absolutely want the toilet in a separate room from the sink, whereas Americans typically do not," observes architect Robert Cole in the *Washington Post* article. Accepting such differences lies at the heart of understanding your housing history and preferences from your housing profile. And what about a partner who initially does not want a tangible feature but turns out to love it later—something I suspect Tony will not do? Chapter 9 deals more extensively with how to handle couple disharmony in any of your pending or future real estate transactions. First, however, it is essential to know and understand exactly what it is that *you* really need and value in your home.

Environmental Comfort

Our environment, very simply, consists of all that surrounds us and affects our lives. It is the climate, the topography, the scenes we see, the sounds we hear, the safety we feel, the air we breathe, the water we drink, and many other conditions that we encounter every day in our neighborhoods, communities, towns, cities, and nation. We often take these conditions for granted and can easily get used to disagreeable, even unsafe conditions, without noticing. When we are in tune with our environment, however, we are most comfortable. Beth's story illustrates one of many ways we can feel "in sync" with our home environment.

Beth was entranced by a city street scene. In a hurry, she had taken a shortcut through a neighborhood she had not seen before. It was springtime in Washington, D.C., and she happened upon a two-block street lined with old trees and two-story row houses. Stippled sunlight played on tiny yards full of pink and white azaleas in full bloom. Suddenly, time didn't matter. Beth double-parked, got out of her car, and stood on the sidewalk looking around and smelling the spring fragrance. She wished with all of her might that she could live in a house—any house—on that street. She heard city sounds a block or so away and realized that she could walk to work or take the bus on mornings if she were running late.

When Beth returned to her rented suburban apartment, she could not get that street scene out of her mind. For days it lingered. Beth realized that she "belonged in the city" and started scouring "For Rent" ads in the newspaper. Incredibly, she found a house on that very street and rented it with an option to buy. Two years later, with a lot of help, she bought her home and became a first-time homeowner. When a job transfer took her to New York several years later, she left her beloved city neighborhood and home. Even now, she still cherishes the memories of her years there.

Beth's brief stopover in what later became her neighborhood clearly touched a nerve. It brought her face to face with some important lessons about herself. Significantly, Beth—now a single mom—had grown up in similar city locations. The tree-lined street, the flowers, row houses, and city sounds were familiar and welcoming. Although she had not acknowledged her discomfort, she felt out of place in her suburban location. The apartment complex housed mostly small families, some stay-at-home moms, but few single parents of very young children. After her unscheduled visit, Beth increasingly longed for the vitality, convenience, familiarity, and relative anonymity of an urban environment. Her move to the city achieved all that she hoped for and more. By carefully analyzing her instantaneous "heart connection" to two city blocks, she realized her true housing values. She was able to change her life and achieve real joy in urban living—something she did not even know she desired before her detour on that beautiful spring day. In the next chapter, we take a look at how Beth handled the "Money Factors" of this move and her ultimate purchase, but for now we can leave Beth, knowing that she was secure and happy in her "native" environment.

Dealing with Being Uprooted

What happens when someone is wrenched from his or her home, or voluntarily leaves an area or country because of some pressure or changed set of conditions? This situation is quite common and happens to nearly everyone at some point in life. It has happened to everyone who ever left home and to every immigrant who had the need and the courage to seek a better life. It can occur because of a job transfer, a new marriage or partnership, college or university education, financial upheaval, illness or frailty, or when a government agency condemns or "takes" your property.

Cynthia left home to join her new husband in another city. For nearly three years, she revisited her old home every chance she got. She often complained about having moved, and she grieved openly for the familiar places of her childhood and youth that she was sorely missing. The love and patient understanding of her husband, a great new job, two young sons in just a few years, plenty of social support, new communities of interest, and her desire to make a beautiful home for herself and her family slowly but surely replaced the old homestead. Cynthia is now a "native" in her new surroundings and so are her children, who have never known the home Cynthia left behind.

Although the tangible dimensions of your housing choices are clearly important, as they were for Cynthia, they do not exist in a vacuum, but in concert with the other deciding factors that make up your unique housing profile.[2] The personal and social factors, and the Money Factor, as you will soon see, eased the way for Cynthia to settle down comfortably at long last in her new home and her entirely new surroundings.

Points to Ponder

Your Tangible (T) Factors include the following:

- Physical comfort with all of the features in a home
- Environmental comfort with all of the features that surround a home

If you want to avoid a decision that could lead you to buy or rent a housing lemon, you must know and understand your housing psychology. Be alert to the differences between and among the following:

- Cherished housing values

- Basic or leftover childhood housing needs

- Stubborn housing wants

- Somebody else's housing shoulds

End Notes

1 Kahlenberg, Rebecca R. "He Loves It, She Loves It Not," *The Washington Post*, Real Estate, Section F, July 10, 2004.

2 In their classic 1976 study, *Social Indicators of Well-Being: Americans' Perceptions of Life Quality,* authors Frank M. Andrews and Stephen B. Withey (New York: Plenum Press) confirmed the idea that people can and do divide their lives up into domains that, although not isolated, are separate enough to be identified and evaluated as distinguishable parts of life. Housing satisfaction is both a domain of subjective well-being within the quality of life (QOL) research tradition and a tradition within the housing field that is aligned with housing preference and residential mobility research. In QOL research, satisfaction with neighborhood, community, and environment is held in common.

8

THE REAL DEAL ABOUT FINANCES—THE MONEY FACTOR

When it comes to money…what we have begins with what we think.

—Suze Orman

Buying or renting a home, trading up or down, remodeling, refinancing, or investing in a second home is all about cost and affordability, right? Absolutely yes and no! But aren't price, monthly payment, interest rate, and tax consequences the *key* decision factors in any housing transaction you undertake? Of course they are, and no, not as often as you might think. Confusing? Yes, but so is the way many people go about making financial decisions. Although it is true that your finances inevitably constrain, shape, and facilitate your housing transactions, *the importance you attach to your finances in general will show up as clearly as your fingerprints on the homes you are likely to choose.*

"Buyers are liars," is an old saying among real estate professionals. Why? Because many buyers insist that the upper limit they have just given their agent is fixed and unchangeable. Then they will buy a home that exceeds their budgeted price. This tendency gives agents a large headache, especially if they have lost the sale to another agent who was not aware of, or ignored, the buyer's limit. But buyers usually are not lying—to themselves maybe, but not to their agents. What this saying really suggests is that people often jump into the marketplace with little awareness of their underlying financial needs and values, so perceived financial constraints are not always valid. If this feels familiar, be aware that your tendency to rush ahead without adequate preparation can lead to even more serious complications. Understanding how your needs and values on the personal, social, and tangible factors inevitably intersect with the ever-present M Factor might very well spare you financial grief later.

In previous chapters, you examined the two important human relationship areas that figure into all of your housing decisions: Personal Factors and Social Factors. You have also reflected on how Tangible Factors affect your actual housing selections. The fourth and last area in your values system that influences all of your housing decisions is your relationship to the "Money Factors" in your life. Your M Factor not only reflects your attitudes and beliefs about money, but also your approach to personal financial management. Your housing history also makes its appearance in connection with the critical M Factor and will either show up as the "money baggage" or the "money savvy" you bring with you to all of your housing transactions.[1]

Some people try hard to ignore or circumvent altogether the importance of money issues. They believe if they work hard and say their prayers, the money will follow. Others get knotted up about money because "money" is about so much more than dollars and cents. It ties into our conscious or unconscious needs for love, independence, power, security, control, and self-worth. But one thing is certain. Money is ever present and ever changing in all of our lives, and we must make our peace with it, especially where our housing is concerned. That means setting aside any money baggage you still carry, so you can lighten your load as you approach housing decisions. It means talking about money even though that makes you uncomfortable. It means honoring the money concerns of others who will be moving with you. It means keeping your head and suspending money emotions that can spoil not just your housing search, but also your ability to negotiate wisely and well. It means overcoming resistance to doing at least *some* financial planning. Finally, it means anticipating any possible housing losses so that you can adequately protect against them to the extent you can.

If you are prone to anxiety about your finances, you may feel the sheer enormity of your pending housing decision as almost unbearable. If, on the other hand, you are pretty comfortable with money issues, you will take the financing part of your housing transactions in stride. Everyone else will fall somewhere in between these two extremes. To learn what the M Factor means to you in your housing values system, look for clues in your own housing history as you review your money values and needs in connection with your future home.

Your Money Values and Needs

If you scored a high M, finding a "good deal" is of paramount importance whether you buy or rent your home. If you are a buyer, the home you choose must be fairly priced, well located, and have the potential for good appreciation (and possible rental) during the years to come. You are likely to care a lot about sticking to a budget, even if it is only a mental budget. You will want to be able to afford your monthly payments and to feel confident about the future resale potential of your home. If there is an extra room, an au pair apartment, or some other space that can be rented out in case you get into financial trouble, so much the better. If you have a low M score, you are more focused on the psychic or physical features of the home you seek. You care more about the "feel of the place" than you do about its price tag, and you want to be "wowed" by its charm. You value a home that will nurture you and reflect your chosen lifestyle. Home for you is a haven, not an *investment*. Oh sure, it will probably appreciate—most everything does—but appreciation is not what is most important. Primarily, home is the place where you spend your most intimate and personal time—the place that shelters your *family*. Thinking about home in the context of money seems to you somehow intrusive if not downright offensive.

The story of Warren and Christine illustrates how the M Factor facilitated their family housing goals and intersected with their other three deciding factors to ensure their housing success. It also illustrates how Warren's childhood experience set the stage for his interest in fixer uppers today.

Buying their first home was a big plunge for Warren and Christine. "I had to keep switching jobs so we could afford it," Warren told the interviewer. "That's what it took, so that's what I did for six years." They bought the house as a fixer upper, something Warren found very familiar. When he was 12-years-old, his family moved into an old Victorian badly in need of repair. Warren and his two brothers helped their dad fix up the old house. "My father would come home from work and we'd go outside and paint until late at night. People would look at us like, whoa, these people are weird…today, all of us are fixers."

Warren explains, "The way I see things, a home is a big financial responsibility. It needs constant care, but you have your own place. You can fix it the way you want, and you can get financial rewards as well. The work is like a hobby for me, and at the same time I've provided my family with a really nice place in a safe environment." Now Warren and Christine are planning to move to a larger home in the same neighborhood. "We had two children while we were here, and the new house has more room plus a garage." Thanks to the improvements Warren made to their first home, they are buying their next home with a large down payment and even lower monthly payments than before. "We are so excited about going to a new home. It is like a new adventure, you know, something new to start fixing up, and hopefully, cash in on some day in the future."

Warren and Christine have compatible housing goals and are comfortable with the role that money plays in their lives. Christine's childhood was nothing like Warren's—she grew up in a West Coast suburb and lived in one home until she left for college. But Christine's go button is staying home with the kids as her mom did for her. She is happy to honor Warren's fixer-upper skills that make it all possible. They budget, pinch pennies, watch the markets, and plan for their kids' education and for retirement. Most important, they have learned to talk to each other about their money feelings, disappointments, fears, and aspirations. They know if they hang tight, take on extra work when necessary, and tolerate the inconveniences of fixing up their homes, they will achieve their housing ambitions—and much, much more.

What if, unlike Warren and Christine, you are not so comfortable about the money issues in your life? Can you still create your own housing successes? Here are the experiences of Karen and Dan. Although they offer a different set of circumstances and different motivations, they too have been financially savvy—and successful with their housing choices.

Karen and Dan, a medical corps veteran employed by a local hospital, married in 1962 and began looking for a home. A neighbor told them of a new development going up near their apartment. "I wanted it to be like it was when I was young," Karen said, "close to everything, so our kids could walk to school." They decided to sign up when they first saw the new homes, and the GI bill helped them make their purchase. "To have a home of your own to me is made by God, that's all I can say. I mean it, really. Once you get a home of your own, you have reached a goal of your lifetime."

Once settled, Karen became a real estate broker. She had helped her mother manage rental houses when she was growing up, so she was confident she could succeed at real estate. Karen worked around her family's schedule, showing and selling on weekends. She and Dan also began buying houses and renting them out. "Karen has a knack for finding homes that suit her clients—both buyers and renters." Dan likes to say. "I'm emotional about houses." Karen adds. "The thing that is important to me is that certain people need certain houses, and I help them find what they need."

Although they have moved into bigger and better homes over the years, their motivation, Karen and Dan insist, is not the prestige or financial advantage that comes with the larger home. "Listen," Karen says, "when it comes to home, it is your friends and your family that are most important. That's what home is always all about."

Karen and Dan do not like to deal with the money issues in their day-to-day lives. They do not like to think about money or even to plan, but they do not dismiss the issues either. Years ago, they agreed to take turns paying bills and to hire an accountant to handle the bigger picture. Like it or not, several times a year they sit down with their accountant and make major decisions. And how do they make their housing choices? "That's part of what we like to do together, and we have fun working with the people involved," they will tell you.

Clearly, these two couples measure by different yardsticks. Whereas Warren and Christine take a straightforward approach to dealing with their financial affairs, Karen and Dan think of money as a way to facilitate their housing investments and to help other people. Neither approach is "right" or "wrong," but it is crucial to know your money styles and feelings so you can deal with them as you are making your housing decisions.

Your Financial Well-Being

For most of us, home is the most important financial resource we will ever have. However, our housing decisions are only partly based on the financial terms and conditions that frame the contracts we sign to purchase, rent, and mortgage our homes. This is true for almost everyone—*irrespective of our knowledge or education level*. How can that be? There are four main reasons:

1. Old-fashioned economic theories that good decisions are objective, free of emotions, and devoid of intuition are dead wrong. People's homes have always been about more than money.

2. Anyone schooled later than WWII must play "catch-up" unless these skills were taught them by their parents. Before then, public schools prepared students in the *lower grades* to enter the adult world by teaching them basic financial skills. Kids learned to budget, to value thrift, to use credit, to save money, and to invest.[2]

3. Financial complications and financial responsibilities exist today that our better-schooled elders never dreamed of. Most of us do not understand our telephone bill, much less the barrage of other contract language we are expected to know and navigate.

4. Many people have no *desire* to master the level of personal finance that is required today. They have other interests: the arts, children, spiritual endeavors, helping others, and developing their creative potential along other lines and in different pursuits.

These realities, however, do not excuse the need to manage the money, areas of our lives. As you probably know by now, your ability to make competent housing choices depends on how well you incorporate the M Factor into your housing decision-making process.

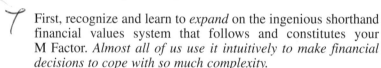

Size Versus Neighborhood Quality

Most buyers face budget limitations when shopping for a home. In 2003, according to the National Association of Realtors' "Profile of Home Buyers and Sellers," more people who purchased homes compromised on the size of their home (21 percent) or the lot size (18 percent) than on the neighborhood quality (12 percent).

If you, like Warren and Christine, manage your finances routinely and comfortably, this fourth dimension of your housing value system can be taken in stride. For everyone else, the central lessons to be learned are these:

First, recognize and learn to *expand* on the ingenious shorthand financial values system that follows and constitutes your M Factor. *Almost all of us use it intuitively to make financial decisions to cope with so much complexity.*

Second, promise yourself—especially if you have scored a low M Factor—to do some financial planning in connection with your housing decision making. Use the following financial values system to guide you. *Your future well-being and the well-being of those you love depend upon it*!

How the M Factor Works: Your Financial Values System

Suppose we lived in a world where we had to understand our telephone bill before we could have a telephone. Suppose we were required either to know the details of our credit card contract or forego the use of credit. Imagine the same scenario with our car title or lease. And the same with the deed and mortgage on our home. One of two things would happen: Either few of us would have telephones, credit cards, vehicles to drive, and homes to own; or the agreements would be framed so that we all understood exactly what we were signing. Because legal complexity is not likely to morph into candor and simplicity anytime soon, this system is not likely to emerge. Nevertheless, we have learned to cope—so well, in fact, that many of us no longer ask for explanations of financial details we do not understand. Instead, we created an ingenious "mental" financial values system to navigate financial complexity in our lives. We use it in a manner that matches our skills and interests with our cherished ideals. *It also facilitates our ability to obtain telephones, credit cards, vehicles to drive, and homes we can own.*

Three overarching values intersect our financial life and also form the essence of the M Factor area of your unique housing profile: *sufficiency, sustainability, and appropriateness.* We keep these values in mind as we go about navigating the financial details of our everyday lives. Most of us use these standards to compare prices and terms, to determine how much we can afford, and to weigh the risks and rewards of our credit management, our jobs and careers, health coverage, homeownership, education, retirement, and other big-ticket items and issues. Embedded in these values are our requirements for equity and fairness in our financial dealings. We take a lot as consumers because we are basically trusting. But when we have finally had enough, we will push back. Many changes that counter unfair practices in real estate were made because consumers and their advocates pushed back.

Sufficiency—Will There Be Enough?

We value having enough money to obtain what we consider the necessities in life, a perception that varies widely from person to person. *Do I have enough?* A direct relationship exists between this question, how frequently you think about it, and the balance in your bank account. It is a (more or less) constant part of your financial mental accounting. It applies both to everyday and to big-ticket decision making: earning your living, paying bills, buying goods and services, saving and investing, paying your taxes, buying a home, and settling accounts. "Is there enough?" will run through your mind, "to pay what you owe, to educate yourself or your kids, to provide for your family, to buy food or medicine, to pay the mortgage, or take a vacation."

If you have a low M Factor score, you may need some encouragement here. The question of "is there enough?" is measurable. In later chapters, you will take pencil to paper and check it out. In some circles, this is part of your "budgeting"—others call it your "spending plan." Whatever it is called, this dimension of your M Factor plays heavily into your housing profile and your housing decisions. In collecting the financial details you must gather for your landlord or mortgage lender, you are required to give up some of your mental accounting habits for actual written calculations in black and white. No guessing. No mental estimating. You need to come up with actual numbers, so why not make this the beginning of some actual planning. That way, you will always know what kind of housing you can afford. And you will feel better, too, because you will be squarely facing whether, and under what conditions, you will really have enough!

Sustainability—How Long Will It Last?

Sustainability is the kissing cousin of sufficiency. *How long will my money last?* This too is often part of your mental accounting system, and there is a direct relationship to the balance you have in your *savings* account. If you have little savings, this question can wake you up at night, especially as you grow older. We value knowing that we can make our payments and meet an emergency that interrupts our income stream or costs more than we ever dreamed. Many cannot meet an emergency. They are one paycheck away from financial disaster, some from even losing their home.

You may ask this question in different ways. How long will my paycheck, savings, or resources last? How many payments do I have to make? Will I be able to retire? Will I have to go without? Whatever form this question takes, it too is a crucial dimension of your M Factor and it too can be measured. Without being skilled in high finance, you can add up your savings and take note of how long your funds will last in an emergency. If you have not yet formed a savings habit, go to work on it *now*. It is the question mortgage lenders ask when they consider your loan application. It is the concept that underlies our need for financial planning. Use it as a guideline for framing your financial picture—how long will my money last?

Appropriateness—Is This Home Right for Me?

Learn to apply this dimension of your M Factor, and you are likely to stay out of financial trouble. Picture this: Your son has a job delivering publications and he needs a car. You are willing to help him buy one, but would you choose a new Mercedes? Even if you could afford a new Mercedes, it would be an inappropriate choice. No other dimension of your M Factor—or your personal, social, or tangible factors—is more important than this question when it comes to your housing finances: Is this home appropriate for me?

In Chapter 7, you encountered the story of Beth, who exchanged her suburban apartment for city living. She found a row house on a street and in a neighborhood she fell in love with. "Love," as the old saying goes, however, was "not enough." There had to be benefit in the financial transaction that made the switch in home and lifestyle a positive choice for Beth—she was a single mom and the sole supporter of her three children.

Although the monthly rental for her row house was twice the cost of the suburban apartment, Beth quickly calculated the value of the upper floor as a rental unit. Luckily, it had a partial kitchen, and she could install a used refrigerator, which was all that it needed. That done, she took a serious look at the first floor and basement, which would be the living space left for her and her three children. The basement was too gloomy to be sleeping space, but Beth thought of a way to utilize the space and keep the main floor clear of clothing at the same time. She converted an enclosed porch to the family "living room" and used the other two main rooms on the first floor for sleeping. Then, she arranged the basement into a large dressing area, complete with everyone's dressers and open-air closets. Because there was a bathroom in the basement, this made an ideal dressing area for everyone and kept the children's messes to a minimum upstairs. When she tabulated the costs of her new housing, after the rental income she received from her second-floor tenant, it was half what she had been paying in the suburbs. In addition, she could often leave the car at home and walk to work and shopping instead of always having to drive.

Beth signed a two-year lease on the row house and moved in with her children. She had made a sound housing decision. Her decision was based on her calculations (1) that her income from her employment was *sufficient* to afford her new home, (2) that the rental income of the second-floor apartment would be *sustainable*, and (3) that she was moving to a home in an area and bearing a net price tag that was *appropriate* for her lifestyle. In short, Beth's M Factor was in sync with her T Factor. Because she was honoring her personal values about city living, her housing decision and lifestyle change was much more in tune with her P Factor as well. As for her family, Beth shared her feelings and prospects with them even though they were all under 10 at the time. Together they visited schools, neighborhood merchants, the public library, and local eateries. Clearly her S Factor was working in her children's favor, too. It took several months after Beth "fell in love" for her to figure out *what her attraction was all about* and then to work out the details of a move. Through it all, she kept her head, and her value system delivered the housing and personal value she was after.

Points to Ponder

Your money factors include the following:

- **Sufficiency**—Do I have enough?

- **Sustainability**—How long will my money and other resources last?

- **Appropriateness**—Is this an appropriate home for me?

Questions to ask about your M Factor as you make housing decisions include the following:

- Is my M Factor compatible with the M Factor values and needs of my significant others? Am I willing to trade-off values to make them more compatible?

- Do I have sufficient resources to cover the housing I am considering? What can I do to change my financial picture?

- Will I be able to afford my housing choice over the long term? Is my housing decision sustainable? What about an interruption in personal income? Do I have emergency funds tucked away?

- Does this home purchase (rental) make sense given my current and foreseeable financial circumstances?

End Notes

1 Home is an *expense* if it is rented, or an *investment* if it is owned, the result of two financial decisions: how much housing to acquire and whether to rent or buy. When housing is owned, it can become a financial resource. If there is accumulated equity, it probably constitutes the single major financial resource available to its owner. As an investment, it is possible to quantify the expected performance of a home purchased today, so the return to the owner can be calculated and compared with returns on other assets, such as stocks and bonds.

2 Bowditch, Deborah J. and Nan Mead. "The Greatest Generation's Advantage." *Credit Union Magazine,* January, 2004.

Chapter 9

Secret 4

Your partner's housing value system is as important as yours.

9

WHEN HOUSING
VALUES DIFFER

If you feel that those raising objections do not understand your position, remember it is likely that you do not fully understand theirs.

—Robert Heller

In *Warm Hearts and Cold Cash*, Marcia Millman writes, "No wonder couples remodel their houses just before they break up. It's a final effort to keep their relationship patched together."[1] However, a relationship does not have to end in a break up. In fact, remodeling or moving, or any other joint housing decisions, can be a restorative process instead.

A major purpose of the information and exercises in earlier chapters was to prepare you to work productively alone or with loved ones as you make housing decisions that impact your life and the lives of those you care about. Now, with the experience of having recalled your unique housing history and with the results from your housing profile, you can compare, negotiate, and make trade-offs that result in a joint housing decision that satisfies your needs and values.

Psychological Risks of Moving

If you are single, you benefit by being able to have it all your way. You suffer by bearing the responsibility for your housing decisions and for the consequences of your decisions. You also bear all the responsibility for getting the many-faceted job of changing homes done. In your initial housing decision planning, identify trusted friends and others who might be able and willing to advise you as you ponder your choices and moving options. If you decide to move, have a deadline for asking them for help. Yes, bribery is allowed and encouraged. If you are single and contemplating a move into unfamiliar territory, make sure you thoroughly research the terrain first. Identify, *in advance of making your decision to move*, where you will find emotional support and physical assistance when you need it. If someone— a parent, child, or significant other—disapproves of your contemplated move, and you are arguing or having second thoughts, the rest of this chapter is for you.

Couples, in theory, benefit by sharing both the decision-making process and the responsibility for the consequences of decisions. After all, you have someone to help you get the job done when you decide to move. Unless you prepare up front, however, any dysfunction in your relationship is certain to arise during the process of your housing decision and again as you actually do move.

One or more of the following challenges are likely to be encountered:

- Unresolved feelings about the decision to move or the choice of new residence might erupt as pressures increase.

- Long-standing disagreements over spending habits might surface.

- Underlying feelings about the usual distribution of labor in the relationship might be revealed.

- Competition and resentment over unequal employment success after relocation might arise.

- Tendencies to blame one another heighten when things go wrong.

- Unexpected or unfamiliar behavior might be triggered by the losses experienced in the current move.

- Differences in how partners experience and react to the move might fuel an already stressful situation.

Being conscious of these potential pitfalls as you venture into the housing-decision process can help to lessen the negative impact on your relationship. Moving can be the breeding ground for anger and resentment, or it can be the proving ground for love and compassion. Keep the lines of communication open. Be kind to one another.

If a housing decision is motivated by a job or career change for one partner and the other partner is "following," relationship issues become more complicated, because the gains and losses associated with a move might be perceived as unequal. Perceptions of inequality are frequently a source of anger and resentment. Although beginning a new job is a stressful life transition in its own right, it provides the mover with an immediate source of identity and a ready-made sphere of meaningful social interaction through which to experience recognition and accomplishment. In contrast, the "following" partner (sometimes less favorably referred to as "the trailing spouse") can feel socially isolated and experience loss of identity and a diminished sense of self. This partner might feel invisible in the new community, abandoned by a partner who is preoccupied with the demands of exciting new employment, and insecure about his or her ability to find meaningful work and social contacts.

The waiting was finally over, and Will had been offered his dream job as general counsel of a nonprofit organization dedicated to land conservation. Although her own career as a fund manager would need to be sacrificed, Anne Marie was certain she would find comparable work as they packed up to move to Washington, D.C. from California. Will had been summoned to Washington as a condition of employment. He expected to live and work there for two or three years before returning to the California offices of the same organization. So he and Anne Marie rented out their California home and became transition renters in the D.C. area.

The general economy was faltering that summer, and Washington was headquarters for few investment houses, but Anne Marie optimistically began her search for employment soon after settling into their new home. Weeks went by and then months. While Will was happily engaged in his new job, Anne Marie found nothing comparable to the executive position she enjoyed in California. To fill in, she began accepting temporary jobs. At the end of two years, they returned to California, but Anne Marie's career interruption had taken its toll. Depressed and anxious, she began an affair and soon after that the couple divorced.

Although a lot of individuals in Anne Marie's position are able to change homes, geographic locations, and jobs successfully every day, as Audrey McCollum and her colleagues[2] aptly state, "Feeling invisible, unknown, or useless are lonely and frightening states" for those who do not. This moving dynamic is fertile ground for anger and resentment to build and for estrangement or depression, or both, to take root.

These researchers also provide a thorough discussion of the common societal "Myth of the Transportable Homemaker," which presupposes that the work of a stay-at-home partner can be relocated with ease. After all, your job description stays the same, and you will be working with the same people, right? This myth overlooks the web of neighborhood and community relationships that support and facilitate the performance of this occupation.

Stay-at-home partners (and anyone like Anne Marie, who has experienced his or her own unresolved career transition) take note: You need to educate yourself about the psychological risks you face during the process of a move. You must implement appropriate strategies to meet your physical and emotional needs:

- If staying at home *is* your career, you cannot perform your usual job of taking care of everyone else and helping them "adjust" if *you* are not adjusting.

- If "staying home" is expected to be a temporary condition while you look for work outside the home, you need to become familiar with local employment markets and services as well as support networks in your new location before your move.

- For anyone in either of these situations, plan to take action *in advance of your move if possible* to scout out new connections and activities that will help you reestablish a positive identity after your move.

- As a minimum, be aware of the potential pitfalls, discuss them thoroughly with your partners and other loved ones, and be prepared to support one another should they arise.

The Housing Encounter for Couples

One of the more successful programs for couples who want to enrich their relationship is the Marriage Encounter. Usually sponsored by a faith-based organization over a weekend, structured sessions inspire couples making the Encounter to become aware of their own feelings and to express them in private to each other. During my work with individuals and couples on housing decisions, what I now refer to as the "Housing Encounter" began to unfold.

Like the Marriage Encounter, there are two secrets to the success of the Housing Encounter. They are a couple's willingness to

- Set aside the time needed to devote to pending housing decisions

- Engage in personal reflection and mutual sharing in an honest, face-to-face, heart-to-heart manner.

Let's examine these a little closer.

Taking Time Out

A business that is in the process of deciding whether to relocate from one area to another will progress through weeks, months, and sometimes years of—often confrontational—meetings and consultations to assess the consequences of the relocation. Only the most poorly managed business would actually move without taking time to review all the variables—both human and practical. In contrast, couples can get swallowed up in the busy details and pressures of everyday life. They allow even major issues in their lives together to be decided by default. But as we have seen, a housing decision involves everything that really matters to them, both individually and as a couple.

The first secret of a successful Housing Encounter involves picking a time and place conducive to having thoughtful conversations about your housing-decision problem. Whenever possible, this means leaving behind your everyday hassles for a weekend (or even several days) away from where you live.

The second secret involves *structuring* time away so that you and your partner can consciously commit to individual reflection and face-to-face, heart-to-heart sharing.

If the decision is particularly difficult, you might need to schedule *more than one weekend away* to face the importance of the issues involved and your feelings about them, separately and together. Does taking this time away seem unrealistic given the complexities and constraints of your life? Consider again the months, weeks, even years of meetings and planning time a business will structure to make a decision about the possibility of moving. Then, if you are still not convinced, list the possible consequences of your own housing decision gone wrong.

The Five Essentials of Joint Housing Decision Making[3]

Whether or not you choose to go away, if you and your partner can incorporate the following five essentials into your housing decision interactions, chances are you will enjoy working together on the moving or housing decision:

- **Know What you Really Need and Value**

  Understanding yourself—including your housing history, your housing needs and values, your spending and saving habits, financial goals, and your approach to communicating about those issues—is essential to a housing-decision process that is enjoyable and an outcome that will make you happy. If each of you understands your inner needs and values and maintains self-awareness throughout the process, you will not have to wonder where you each stand on the issues.

  ### First Things First

  If you are unsure about what *your* housing needs and values are, or you are unwilling to accept and negotiate the differences between yourself and those you love, you might want to return to Chapters 2 through 8 *before tackling joint decisions.*

- **Communicate Effectively**

  In uncovering your housing history and completing your housing profile, the unique "you" evolved, and so did your housing preferences. You became aware not just of what you need and value in a home, but *why* you need or value it. This can lead not only to new self-understanding (Essential 1), but also to new respect for the past and present circumstances, objectives, and values of your partner. Joint housing decisions are not a one-way street, however. Now it is up to you and your partner to communicate your preferences to one another.

  Effective communication (Essential 2) is at the heart of any decision that requires mutual understanding, and a housing decision is well worth the effort to communicate clearly and effectively with one another. With results of your housing profile in hand, you should find it easier to talk about your feelings and motivations. Share these results one by one with your partner. Compare notes, check differences and similarities, and use both the profile and your history to relate stories about events that might have remained unknown between you until now.

- **Accept Your Differences Graciously**

  Being able to accept and appreciate the ways in which you and your partner differ is Essential 3. It is key to successfully negotiating and accommodating differences in your housing needs and values. Dr. Nathaniel Brandon, author of *The Art of Living Consciously*, tells the story of two men in the same therapy group. Alex was a 38-year-old lawyer who was contemptuous of any pursuits unrelated to money. Jim was a 40-year-old psychotherapist who specialized in "spiritual healing" and expressed distain for any form of commerce. The two men disagreed on almost everything and openly disliked each other. Through therapy, they became aware that they were each other's "disowned selves," the secret part of themselves they were so intent on denying. With this realization, both men began to change. Alex began to shift attention to his forgotten "spiritual life." Jim raised his fees for therapy sessions without feeling guilty for the first time in his career.

  The point of this example is that there is much to learn about ourselves from our seeming differences. By encouraging wider expression from our partners, we become more creative and multifaceted in our own outlook. On the other hand, we close down our creativity and halt the process of good decision making when we take a scornful position about our differences. This is particularly important because creative decision making invariably requires us to consider creative solutions.

- **Negotiate Patiently**

  You are two different people, from different family backgrounds, with different housing histories, housing preferences, and possibly financial circumstances. There are bound to be some issues that you will need to negotiate to a satisfactory conclusion. Here's how:

  - Strive above all to be *fair*. A housing decision is fair if it meets two criteria:

    1. What you agree to benefits both of you. It is not one-sided.

    2. Your agreement is negotiated without undue pressure or coercion by either partner.

- Give a nod to your housing emotions, but refuse to be carried away by them. Remember they are rooted in childhood experiences and that you are negotiating today by focusing on your adult housing *values* as your priorities—not your *needs, wants,* or *shoulds.* You can do this by:

  1. Telling each other stories about your housing history and listening patiently to one another.

  2. Trying to establish whether your emotion is tied to a genuine housing need from your childhood. If it is, can you let it go?

  3. Recognizing it as an unresolved childhood need (not a should or want) and seeing how you and your partner can agree to accommodate it.

  4. Returning to this issue at another time if necessary until you both feel more comfortable discussing it.

  5. Seeking assistance if it continues to cause trouble during your negotiations. You need someone qualified to mediate the issue and help you to a satisfactory joint resolution.

- Admit it if you don't have enough information to make a decision and then follow up by getting the information that you need:

  1. Go on a fact-finding mission to gather numbers, mortgage terms and conditions, help from real estate agents or other advisors, books and periodicals, or other information resources. (See the "Recommended Resources" appendix.)

  2. Share the fact-finding methods, timing, and type of information you need to be more knowledgeable about decisions you are facing.

  3. Enjoy the process of gathering more information.

  4. Come together again when you are better informed.

  5. Remember to be fair and stay patient during the negotiation.

• **Maintain a Positive Outlook**

Psychologists M. F. Scheier, J. K. Wientraub, and C. S. Carver[4] indicate that people who have general expectancies of good outcomes of a situation experience fewer physical illnesses during times of stress. Because negotiating joint housing decisions can be a stressful endeavor (until you get used to it and see how enjoyable it actually can be), those who cope best enter into it optimistically.

1. Look at differences as challenges. Do not demean them.

2. Discuss differences in terms of how they can be merged and resolved creatively, not how terrible they are or how awful they make you feel.

3. Get help from trusted friends, counselors, or advisors to mediate or otherwise help you deal with some of the stickier challenges or particularly heavy problems that need solutions.

4. Make very specific plans. You can always change them later, but remember that they are joint plans. Do not sabotage all your good work as a couple by making changes without joint agreement.

5. Carry out your plans as quickly as possible.

If your housing decisions include children, it is wise to acknowledge up front that everyone is likely to have a different set of concerns. Although approaches with family members can vary, it is especially important that you and your partner resolve any housing incompatibilities first. We examine some effective ways of handling a pending move for family members more extensively in Chapter 17, "Overcoming Moving Stresses."

While keeping the "five essentials" in mind, here are two other ideas for you and your partner to consider at the outset. First, the solutions that best satisfy your *mutual* concerns are those that address and resolve your *individual* concerns. Second, working together with a partner to set priorities and housing goals that you know satisfy you both can significantly strengthen your relationship. To illustrate this, we will return to the dilemma facing Megan and Ron, the Boston couple caught a few chapters back in a quagmire of housing indecision so serious that it threatened their relationship.

Still living in an apartment they rented during graduate school, Megan and Ron were eager to move. When they tried looking for a home in another location, however, their housing and lifestyle values collided. Ron wanted to live in a luxury condo in Boston. He was now a successful investment banker and wanted to live in the city near his work. Megan wanted to settle in a more moderately priced suburb. She was unhappy to think that so much of their income would go toward luxury living with little left over for the family security she was ready to start building. Their discussions became so contentious that for a while they just stopped looking.

The impasse between Megan and Ron was rooted in their childhood. Megan grew up in a rural, midwestern community and shared the deeply conservative values of her parents. An assistant director of a nonprofit firm that teaches immigrants how to navigate the practicalities of life in the United States, Megan's job today reflects the restraint and moderation she was brought up with and what she desires in her home surroundings. In contrast, Ron grew up in a Brooklyn neighborhood that became a slum. His parents clung to their old ways and to "the old neighborhood" while the families of all of Ron's friends left for the prosperous suburbs before he finished junior high school. His penchant today for high-stakes earnings and living reflect his childhood desire to flee what he remembers as an unsafe and depressing past.

Megan's and Ron's Nesting Profiles

Here are the scores from Megan's and Ron's nesting profiles:

	Personal	Social	Tangible	Money
Megan	3	8	3	6
Ron	4	7	6	5

Megan's keen interest in having a family and creating community ties showed up in her very high Social Factor (8) score. She also highly values financial security, as seen by her strong showing on the Money Factor (6) score. Both her Personal Factor (3) and Tangible Factor (3) scores are modest. Her personal goals include having a "nice home" for her future family, but Megan is not focused much on its details or style. Instead, Megan's tangible requirements primarily consist of having a home that is located in a safe neighborhood with good schools.

Ron also has a high Social Factor (7) score, followed by his Tangible Factor (6), Personal Factor (4) and Money Factor (3) scores. Ron's interest in having a family and developing community ties is nearly as high as Megan's.

However, Ron grew up in the city and has an eye for urban architecture, mixed-use developments, and vibrant neighborhoods—something Megan has never really experienced. This is reflected in his strong Tangible Factor (6) score. The big surprise is Ron's low Money Factor score. Although he is a financial services representative and knows how financial security is achieved, he does not apply his knowledge to his own life circumstances and even admits he tends to be a spendthrift.

Like many couples, Megan and Ron had fully shared the life circumstances under which they met, courted, and married. In graduate school, they had common interests and a mutually enjoyable social agenda. They pursued similar educational and career goals, and they easily supported each other whenever the pressures of study or pinched finances got in the way of their life together. When it was time to find and settle into their first "real home," however, raw emotions surfaced. Small value differences they had overlooked earlier seemed suddenly huge. Fights and bitter silences followed every real estate outing, and they blamed each other's "unreasonable" attitudes and desires for their failure to agree on when and where to move.

"Unreasonable" Reasoning

As long as we fight and maintain long silences over our differences with a loved one, we literally *hold on* to the surface reasons we differ and never resolve and get past the real underlying reasons. When our difficulties about money, children, jobs and careers, or a move to a new home lead to angry, painful, or passionate exchanges, you can bet there is more going on and the trick is to find out what it is as fast as possible. That is what Megan and Ron did. It is how they ultimately resolved their housing impasse, and in the process they strengthened their whole relationship.

The couple's housing histories and housing profiles revealed serious values differences that affected not only their pending housing decision but their entire married life. The exercises helped Megan and Ron realize the roles their past were playing in the present. They were able to articulate their life values and to regard the housing dilemma they faced from each other's perspective. Ron viewed Megan's conservative background and her need for financial security with new respect. Ron's recollections about growing up in a Brooklyn slum helped Megan understand why his "upscale urban condo" held so much appeal. The exercise also confirmed their strong mutual desire for family and community, and it was this focus that framed the solution to the couple's housing stalemate.

Prices in Boston were so high that the condos Ron had previously considered were literally off the charts for Megan. Her insistence on moving to a suburban community, Ron learned to his surprise, was almost entirely financial. (Megan's smaller objection to city living—that she had lived in the suburbs as a child—seemed silly and she easily let it go.) Ron realized that his deprivations in Brooklyn were over for good, and he no longer needed to compensate by reaching for the "high life." When Ron agreed to look for more modest city housing, Megan was content and even excited by the prospect of finding an urban neighborhood where they could start a family.

Megan and Ron each used their housing history and profile to help them solve their stalemate and joint-decision dilemma. The exercises worked because they no longer blamed each other for their mutual disappointments. They concentrated their attention instead on their value differences and then came together to compare and work together to resolve the real underlying problems. Simply put, their problems are rooted in the fact that they are individuals with different pasts, influences, tastes, attitudes, beliefs, customs, and behaviors that needed to be celebrated not denigrated.

Like Megan and Ron, you can follow the five steps I have recapped here to process your differences and arrive at a solution that will satisfy you and your partner if you now disagree. They form the foundation for good joint decision making in general. They are crucial when it comes to selecting a place to live, whether you live with a partner and/or with other family members. If you are surprised that these essentials seem general, hold on! Remember that what you need and value for yourself includes *everything in your life that really matters to you*, just as the needs and values of those with whom you share your home include all that matters to them.

Five Essentials for Successful Joint Housing Decision Making

1. Know what you really need and value.
2. Communicate effectively.
3. Accept your differences graciously.
4. Negotiate patiently.
5. Maintain a positive outlook.

End Notes

1   Marcia Millman speculates that people beautify their houses in midlife in place of
the attention they once devoted to their physical appearance. Although her views
tend toward the cynical, I value them nevertheless, because Millman, a professor
of sociology, spent several months observing trials that involved contested wills
and divorces. (See Millman, Marcia. *Warm Hearts and Cold Cash:The Intimate
Dynamics of Families and Money.* New York: The Free Press, 1991.)

2   McCollum, Audrey, Nadia Jensen, and Stuart Copans. *Smart Moves: Your Guide
Through the Emotional Maze of Relocation.* Smith and Kraus Publishers, Inc., 1996.

3   These "five essentials" have been adapted from Katherine E. Stoner and Shae
Irving's book, *Prenuptial Agreements,* published by Nolo Press in 1994, on how to
write a fair and lasting prenuptial agreement. Aside from housing decisions, there
is perhaps no other couples negotiation that holds the seeds for emotional upheaval
(as well as productive learning experience and relationship benefit) than creating a
prenuptial agreement. My thanks to these authors who have written a book that can
be used productively for any difficult creative process between two people who care
about one another and a future together.

4   Scheier, M. F., Weintraub, J. K., and C. S. Carver, "Coping with Stress: Divergent
Strategies of Optimists and Pessimists." *Journal of Personality and Social
Psychology* 57:1024–1040, 1986.

Part 2

FINDING SOLUTIONS THAT WORK FOR YOU

Chapter 10
Secret 5

**You can use your housing value system
to make your best choices.**

10

WHETHER TO MOVE
AND WHEN TO MOVE

When we value something, it has a positive tone. We prize it, cherish it, esteem it, respect it, hold it dear. We are happy with our values...We prize and cherish the guides to life that we call values.

—*Louis E. Raths*

Researchers generate theories, forecasts, risk assessments, and behavioral studies about the decision process. Businesses—big and small—thrive by using this research for effective decision making. In *Values-Focused Thinking*, decision analyst and professor Ralph Keeney, asserts that *values* drive our best personal decisions as well as our business decisions.[1]

Your housing value system consists of all that you value about where and how you live, as indicated by your personal housing history and the results of your housing profile. This chapter explains how to turn your housing value system into a tool for making your best housing decisions. As a decision tool, it can help you do the following:

- Structure real-life scenarios under differing circumstances.

- Solve complex housing or moving problems as a single, with a partner, and/or other family members.

- Stay focused and maintain your objectivity.

- Guide you through all that really matters to you.

- Counter the frustration and anxiety of indecision.

- Sort through alternatives to make your best decision.

A Nation on the Move

Nearly 50 million of us will move this year. We will leave home for college or new careers, begin married life in cozy apartments, trade up for growing families, trade down, or find homes for retirement. Our reasons will vary with age and life situation.[2] Some moving decisions are straightforward: Your home is too small and you would like more room. Do you move or remodel? Others are complex: Your employer is expanding to another city and offers you a job in the new location. Do you and your family move or stay where you are? Still others are heart wrenching: Your partner has died of a sudden heart attack and your living costs without his or her income are out of sight. After weeks of soul searching, you still cannot decide whether to move from the home you shared with your partner. Where to go, what to do?

When you choose to move, you commit yourself and your loved ones to multiple processes that can temporarily, but simultaneously, disrupt your equilibrium in every life sector. All that matters to you—your personal, social, tangible and money affairs—will be affected by the life transition we call "moving." Just *thinking* about a possible move can be upsetting and so can trying to make wise decisions. Here's why:

- **Personal Factors**—Moving challenges your feelings of identity, security, and being in control. It taxes your emotional and physical stamina and expands the pressure of your overly long existing to-do lists.

- **Social Factors**—Moving disrupts all that is socially familiar about your life. It can cause you to grieve about leaving family members, friends, neighbors, and communities. It can also stir up bittersweet memories of childhood or other times past.

- **Tangible Factors**—Moving rearranges all that is physically familiar about your life. Even though you may be initiating the change, there will be new people, places, customs, and environments to get used to.

- **Money Factors**—Unless you have planned in advance and have the resources for a smooth transition, moving can mean financial uncertainty or even financial upheaval.

As the moving process gets underway, you may ask yourself the question my daughter Elle recently asked when she called in a panic, knee-deep in an across-country move to the next home of her dreams. "Mom, what was I thinking? What am I doing? Have I lost it, or what?"

Whether we are 5, 15, or between 20 and 90-something, whether we are thinking of moving across town or across the ocean, whether we are partnered, with children or on our own, changing the place we live can be a stressful time. Even if we can hardly wait to move into our next home, the shift and the details we must balance can play havoc with our emotions and our finances.

Some of us will not actually move, but will nonetheless be in the grips of complex housing decisions. We will refinance mortgages, upgrade present living space, buy a second home, or buy a home for investment. Older adults will use home equity to borrow funds through reverse mortgages that help supplement income during later life. If you are one of the millions who will move, refinance, invest in real estate, or otherwise make a housing decision in the foreseeable future, it is time to take stock of your housing and moving decision-making skills and approach.

Turning Your Housing Profile into a Decision Tool

The desire to move is almost always triggered by a feeling of dissatisfaction (discomfort) with your present housing. What is happening is that your housing value system has been upset, and you are experiencing a state of disequilibrium in your life—however vague or intense. That condition as we have already seen can jumpstart your search for a better home. If you should find your better home first, you will soon feel that discomfort stirring in support of your decision to move. Like Beth, who fell in love with a city neighborhood, you will become aware of the inadequacies of your present home only after you start thinking about changing it. The *irritant of change* is introduced and your discomfort begins. You will think up and tally the reasons for and against your possible move, and when you have made your decision (or abandoned the idea of moving in favor of some other solution), you will feel satisfied and your discomfort will end.

In previous chapters

- You recalled your personal housing history and learned to discard any negative influences of your leftover *childhood needs* whenever possible.

- You learned how everything you really value can be categorized for simplicity's sake into one of four Decision Factors: "Personal Factors," "Social Factors," "Tangible Factors," and "Money Factors."

- You created your unique housing profile, which helped you rank the importance of your housing *values*.

- You discovered that your housing psychology incorporates competing values, needs, wants, and shoulds. Because you're the executive director of your own internal decision dialogue, you learned that *you can consciously choose your housing values as the guiding principles in all of your housing decisions*.

Categories of Housing Decisions

Housing decisions fall into four categories: routine, emergency, relationship, and strategic. *Routine* decisions include locking your doors, basic care and maintenance, and keeping your house payments current. You hardly think about them—you make routine decisions every day multiple times. Three other types of housing decisions include: emergency, relationship, and strategic decisions. When the basement is flooding in a downpour, it is time to make an *emergency* decision. Chapter 9, "When Housing Values Differ," examined the many ways in which a *relationship* decision can be addressed to smooth inevitable differences between partners. In addition to relationship decision making, moving, buying or selling, choosing to build or remodel, or investing in real estate all require you to follow the six essentials of a *strategic* decision:

1. Decide among priorities.

2. Assess your financial picture, present and future.

3. Adjust your priorities.

4. Set goals.

5. Turn goals into a specific plan of action.

6. Adjust and reset goals and plans as necessary.

Your first and most important step is to decide among your priorities.

Evaluating Your Desire to Change Your Housing

Use the worksheet on the following pages to turn your housing value system into a decision tool that will make the process faster, easier, more pleasant, and more effective. From your housing history and housing profile, you should have a good idea of how the four deciding factors (personal, social, tangible, and money) filter and contribute to the following:

- The features and issues that frustrate or please you about your present home

- The features and issues that you are seeking to change by remodeling or moving to a different home

By incorporating what you have learned about your needs and values into the decision process, you will know what you really value about your housing and *why*.[3]

You will be able to determine through this exercise exactly what may be going on that feels "out of sync." Perhaps you will find that your discomfort is due to *something other than your housing*. Recall Juliet's experience in Chapter 1, "Introduction to the Ten Secrets." Juliet wanted to move to a mountain cabin in the country when her real concern was her separation from her husband, Paul.

Proceed carefully through each deciding factor and think hard about your dissatisfactions in every life area. If you discover that you are really feeling discomfort about a family member, or your job, or a colleague, or any number of other life situations, moving—or even remodeling—will not solve the problem. You will have to address what is really at the heart of your discomfort. Try asking yourself "why" questions each time you uncover a problem. If you are unhappy about what might be happening in your neighborhood, ask yourself why. When you uncover that answer, ask another "why" question until you are confident that you have reached the real problem.

You may be seeking real personal change, and if so, modifying your environment might make all the difference. Harvard-trained psychologist Dr. Robert Epstein states that "the simplest way to change yourself is to change your world." His book, *Self-Help Without the Hype*, relates the story of Uncle Fred, who changes his living space so that he can become a writer:

> But you see, I created that me—that person who loves to write—
> the person who sits here before you. And I did this in large part
> by modifying my environment.

Ask anyone who works at home how they do it, and they will tell you about dedicating rooms or parts of rooms to their work or creative endeavor. Sales of exercise equipment, garden spas, swimming pools, artist easels or kilns, and backyard grills—to name just a few items—all are purchased to help us modify our behaviors and our lives by changing our surroundings.

Of course, you will also inventory the tangible issues or physical features and constraints about your home that might be causing your restlessness or desire to change homes. Perhaps moving is the answer. If so, let's move on to the Moving Evaluation Worksheet to find out.

Approaches That Will Solve Your Housing Dissatisfaction and Discomfort

Because everything that matters to you happens in one or more of these areas, your dissatisfaction (discomfort) with your present home is also occurring in one or more of these life areas. By reviewing them in the Moving Decision Evaluation Worksheet, you will be able to easily identify (1) exactly where and why you are feeling uncomfortable, and (2) the best way to solve your discomfort. Here are the steps to follow to complete the exercise:

1. Identify your housing dissatisfaction triggers. They are your inner urges that range from vague to intense and cause you to start thinking about changing where you live. Check off the ones on the sheet in each of the four categories or add others of your own.

2. Make the decision process *conscious* by ranking your housing priorities. Your decision goal is to get from your housing discomfort triggers through all four deciding factors to your housing solution. You may

   a. Assign a numeric value to each factor and each alternative.

   b. Mark them with pluses and minuses (+, ++, +++, ++++, or –, – –, – – –, – – – –) to indicate their degree of importance to you.

3. Assess your alternatives and the future consequences of your decision options on each life factor (Personal, Social, Tangible, Money). The question to ask yourself as you assess each alternative is this: Will choosing this alternative help me or hurt me?

4. Select the solution with which you are most comfortable. This is your fundamental housing decision objective.

5. Be as creative as possible with your alternatives. You might want to assess remodeling options, different home types and lifestyles, different locations, moving in with others, staying where you are, or sharing your present or a future home and expenses.

Moving Decision Evaluation Worksheet

Housing Triggers	Present Home	Alternative #1	Alternative #2
Personal Factors: Safety and security Autonomy and control Identity: the real me Spirituality			
Social Factors: Family Friends Communities of interest: local, national, and global			
Tangible Factors: Comfort and beauty/ location Environment: Inner (health) Outer (air, climate, and so on)			
Money Factors: Sufficiency: Do I have enough to handle all costs? Sustainability: What about future costs and other financial consequences? Appropriateness: What is the appropriate financial choice for now?			

If you cannot come to a decision, look for possible life problems that will not be solved by changing your living space. If housing remains the real problem and you still cannot decide, set the exercise aside, gather more information, and return to it in a day or so. Copy and use this form to guide you through this exercise as many times as necessary until you are confident that you can clearly see and assess your alternatives and make your best decision. If there are several different alternatives, add the necessary number of columns by drawing or cutting up two or more forms to give you the extra workspace.

If there are two or more involved in the decision, copy the exercise for each person and repeat the exercise until you are satisfied that your joint or group decision is in everyone's best interests. Discuss each difference that arises and follow the suggestions in Chapter 9 for dealing with joint decision making.

Assessing the Financial Details of a Housing Decision

Even though you will be using "mental accounting" to quickly assess the money factors in connection with your housing decision evaluation exercise, you must also calculate actual numbers and assess the real or projected costs of any housing transaction before you proceed with it. Recall that all of the people who made poor housing decisions in earlier chapters faced the inevitable financial consequences of their choices. Although the exercise you just completed is helpful in guiding you through all four deciding factors to arrive at a satisfactory decision, nearly all housing decisions are by definition also financial decisions. Calculate your actual decision costs carefully by completing the second exercise here: the Comparative Housing Cost Analysis.

If you had a high M Factor score on your nesting profile, chances are you have already calculated the following information. If not, now is the time to put pencil to paper so that you can see the financial consequences of your decision to move, remodel or redecorate and stay put, or find some other solution to your present housing discomfort. Find the answer to your first Money Factor question as you complete the following worksheet: *Do I have enough?* Then return to your Moving Decision Evaluation Worksheet and make the necessary adjustments to your housing values system priorities.

Comparative Housing Cost Analysis

I. Monthly Costs Comparison	Current Expenses	Alternative #1 Expenses	Alternative #2 Expenses
Housing Costs			
Rental payments			
First mortgage payment			
Second mortgage payment			
Condo, co-op, homeowner association fees/dues			
Property taxes			
Utilities			
Gas/oil			
Electric			
Water			
Trash pickup			
Phone			
Cable TV			
Furnishings			
Maintenance/repair			
Commuting Costs			
Car payment			
Gasoline			
Repairs and maintenance			
Registration and fees			
Taxis			
Tolls and parking			
Public transportation			
Taxis			
Other debt payments			
1.			
2.			
3.			

continues

Comparative Housing Cost Analysis   *(continued)*

I. Monthly Costs Comparison	Current Expenses	Alternative #1 Expenses	Alternative #2 Expenses
Insurance			
Homeowners/renters			
Auto			
Other			
Income Taxes			
Federal			
State			
Local			
Other Costs			
Monthly increase/decrease of costs to move			

Housing Discomfort Triggers

Several types of events can trigger your housing discomfort. Some dissatisfactions will be vague, and you can obsess about others. Your discomfort about wanting a better-looking home may result from one or more of a huge variety of reasons—you live in a declining neighborhood, you cannot afford to decorate your home the way you want, newer homes in the next town seem suddenly more attractive, you have had an increase in pay and now you are ready to buy the beautiful home of your dreams, and so on.

Roger bought a home overlooking the river on a bluff. It was a lovely spot, private and secluded. The house was old, small, and unkempt, but Roger did not care. The location was ideal. He remodeled the house, decorated it, and landscaped the property into a showplace. He was the proud and contented owner of what was for him, the most beautiful home in the world.

A few years later, the lot next door was sold to new owners, and they broke ground to build a large house. To Roger's dismay, the house was sited much too close to his own small home. Although he tried to landscape it away, the neighbor's house caused him increasing discomfort. Roger's view of the river was somewhat spoiled, and his sense of privacy had been disturbed. He also was convinced that the market value of his home had been impacted negatively.

In reality, the house next door increased the price he was able to get for his home, but for Roger the home lost its value and he was no longer comfortable living there. He initially decided to implement "Alternative 1" and tried landscaping to "plant out" the house next door, but that proved to be an inadequate solution. So Roger decided on "Alternative 2," which in his case meant moving. He has just started searching for a new home that satisfies his underlying values on all four deciding factors. Fortunately for Roger, money will not be one of his constraints. He will easily be able to afford his next beautiful home, thanks to the excellent price he got for the home he is leaving.

Roger made his decision process conscious, and that will be your challenge as well. Start by setting your housing priorities. Your decision goal is to get from your housing discomfort triggers through all four deciding factors to your housing decision. You will want to assess your personal, social, tangible, and financial options, and the future consequences of your decision options on each of these life dimensions, until you can feel confident that you are making the choice that will bring you the most personal satisfaction and happiness.

The Six Essentials of a Strategic Decision

1. Decide among priorities.
2. Assess your financial picture, present and future.
3. Adjust your priorities.
4. Set goals.
5. Turn goals into a specific plan of action.
6. Adjust and reset goals and plans as necessary.

End Note

1 Keeney, Ralph L. *Value-Focused Thinking*. Cambridge, Massachusetts: Harvard University Press, 1992. The author, a scholar and consultant on judgment and decision making, unmasks pure "rational man" methods and emphasizes instead the fundamental values that underlie all of our decisions, both personal and professional.

2 In housing scholarship, satisfaction, preference, and residential mobility research, all try to anticipate what makes people want to (or decide to) move, and why people prefer or derive the most satisfaction from one housing situation and/or location over

another. These research areas are of obvious importance to demographers, geographers, economists, and market researchers. The research tradition seeks to learn why one tenure may be preferred over another (owning over renting) preferred living arrangement (type of dwelling unit, number of rooms, neighborhood), and on satisfaction with dwelling, neighborhood, community, region, and city. Other studies assess the housing desires of people in various life stages, ages, and classes, as well as housing expectations defined by Morris and Winter in 1975 as the "realistic assessment of future conditions…what is felt to be plausible in the future." See Morris, Earl W. and Mary Winter. "A Theory of Family Housing Adjustment," *Journal of Marriage and the Family,* February, 1975: 79–88.

3   If, at this point, you are still not so sure about your housing needs and values, return to earlier chapters and retake the housing history and housing profile exercises, or take them for the first time if you skipped them earlier.

Chapter 11

Secret 6

**Self-knowledge is personal power.
Housing knowledge is financial power.**

11

TO OWN OR NOT TO OWN, THAT'S A GOOD QUESTION

The deepest American dream is not the hunger for money or fame; it is the dream of settling down, in peace and freedom...and cooperation, in the Promised Land.

—Scott Russell Sanders

More than any other life factor, your savings and money habits will influence what sort of home you will be able to rent or buy, not just today but in the future as well. Your housing value system, as you know well by now, consists of four categories of deciding factors: personal, social, tangible, and money. To make a buy or rent decision, reorganize the order of these factors and prioritize them so that your Money Factor is first. Then add the rest in the order of their significance to you.

If you scored low (4 or below) on the M Factor, or you have otherwise put off confronting the money issues you know you must address in your life, you can shortchange your housing decision making. Your ability to make competent housing choices, including the decision to rent or to buy, depends on how well you incorporate the Money Factor into your overall housing values system, and this fact of American life is not new.

Bottom-Line Lesson

Although there is so much more involved in making a homeownership decision than just the Money Factor, choosing whether to buy or rent your next home is fundamentally a financial decision.

How the American Dream Really Works

Why does the idea of the "American Dream" touch us at our core? Is it wish fulfillment, a get-ahead ambition shared by most of us, or a term hyped by smart housing marketers? It is all that and more. The American Dream is as old as the founding of the nation. A missionary in the eighteenth century had this to say about Americans as he toured the colonies:

> *The American can never flourish on leased lands. They have too much enterprise to...remain tenants.*[1]

Most of us have a personal mission to have a home we own. We strive to "make a home" for ourselves and our loved ones as the place we want to "hang out," "putter around," or "just do things together" when and as we please. We also seek the security, social recognition, and financial rewards that homeownership bestows. With so much symbolism, tradition, intimacy, and social activity connected with our home, there is little doubt that our desire to become homeowners crosses every cultural, social, and economic boundary. However, the key value the missionary noticed about Americans so long ago was their *enterprise.*[2]

Who We Are

...James Amato... Siew-Nya Ang... Laura Angilletta... Patrick Michael Aranyos... Janice Ashley... Eustace Bacchus... John James Badagliacca... Tatyana Bakalinskaya... William Bernstein... Anil T. Bharvaney... George Bishop... Susan Mary Bochino... As I listened carefully to these and other names read at the World Trade Center memorial service, I was struck by America's amazing diversity.

My grandparents, my husband's parents, your ancestors, or perhaps you yourself came to this nation dreaming of a better life. Many brought Old World goals and new ideals:

> *"...owning a home allowed Italians to uphold traditional community ties by renting apartments to their relatives."*
>
> *"...Slavic immigrants, peasants without property in the old country, eagerly sought homes in America...."*[3]

They all sought a level of freedom, security, dignity, and comfort they could not achieve in their native country.[4] Many scrimped on meals, took in boarders and laundry, became servants, saved, and sacrificed to make their dream of homeownership a reality. Today foreign-born Americans are just as likely to buy homes as native-born Americans, demonstrating they are working just as hard to realize the very same dream.[5]

Achieving the American Dream

Renters say their number one reason for saving is to buy their own home.[6] When asked to define "the good life," more than 85 percent of us rank "owning a home" first.[7] But the American Dream is not just about houses. It is a set of get-ahead values by which we all live. It is about working hard to achieve financial security. It is having a sense of purpose and feeling useful. It involves having the opportunity for advancement at work or for starting our own business.

At its most basic, American "individualism" is not self-interested indulgence. As the missionary observed, it is an enterprising spirit that flourishes when people have personal freedom, control over their social and natural environment, and the chance for self-development. For most people, homeownership is the most accessible means of maximizing freedom and control and reaping the rewards of their hard work and planning. Although not the whole of the American Dream, becoming a homeowner is the dream's most satisfying and transforming achievement.

Homeownership is also the starting point for accumulating wealth. Even when actual ownership is held by the bank to secure a mortgage, having your name on the deed transforms your financial and social status. At last you have begun your climb up the housing ladder. It is an ideal that can enhance your ability to become financially secure whether you were born and grew up in America or came here from somewhere else in the world.

Renting Your Way to the American Dream

Historically, renters were seen as second-class citizens. It was 1860 before they were allowed to vote by overcoming opponents who argued that "moderation, frugality, order, honesty, and a due sense of independence, liberty, and justice" were traits only of landowners.[8] Some prejudice against renting still exists, but this is an attitude with little foundation because nearly all homeowners have been renters at one time or another. The trend is for renters to become homeowners when the time is right and circumstances permit. If you are a renter, you can take some comfort in the following numbers from 2003:

- A whopping 92 percent of all married couples 65 years old and older were homeowners.

- Of all householders 65 years and older, whatever their marital status, 80 percent were homeowners.

All—or nearly all—of older homeowners were once the nation's renters, but today 77 percent of them own their homes free and clear of mortgage debt.[9] Anyone still holding the old-fashioned view that renters are somehow inferior to homeowners has a lot to learn about the American character and the powerful pull of the American Dream.

While we are young and not yet established, when we are newly divorced or in some other life transition, or if we are newcomers to America, we will wisely choose to rent our homes. Sometimes for tax, work, retirement, or other related purpose, we rent as a more-or-less permanent alternative to homeownership. Despite shared personal and social values about owning our home, sometimes common sense or life circumstances guide us—or dictate—that it is better to rent. When you cannot find affordable housing, do not know the area, or the timing does not feel right to buy a home, renting is a lot smarter than blindly following societal trends or the advice from well-meaning, but wrong-minded, family members and friends.

Although you must budget, save, maintain good credit, and gauge your timing, the rewards of planning for homeownership can be considerable. There are also some surprising resources that can help you. Take the case of Geraldine and Fred.

Geraldine and Fred had both been homeowners in former marriages and hoped to have their own home again. Although they brought steady income from Geraldine's nursing career and Fred's position as a soccer coach to their new marriage, they were reluctant to stretch an already tight budget to purchase a home. Geraldine was carrying high costs for twin girls in college. Fred was paying temporary support to his former wife and helping his elderly dad make ends meet. This was definitely not the right time for them to consider homeownership. They had neither the resources nor the inclination to take on the responsibility of owning a home. For now they looked forward to renting an apartment and having the freedom to take frequent trips to visit the twins and to check on Fred's dad, who lived in another city.

Four years of modest apartment living gave Geraldine and Fred the transition time they needed. After the girls graduated, they made the decision to move closer to Fred's dad. Geraldine easily found employment at a local hospital, and Fred was hired as athletic director at a private school. To their surprise and delight, the school headmaster explained to Fred that an endowment fund existed to help new faculty relocate. Geraldine and Fred were able to supplement their savings by borrowing the remaining funds needed to make a down payment at a very low interest rate. They chose a small home with future expansion possibilities in an excellent location close to the school. They were rewarded for having made wise transition and long-term planning decisions that they were disciplined enough to follow.

Even though the American Dream is part of the fiber of American life, as Geraldine and Fred's story clearly illustrates, it takes planning, hard work, foregoing some immediate pleasures, cash, steady income, and the willingness to accept the responsibilities involved. Homeownership is a worthy economic and emotional goal, but its accompanying promises of wealth and increased social status can be a lure and a trap for the unprepared and the unwary. The wrong time, the wrong price, the wrong home, the wrong location, the wrong mental set—any or all of these factors can bring to your doorstep the unwelcome twin of the American Dream—the American Nightmare.

Contrast the story of Geraldine and Fred with this account told to me by Lourdes, who with her three-year-old daughter immigrated to the United States from Columbia in 1987.

"It took seven years to become legal," Lourdes said, "and even longer for my husband, who immigrated later. Although we both had jobs and lived in a comfortable, small rented apartment in a Washington, D.C. suburb, life seemed unsteady. When Andy told me he wanted to buy a house, I was afraid." Andy worked as a cook at a restaurant, and Lourdes was a receptionist for an employer who was having trouble meeting the payroll. Lourdes told me that she and Andy "had really bad communication problems about money," and so she did not tell Andy about her misgivings or "stand up to him" when he took the lead in buying their townhouse. Soon afterward, their world fell apart. Andy's boss announced he was moving to Phoenix and wanted Andy to go with him to help open a new restaurant. Lourdes was laid off, as she had feared. Rather than look around for new work locally, Andy and Lourdes rented their new home to a tenant who "trashed the place before it was finally foreclosed."

Moving to Phoenix did not solve the tumultuous personal and financial difficulties in their marriage. Lourdes eventually filed for divorce and then bankruptcy to get a fresh start. She is a transition renter now and wiser about financial planning and setting goals. She is working at a great new job and is busy rebuilding her savings and credit to buy her next home.

Reversing Your Focus to Make a Rent-or-Buy Decision

Do you have enough in savings and monthly income to become a homeowner? As both of these cases show, you must first build and follow a financial road map to reach the home you really want. Only you can decide among the pros and cons of buying or renting a home as you analyze your money factors first, and then the rest of your housing value system to find a good match for your current life situation. Although that dream home could be within tomorrow's reach, you might have to be willing—like your ancestors and mine—to scrimp a little today in order to get it.

If you had a high M factor score on your nesting profile, chances are you have already calculated the following information. If not, now is the time to take pencil to paper and complete this financial analysis so that you can learn the details of whether you should rent or buy your next home. Notice that there are three columns: (1) Current Expenses, (2) Expenses If I Rent, and (3) Expenses If I Buy. These columns will accommodate your present situation whether you are still living at home with parents, sharing a home with housemates, or contemplating a move after a divorce. If you are presently renting, and your current expenses will stay the same unless you decide to buy your next home, simply skip the column that does not apply. Better yet, use it to discover where you might be able to save on current expenses to beef up your savings for your down payment. Then find the answer to your first Money Factors question as you complete the following worksheet.

Money Factor Analysis: Do I/We Have Enough?

I. Income Analysis	Amount
Monthly Income	
Job or business	
Savings and investments	
Alimony	
Child support	
Social Security	
Other	
Total Monthly Income Before Taxes	
Taxes (Estimated Average Monthly)	
Federal	
State and local	
Total Monthly Income After Taxes	

II. Monthly Living Cost Analysis	Current Expenses	Expenses If I Rent	Expenses If I Buy
Housing Costs			
Rental payments			
N/A			
First mortgage payment			
N/A			
Second mortgage payment			
N/A			
Co-op, condo, or homeowner's association fees			
Real estate taxes			
N/A			
Utilities			
Gas/oil			
Electric			
Water			
Trash pickup			
Phone			
Cable TV			
Furnishings			
Maintenance/repair			
Food and Meals			
Groceries			
Restaurants and takeout			
Transportation			
Car payment			
Gasoline			
Repairs and maintenance			
Registration and fees			
Tolls and parking			
Public transportation			
Taxis			

continues

II. Monthly Living Cost Analysis	Current Expenses	Expenses If I Rent	Expenses If I Buy
Healthcare			
Doctors			
Dental			
Drugs			
Eye care			
Fitness expenses			
Other			
Personal Care			
Clothing			
Hair/nails care			
Dry cleaning			
Makeup			
Other			
Child Care			
Daycare			
Child support payments			
Sports expenses			
Toys			
Pet Care			
Food			
Medications			
Grooming			
Boarding			
Debt Payments			
Credit and charge cards			
Card 1			
Card 2			
Card 3			
Card 4			
Card 5			
Student Loans			
Loan 1			
Loan 2			

II. Monthly Living Cost Analysis	Current Expenses	Expenses If I Rent	Expenses If I Buy
Other Installment Debt			
1.			
2.			
3.			
Insurance			
Homeowner's/renter's			
Auto			
Health			
Life			
Disability			
Long-term care			
Education Costs			
Tuition costs			
Books and supplies			
Recreation			
Entertainment (movies, outings)			
Vacations			
Gifts			
Other			
Professional Expenses			
Tax preparation/accounting			
Legal fees			
Financial advisor			
Charitable Donations			
1.			
2.			
3.			
4.			
Other			
1.			
2.			
3.			
Total Monthly Living Costs			

Analyze how much you are earning, what you have in savings, and how much long-term debt you have accrued. When your savings are not great, you have high debts, or you lack a record of steady income, you will have a hard time finding a home you can afford to buy and a lender who will help you finance it. So the wise course of action is to pay down your debts, establish a steady record of earnings and good credit, and initiate a savings habit while you are renting. This means foregoing high-end rent so you can accumulate the minimum down payment of 5 to 10 percent of the home you someday hope to buy.

This analysis will give you your income baseline. After you have benchmarked your true financial position and feel ready to pursue the decision to buy, you can start researching your financing alternatives: You will find there are many good ways to lower down payment and housing payments. Sound approaches by knowledgeable authors are outlined in the books, magazines, and other resources shown in the appendix. With the results of your Money Factor Analysis Worksheet, you can learn how much mortgage loan you can carry before you start shopping. And don't forget to include any costs and expenses that you incur each month if you are in business for yourself.

Make a Homeownership Decision While You Are Renting

Whereas some financial advisors and writers counsel that it is always better to buy a home if you can, others advise caution. Homeownership benefits, they point out, can be offset not only by costs in terms of money, but also in time, responsibility, and effort. As I write about the pros and cons of renting versus owning, you should know that my preference is that you decide right now to become a homeowner.

That does not mean go right out and start looking for a home to buy instead of rent, unless you are already on a track to homeownership and are financially able and emotionally in a good place. What I am advocating is this: You do not just have the option of dreaming about buying a home someday. Unless you are an avowed renter, love the carefree lifestyle, have a financial plan and are steadily accumulating alternative investments that will finance your retirement years, you owe it to yourself and your family to become a homeowner as soon as you possibly can!

Otherwise, where and how will you live at age 65, 75, 85, and beyond? Think carefully about your answer. If you are between ages 35 and 55 now and are continuing to rent, have you taken the necessary steps to start planning for where and how you will live during your later life? How will you make home payments? Where will the money for day-to-day expenses come from if you do not own your own home?

If you are just starting out, are a former homeowner and now a transition renter, or for any other reason you decide that it is wise for you to rent, it is also important that you

1. Accumulate savings while you are renting.

2. Buy your own home as soon as you can.

3. Never, ever spend your built-up equity except to meet emergencies or to leverage your retirement investments (more about this later).

Bottom-Line Lesson

Equity—In real estate terms, equity is the difference between the market value of your home and what you owe on any mortgages or other debts on your home. Equity includes the down payment, all payments against the principle balance, plus any appreciation in the market value of your home that occurs after you buy it.

Of course, the decision to buy or rent will depend upon market considerations, not only in your town or community but also in the overall economy. Your choice will also depend upon your job, the rest of your financial picture, your life situation, and your preferences and goals. Is your market timing right? Is homeownership, with all of its responsibilities, something you want to take on right now? Are you willing to lower your housing expectations if you must? Would you trade style and dwelling condition for value? How about convenience and location? These and many other factors will play into your decision.

Renting Can Be Your Best Choice

There are several financial advantages to renting, including the following:

*   You will not need a large down payment up front—merely a security deposit.

*   Compared to monthly payments to own a home, the amount of rent usually—but not always—is lower.

- You can pack up and leave more readily and with less financial risk when an opportunity in another location comes along.

- In some cases, utility costs are paid by the landlord, usually water and sewage, but even electric and other utilities are on occasion included in your rent.

- You are usually not responsible for the costs of major maintenance or repairs that need to be made to your rental space, so long as you have not caused any serious damage to the property.

- You have no financial risk in your rental investment. If the economy is in recession or the neighborhood surrounding your home deteriorates quickly, the problem of loss of property value belongs to your landlord, not to you.

There are financial disadvantages, too:

- Unlike mortgage payments, rental costs do not contribute toward home equity buildup and are essentially "dead" payments.

- Rent tends to rise with inflation.

- Your landlord can increase your rent each time you renew your lease.

- A landlord might have plans that involve changes or upgrades to your rental unit and refuse to renew your lease altogether, requiring you to incur the expense of finding a new home.

The past few years of low mortgage interest and somewhat relaxed credit guidelines have made buying a home affordable for many more renters. As a result, the nation's homeownership rate soared to an all-time high of 68.6 percent in the fourth quarter of 2003. If you can afford to rent, if you have cash for a down payment, and you want to buy your own home, most real estate experts will tell you that you can probably afford to do it.

Reclaimed Homeownership Status

In 2003, 20 percent of buyers were renters in transition who had previously been homeowners and were able to become homeowners again.[10]

Market Timing Is Important

Whether you are leaning toward buying or renting a home, consider the effect market timing has on your decision. When the market is rising or at the start of an upswing, it is wise to start looking around. When interest rates (or rents) are sky high, you might prefer to wait. Certain times of the year are traditionally better for selecting your next home. Some experts advise prospective buyers or renters to wait until year end, when historically there is less activity in the marketplace.[11] The best time to buy or rent may be between Thanksgiving and New Year's Day, when most people are preoccupied with the holidays. Sellers and landlords might be more willing to negotiate because few people want to move over the holidays.

You might find stiff competition in the marketplace during the late spring or early summer because the demand for housing is highest at this time. More families move at the end of the school year, and after a long winter homes and apartments look fresh and appealing. It is at this time that people seem more optimistic about their prospects for the year and are ready for a fresh start. Whenever you tackle the housing market to buy your next home though, do your homework. Read, collect information, watch advertisements, talk to advisors in the know, and pursue the rich sources of market data in the region and neighborhood in which you are thinking of buying or renting.

You should be renting now if the following is true of your situation:

- You have no savings.

- You have poor credit.

- You are in the midst of a separation, divorce, or other family life transition.

- Your present job or profession feels unsteady or "temporary."

- You are unaware of the housing markets in your area.

- You expect to move again in a short period of time.

Homeownership may be for you now if the following is true of your situation:

- You have savings for a required down payment.

- You have good or fairly good credit.

- Your emotional life is stable.

- Your employment and financial life are stable.

- You have the discipline to make trade-offs.

- You understand the local housing markets.

- You expect to stay in your home for at least the next two or three years.

The Nonfinancial Factors of Rent-Buy Decisions

Although your Money Factor is primary as you consider whether to buy or rent your next home, the other components of your housing value system actually might end up being the most important, and therefore, the determining factors in your decision. If you are stuck, return to the worksheet in Chapter 10, "Whether to Move and When to Move," to learn why you want to move. Here are a few of the things you might want to consider in your decision. Remember to be as creative as possible while you are considering your alternatives.

- **Tangible Factors**—You now have access to amenities, including a swimming pool, fitness center, underground heated parking, and social and activity rooms. You do not use them very often, but you are glad they are there. You also like the high level of security by means of cameras and on-call security guards in the buildings where you now live. On the other hand, you experience some of your landlord's rules as too restrictive. Homeownership offers privacy, lower noise levels, unrestricted pet ownership, backyards and barbecues, and other comforts not available in your rented apartment.

- **Social Factors**—Your partner has his or her heart set on homeowner-ship. Although you like the relative freedom of renting, you have to admit it might now be time to buy. Your children are thrilled and want to look at homes with you. Your in-laws hope you will move to the same neighborhood, but you are secretly not so sure. On the other hand, you travel on business a lot and you would be comfortable with a home in that community. Good schools are available and great shopping, too—actually your best buddy does not live too far away. Perhaps it is time to move to a home that you own.

- **Personal Factors**—As a homeowner, you can paint the walls any color you want, live whatever lifestyle you choose, enjoy the freedom to be who you really are, and feel in charge of your own living space. You will move "up in the world" when you become a homeowner, even though you will be looking for a not-so-big home at first.[13] Your primary goal is a safe neighborhood, a home that "feels right," and a place you can finally call your own.

As is best said by Lewis Schiff from *Money Magazine*, "Home owner-ship is called the American Dream because it is right for so many people, but that doesn't automatically mean it is right for you. Weigh the pros and cons carefully before taking the plunge." Armed with your new understanding of your housing value system and your knowledge of the deciding factors involved in your rent-or-buy decision, you know well that you will make the right decision for the right reasons.

Points to Ponder

- Make a homeownership plan whether you are a renter in transi-tion or a homeowner. Decide what kind of living arrangement you would like to have in the short term and also when you retire. Set these as goals to work for whatever your age or life stage today.

- Live up to your homeownership plan and modify it realistically as the years go by. Anchor your retirement planning with the home of your dreams and get in the habit of saving regularly to make your dreams come true.

- Don't squander your precious built up home equity after you become a homeowner. Reinvest it, yes. Trade up, yes, but keep your eye on your home equity as an important aspect of all your future financial planning.

End Notes

1   Drier, Peter. "The Status of Tenants in the United States." *Social Problems* 30 2:179–198, 1982.

2   Vitt, Lois A. *Homeownership, Well-Being, Class and Politics: Perceptions of American Homeowners and Renters.* Washington, D.C.: Institute for Socio-Financial Studies dissertation, 1993.

3   Cohen, Lizabeth A. "Embellishing a Life of Labor: An Interpretation of the Material Culture of American Working-Class Homes, 1885–1915," in *Material Culture Studies in America*, edited by Thomas J. Schlereth. Nash-ville, TN: The American Associ-ation for State and Local History, 1982.

4 D'Souze, Dinesh. *What's So Great About America.* New York: Penguin Books, 2002.

5 U.S. Census Bureau data show (as quoted in National Association of Realtors, 12/19/03, "Homeownership," www.realtor.org/publicaffairsweb.nsf/).

6 Ibid.

7 Vitt, Lois A. *Homeownership, Well-Being, Class and Politics: Perceptions of American Homeowners and Renters.* Washington, DC: Institute for Socio-Financial Studies dissertation, 1993.

8 Ibid.

9 Chen, Yung-Ping and Lois A. Vitt. "Reverse Mortgages," in *Encyclopedia of Retirement and Finance.* Westport, CT: Greenwood Press, 2003.

10 *The 2003 National Association of Realtors Profile of Home Buyers and Sellers.* Chicago: National Association of Realtors.

11 Ibid.

12 See, for example, Robert Irwin's *Tips & Traps When Buying a Home,* Second Edition. New York: McGraw Hill, 1997.

13 Sarah Susanka (with Kira Oblensky) started a counter-movement to the trend toward bigger and bigger houses with her book, *The Not So Big House,* published by the Tannton Press, Inc., Newton, CT, in 1998. Her ground-breaking message—that quality should come before quantity—emphasizes downsizing the average American home without sacrificing beauty and comfort for occupants.

Chapter 12
Secret 7

The U.S. Housing System makes your American Dream possible.

12

Your Stake and "the System"

That you have property is proof of industry and foresight on you or your father's part....

—John Hay (Secretary of State 1891–1905)

Whether you are a first-time homebuyer or a renter in transition, an established homeowner or a housing investor, you are a beneficiary of the policies and payoffs that homeownership bestows. The social values and institutions that help you become a homeowner have deep roots in American history. If you, like most Americans, realize that homeownership has the potential to be your best investment, you can thank the remarkable "system" that greases the wheels so you can acquire your homeownership "stake." The system—an alliance of financial institutions, federal and local government, big and small business, and nonprofit organizations—educates you, sets interest rates, reduces red tape, and can save you taxes. It reaches out with special programs if you are underrepresented among homeowners, in particular if you are a first-time homebuyer, a member of a minority group, or a low-wage working family. The system, however, is complex. You must learn your way around it to guard against mistakes and to reap the financial benefits available.

The Politics of Homeownership

Politicians believe that owning a home is good for Americans, just as property ownership was believed to be good for humankind during ancient and Western traditions. Like policy makers today, Aristotle called the right to own property "God-given," and St. Aquinas thought property ownership would provide for peaceful and orderly relations between individuals.[1] These notions are the same as those that initially drove American politicians and business interests to make homeownership more available to working- and middle-class Americans in the 1930s. A partnership of government and business was formed to promote homeownership as a way to put people to work and maintain social stability.[2] One business leader put it this way:

> *Get them to invest their savings in their homes and own them. Then they won't leave [America] and they won't strike. It ties them down so they have a stake in our prosperity.*

Business did benefit, but so have successive generations of working Americans. Every U.S. president has supported the goal of widespread homeownership ever since:

- **Franklin D. Roosevelt**—A nation of homeowners, of people who own a real share in their own land, is unconquerable.

- **Bill Clinton**—Homeownership strengthens families and stabilizes communities. It encourages savings and investment and promotes economic and civic responsibility...It is in our national interest to expand homeownership opportunities for all Americans.

- **George W. Bush**—Owning a home lies at the heart of the American Dream. A home is a foundation for families and a source of stability for communities.

This pro-homeownership social and economic policy revved up in earnest after World War II.[3] For six decades, it has helped millions of individuals achieve financial self-sufficiency as well as financial security as they age. When homeownership is not present as the cornerstone of financial preparation for retirement years, the chance of poverty in later life, particularly for women, increases significantly.[4]

Homeownership—Your Stake in Your Future

Stock market advocates advise that if you are not invested in stocks or mutual funds, you are not really "an investor." "Buy a home to live in—if you want," they say. "But put your real money in stocks." Most Americans intuitively know better, and the hard evidence stacks up in their favor. For starters, investments in the capital markets often fall short by comparison. You cannot live with your family in a mutual fund, maintain forced savings through ordinary living expenses, control the daily management of your investment, or seek legal "insider" information about the market before everyone else knows what is trending up or down.

Like the stock market, the housing market does fluctuate. With the housing market, however, history teaches a lesson that most of us must keep relearning: Home prices are likely to rise over time regardless of how high we think they are today. When housing prices do plunge, they usually do not go down a black hole and stay there like some stocks or mismanaged mutual funds. Of course, there are exceptions. Single-industry towns can become depressed when the company pulls up stakes or folds, and until some enterprising soul thinks up new uses for the abandoned facilities. Admittedly, this can be a long time, and there simply is not a quick fix.

Other geographic areas, however, will experience severe downturns in their local economies that are temporary, and alert homeowners should see this coming in time to decide to bail out, move on, or wait for the upturn that happens more often than not. During the early 1970s, large layoffs at Boeing drove Seattle home prices down by as much as 30 percent. Yet Seattle had a lot going for it in addition to Boeing. The local economy soon recovered, and home prices zoomed. The same thing happened in the 1980s to the oil economy and to home prices in Houston, and most notably in the 1990s to the formerly booming California and Massachusetts markets. Throughout these downturns, homeowners who could hunker down for the duration had a roof over their heads, potential tax-favored equity to protect, and the personal and social benefits of having control over their own space. They could choose to work at home, take a second job, rent out a room for some extra cash, send kids to local community colleges rather than expensive universities, carpool, and find other ways to economize. For those with foresight, faith in the future local economy, and some extra savings, "distressed properties" were available for investment. Many investors were rewarded by watching houses rally to their pre-downturn values and then far exceed them.

Does this mean homeownership guarantees you immunity from loss? No, indeed. Loss is a necessary part of living, and we fail at our own peril to deal constructively with every kind of loss we happen to encounter. Researchers who have studied people living to 100 and beyond have found that one of the four significant traits shared by the "oldest old" population is their ability to cope well with personal loss. (The other three traits are (1) a social network, (2) regular physical activity, and (3) a positive outlook.)

Does this mean you shouldn't invest in the capital markets? Absolutely not. If you work for a company that offers a 401(k) and you are not contributing the maximum, or if you do not invest each year in an IRA, you are missing essential tax-sheltered opportunities on the way to your future financial self-sufficiency.

What I am urging you to do in addition is to establish a regular pattern of personal savings earmarked for a primary home that is right for you at your particular life stage. You have to live somewhere, shelter your partner and family, and pay out your earnings every month to someone. If you are paying a landlord who is benefiting from the system, why not do all you possibly can to benefit yourself instead? When you own your own home, you can make the investment decisions that will help you trade up and branch out—into the capital markets, into a second home, or even into investment housing if you have a desire to try that. With increasing savvy, and your determination to make the system work for you, you can build your stake by diversifying into all three.

The System Educates You

Have you looked at the books on real estate and personal finance in your library or bookstore lately? The choices are staggering, and books on every aspect of buying or selling a home abound. Many books cover the financial nuts and bolts of buying all types of dwellings: single-family houses, townhouses, apartments, condos, and co-ops. Guides exist to help you buy into every conceivable kind of homestyle: urban, suburban, country, vacation, or retirement. Topics include searching for the home that meets your needs, making your offer, negotiating the purchase, finding a mortgage lender, navigating the mortgage market, closing your transaction, and moving in. There are books for "dummies," first-time buyers, the upwardly mobile, pre-retirees, retirees, and housing investors. You can learn how to avoid mistakes; how to protect against losing your nest egg; how to buy, renovate, build, finance, and sell. We cannot possibly handle all of these topics in this small book, but you will find many such resources in the listing provided in the "Recommended Resources" appendix.

So what are you waiting for? Take advantage of this treasure trove of information—and I have not yet mentioned the Internet, or the dozens of popular magazines and consumer guides on personal finance. Interactive Web sites help you browse available homes for sale, calculate a mortgage, play "what-if" scenarios, and amortize your payments. They tell you whether you earn enough to qualify and point you to real estate companies and mortgage lenders. Web sites are available that publish your credit scores and suggest ways to improve them, as well as help you order your own credit report. Whether you are a first-time buyer or a seasoned homeowner, there is no need for you to go blindfolded into the housing marketplace, which is what you risk when you address any financial topic today unprepared. Instead, learn as much as you possibly can about home types, homestyle, risks and rewards, mortgage financing, and negotiations between buyers and sellers. Sort out the differences between fixed-term, adjustable, or variable-rate mortgages. Run the numbers and then re-run them to make certain you understand them. Find out how real estate professionals work, how they are paid, and the differences between a Realtor, real estate agent, a "dual" agent, and a buyer broker.

Marilyn, with her husband Tom, bought a new home a few years ago. They blundered into the real estate market, and experienced all the usual anxieties that most people face on their way to becoming first-time homeowners. They endured the competitive pressures of finding an affordable home, the bewilderment of working with a "dual" real estate agent (an agent who represents both buyer and seller), the unfamiliar process—and long periods of uncertainty—while awaiting approval of the mortgage lender, and the mounds of undecipherable paperwork that greeted them at closing. As Marilyn signed the closing documents, she made a promise to herself that she would never again enter into a real estate transaction without understanding the "deal," the process, the players, and the paperwork. Within a few days after they moved into their new home, Marilyn enrolled in real estate school. The unexpected result of her experience was that she became a successful real estate sales agent specializing in new home sales. Working mostly as a "buyer broker," she has helped hundreds of buyers and enjoys great personal satisfaction in the career she never planned.

Does Marilyn today have book-loads of financing, legal, and other technical information she once hoped for all perfectly stored in her head for ready reference? Not totally, but she knows where to look (or who to consult) to find information in seconds! Marilyn takes courses as required—and other classes she chooses—to keep her current on the huge body of laws and customs that impact her brokerage activities and help her to serve her clients. As for the legal, insurance, engineering, home inspection, financing, title, and other aspects of customary home purchase and selling transactions, she works with the experts who contribute to these processes within a vast real estate industry network. You will be introduced to the types of experts you will need and be able to choose your own advisors and service providers as you wind your way through the system that exists to serve real estate brokers like Marilyn and home buyers and sellers like you.

The point is that you cannot know all the details of every part of the combined multiple processes in every real estate transaction. But you can become real-estate savvy. You can go a long way toward having a better experience than Marilyn had when she and her husband bumbled through their first home purchase. Many thousands of first-time homebuyers, renters in transition, and seasoned homeowners have attended the excellent selection of homebuyer education classes available in every major city and in many rural locations. By tapping into the extensive collection of materials and educational offerings available to you in bookstores, libraries, on the Internet, and from homebuyer and investor educators, you can develop at least a passing familiarity with the engaging world you are about to enter and perhaps re-enter many times.

The System Sets Interest Rates

Interest is the fee you are charged for the use of someone else's money—a finance company's money, the bank's money, the credit card company's money, or your mortgage lender's money. When you pay interest on money you have borrowed to buy a car, or for most other consumer goods and services, it is not tax deductible. When you pay interest on money you have borrowed to own your home, it is tax deductible. Do not take this difference for granted, but do not overvalue it either. Although the purpose of this difference in tax treatment is to help you acquire and own your own home, tax laws have chipped away at the treatments and levels of this benefit. If you are being told that you will receive tax savings from interest deductions, pay a visit to your tax preparer and find out what your actual savings are likely to be.

Until the past 25 years or so, two types of mortgage loans were available, and they both featured a fixed rate of interest: those that were insured or guaranteed by the government, and those that were not. The adjustable-rate mortgages that exist today were developed to make payments more affordable in the early stages of homeownership, so that many more people could become homeowners. Such mortgages allow interest rates to adjust up or down at regular intervals, depending upon the terms of the financing arrangement. The reasoning is that the homeowner's income is likely to increase and will cover any upward adjustment in interest rate over time—a downward adjustment is a happy twist of fate for the homeowner.

The adjustment intervals are key to the financing arrangement and should be carefully studied by any homebuyer considering an adjustable-rate mortgage. Furthermore, the homebuyer should go over the terms with an advisor. Here is what happened to two friends of mine who neglected to read the fine print in the adjustable-rate mortgage loan that financed their home purchase a few years ago.

After earning a midlife law degree, Gene and his family decided to settle down in the midwestern city where he had gone to law school and worked part time for a firm that invited him to stay on. Cash was tight because of student loan payments, but Gene and his wife, Virginia, highly valued homeownership. They signed a two-year lease-purchase agreement that credited part of their rent payments toward a future down payment on a house they believed they could afford within the two-year period.

Interest rates fell and home prices rose in their general housing market, and a few months before their purchase option deadline, Gene and Virginia went shopping for a mortgage to buy their home. To their surprise, lender after lender declined to accept Gene's accruing rental payments as a "proper" down payment. With prospects for loan approval looking bleak, Gene asked around for leads and was put in touch with a "sub-prime" lender. At the eleventh hour, they obtained their financing at a higher rate of interest than they would have preferred—9.5 percent—but they breathed a sigh of relief anyway to have met the contract deadline.

Six months after closing, Gene and Virginia received a notice from their lender that the interest rate was being raised to 10.5 percent. Six months after that, another notice came that increased the rate to a whopping 11.5 percent, despite the fact that interest rates in housing markets across the nation had been decreasing substantially. Gene checked the mortgage and promissory note that he and Virginia had signed at closing and found the terms that permitted the interest rate to increase every six months. He was chagrined and embarrassed to realize that although he routinely drafted and reviewed legal agreements for others, he had not read his own mortgage documents before signing them!

You do not have to be a budding attorney to understand the importance of knowing the terms and conditions of your mortgage loan. There are two variables to know thoroughly—interest rate and mortgage term—what is your rate and how many years will the payment be fixed at that rate? If you have an adjustable-rate mortgage, make certain you have "loan caps," which are safety features that set limits on interest-rate changes. In Gene and Virginia's case, they were lucky. The impact of lowered market interest rates worked in their favor. After a few months of paying their loan at the 11.5 percent rate, they were able to refinance at a market rate of 7.5 percent. Why the big difference? They no longer had to prove where the down payment came from, because the new loan was a refinance of their existing loan. Their new lender based loan approval on Gene's new full-time employment at the law firm and the couple's on-time mortgage payment history over the previous year.

Beware of interest-only, partially amortizing, and balloon loans. Unless you are fully acquainted with these types of mortgages, understand the risks, and have a workable plan for paying them off or refinancing them into more conventional financing in the foreseeable future, do not enter into them. If you do understand them, know your risks, and have such a plan, they can be a wonderful source of financing to acquire a property that might otherwise be unavailable to you. More than once I bought a home where the seller agreed to take back a second mortgage, but I made sure that the loan terms worked for me. Use the excellent resources listed in the "Recommended Resources" appendix to learn more about various types of mortgage financing, and then consult a knowledgeable advisor if you still have questions.

The System Reduces Red Tape

Although the paperwork that Marilyn and her husband signed at closing several years ago appeared to be piled high, it was nothing compared to the forms that are required today. Red tape has increased then, right? Well, yes and no. There are more consumer protections and disclosures today, so there are more forms to sign. At the same time, buying or selling a home and the mortgage loan process have been substantially streamlined. Real estate contracts and the required disclosures can be faxed back and forth between buyer and seller, saving time, anxiety, and complications. Credit reports and credit scores can be obtained in seconds. Mortgage loan applications can be made via the Internet or telephone—we seldom meet the mortgage officer with whom we deal. Nor can we talk to the "underwriter," who more often than not is a computer programmed to spit out approvals or the unsettling news that our application is on hold for more information or has been denied.

Patty and Christopher recently purchased a house, applied for a mortgage loan that was approved in three weeks, and they moved in—all within 30 days. They had sufficient savings and could show the lender the source of their down payment and closing costs. They had good credit and were both employed at jobs they held for a few years. Their combined income qualified them to borrow the amount of the loan they needed. And, they could demonstrate to the lender that they could afford their new house payments in addition to their other regular monthly payments. Patty and Christopher were prepared to become homeowners, and the system got into gear for them.

A house inspector found only a few items that he said needed attention, and the sellers readily agreed to repair the items. The mortgage lender promptly ordered the appraisal, and an appraiser was selected who was reliable and could deliver within the allotted time period. Patty and Christopher obtained homeowner's insurance, selected an attorney, set the date to close the transaction, and arranged to have the utilities transferred. The sellers, who had already moved to a new location and were carrying payments on two homes, were delighted with the timing. Patty and Christopher managed to move into their new home just before the Thanksgiving holidays. They celebrated their good fortune by taking a week off to settle down and experience—with gratitude—their first home together.

There are many examples of contracts, applications for mortgages, and closings gone awry. But most transactions these days proceed fairly smoothly, thanks to disclosure laws; real estate agents and brokers who want to improve their image and career experiences; the enormous amount of consumer information available on bookshelves, in magazines, and on the Internet; stiff competition among mortgage lending sources; and the motivation of others who work in the many businesses that support the home buying and selling process. It is more fun for everyone to be involved in a system that works rather than one that does not.

The System Saves You Taxes

J. K. Lasser's popular tax guide for homeowners refers to the available tax breaks as "finding hidden gold in your home."[5] Author Gerald Robinson is not just talking about interest deductions but about many different homeowner tax breaks that apply when you buy, sell, or rent out your home—temporarily or for an extended term. There is tax advice for special situations ranging from divorce to having a home business, to improving your home, to modifying your home for disability, to obtaining a charitable deduction. Although the most well-known tax-advantaged aspect of being a homeowner in America is the deductibility of your payment of real estate taxes and mortgage interest, your ability to avoid tax on any exempted gain on your home when you sell it is probably your most important.

But Robinson's advice fills a book that should be on every homeowner's shelf for ready reference—not just at tax time, but for all of your housing-related financial planning. Read on and you will understand why.

Peter, a successful cosmetic surgeon, suddenly found his life in financial chaos following a divorce. Because his wife had never been employed outside of the home and Peter still had substantial earning power, the court awarded her a large monthly support payment so that she could continue living in the couple's former home. As for Peter, he was neither emotionally nor practically prepared to support himself separately under the conditions that the court stipulated. He had never budgeted for anything, nor had he developed a savings habit over the years. Like many Americans at every income level, Peter optimistically lived for the present and gave his retirement years little serious thought or planning.

Peter was in practice with two other surgeons. Although the doctors shared the costs of their offices, Peter had owned the unit in which the practice was located for many years. The zoning permitted limited professional use, and Peter liked to say that he "bought his medical suite for a song." With his partners' agreement, Peter sold the unit to their partnership entity to "cash out" his investment and use the money to cover personal expenses. He had fallen behind in his income tax payments and credit card debt, and making ends meet had become a serious problem for him. He reasoned that the cash from the sale of his now-valuable apartment would help to pay some of his skyrocketing personal expenses. What Peter did not calculate into his decision to sell was the whopping capital gain tax (prior to current tax law) that would be due upon the sale of this real estate holding—considered for tax purposes a commercial unit, not a residential dwelling.

After the sale, Peter quickly paid demanding credit card collectors and current living expenses. He had little left from the sale to cover his delinquent taxes, so he let them slide. At tax time his accountant advised that his already high current tax bill would be three times greater than usual—due to the capital gain he incurred from the sale of the medical suite. And that was in addition to his already delinquent taxes that soon enough would become IRS tax liens, accruing penalties, and interest. Peter had no choice but to learn, finally, how to budget for, manage, and climb out of the financial mess his life had become.

The tax benefits (and any tax consequences) of owning residential property should become a knowledge priority in your life. Of course, you do not need to become a tax expert. You just need to understand that there are rules—always changing rules at that—under which the nation's tax system works. It took Peter several years to fully recover from the emotional and financial devastation in his life after the sale of the "apartment" he bought for a song many years before. Learn what is and is not tax deductible before you buy or sell your home or other residential property. Do not let what happened to Peter happen to you.

Become knowledgeable about and plan for the tax benefits you receive from homeownership and avoid the tax traps. Read about them, hire a tax planner, or consult a tax attorney to make certain you are up on the current rules for buying, owning, selling, and renting your home and other property. Then proceed with a clear mind and a freer spirit because you are more confident that you know what you are doing.

Points to Ponder About "The System"

- It educates you to become a homeowner.

- It sets interest rates and other terms related to your home purchase.

- It reduces red tape for you.

- It can save you taxes.

Learn your way around the system!

End Notes

1   Macpherson, C. B. "Property As Means or End," in *Theories of Property: Aristotle to the Present.* Waterloo, Ontario: Wilfrid Laurier University Press, 1979.

2   Kingston, Paul William, John L. P. Thompson, and Douglas M. Eichar. "The Politics of Homeownership." *American Politics Quarterly,* 1984:12 2:131–150.

3   After World War II, homeownership policy formed the means for stimulating growth in the overall economy through increased production and consumption, not only of houses but of all the many related goods and services a nation "on the move" would predictably require. The federal government, in partnership with business interests, infused the housing sector of the economy with massive financial aid and incentives to encourage housing production for owner-occupation. Policies were geared toward increasing the supply of mortgage credit for home purchases and subsidizing home-owners directly or indirectly through tax and other financial interventions. (See Hayden, Dolores. *Redesigning the American Dream: The Future of Housing, Work, and Family Life.* New York: W. W. Norton & Company, 1994; Kramer, Kevin Leslie. *Fifty Years of Federal Housing Policy: A Case Study of How the Federal Government Distributes Resources.* An unpublished dissertation, 1985; Mayer, Martin. *The Builders.* New York: W.W. Norton & Company, 1978.)

4   Davis, Nancy. *When Baby Boom Women Retire.* Westport, CT: Greenwood Press, 1996.

5   Robinson, Gerald J. *J. K. Lasser's Homeowner's Tax Breaks: Your Complete Guide to Finding Hidden Gold in Your Home.* Hoboken, NJ: John Wiley & Sons, Inc., 2004.

Chapters 13–14

Secret 8

Your mortgage is the best tool in your investment toolbox.

13

REFINANCING, REMODELING, AND BUILDING HOMES

...building equity doesn't mean a complete ban on debt. It does, however, mean changing the character of your borrowing from lazy debt to "smart debt."

—John J. Cunningham

Love your mortgage! It is a unique investment tool that is the key to acquiring your own home and improving your quality of life in the future.

Think about it. You can buy a new car, an education, stylish clothing, a vacation, and many other consumer goods and services on credit, but none of these pay you back quite like your mortgage. Thanks to innovations in the housing finance system, the mortgage market is resilient and better able to adjust quickly to changes in the overall economy. That makes mortgage capital more available to you, whether you plan to purchase a home or refinance an existing mortgage.[1] As a result, your mortgage leverages your initial home purchase like no other investment and makes future wealth accumulation possible. You may prepay it; benefit by deducting your interest payments; enjoy periods of price appreciation while your mortgage payments remain level; and tap into previously accumulated home equity to make other wealth-building investments. You can refinance your existing mortgage and change your payment terms. You can "cash-out" home equity under new primary or secondary financing. You can spend your freed up home equity on nonhome-related items or experiences, or you can choose to spend it to make needed repairs or desired home improvements. This isn't news, of course, to homeowners.

Home Mortgage Refinances

In 2003, mortgage refinances increased by an astounding 71 percent. With stock wealth in a state of flux, the lowest mortgage interest rates in 45 years, and appreciating home prices, many people took advantage of mortgage innovations to refinance existing mortgages.[2] Others borrowed home equity through various forms of second mortgages including revolving lines of credit. They used the proceeds of these financial transactions to restructure current mortgage terms, pay off or consolidate debt, tide them over during transition periods, fund college tuition, invest in second or rental homes, and engage in home construction projects. These activities occurred in record numbers.

Refinancing is no different from obtaining a mortgage to buy your home initially. The process of selecting your lender, rate of interest, loan term, and method of repayment involves the same steps as those that were covered in Chapter 12, "Your Stake and 'The System.'" What you want to accomplish with refinancing is what sets it apart from obtaining a mortgage to purchase a home.

You might find this hard to believe with every bank in (and out of) town vying to make you a home equity loan, but not so long ago, your home was known as an "illiquid investment." The equity was locked in and couldn't be touched until you decided to sell the house. Then, as interest rates decreased over the past decade, mortgage companies and other financial institutions made refinancing a staple of their mortgage-lending activities. Like every other shift in consumer finance, this is a good news, bad news evolution.

The good news is that you can refinance to take advantage of low interest rates that you might not see again for many years. If you do refinance, as so many people have already done—some several times—following are some of the most common potential benefits:

- If you can obtain a mortgage with a lower rate of interest, you can considerably reduce your monthly housing costs.

- You can more quickly build home equity by converting to a loan with a shorter term.

- You can convert an adjustable-rate mortgage (ARM) to a fixed-rate loan and have the certainty of knowing exactly what the mortgage payment is for the life of the loan.

- You can convert to an ARM with lower payments or more protective features (such as a better rate and payment caps) than the ARM you currently have.

- You can choose to take cash from the refinancing (cash-out refinancing) to make needed repairs, home improvements, or to remodel your present home.

- If you have no savings for an emergency or for retirement, you can jumpstart these critical financial safety nets with initial deposits from a cash-out refinancing.

- You can choose to buy a second home or a rental property, or you can diversify your investments into the capital markets.

The bad news is that you can refinance your home to pay off your credit cards—what John Cunningham calls "lazy debt"—and then create that debt all over again. You can take a year off and travel around the world or enroll in an expensive two-year course to stretch your intellect. This is bad news? I must be kidding, right? I'm afraid not. Consolidating debt, getting a leisure-time education, and, or learning about other cultures are excellent ways to spend your equity as long as they are part of an overall money management plan for your future financial needs and life events. If you aren't "managing" your home equity as part of a financial strategy for your future, however, you are missing the boat. Soaring markets and low mortgage interest rates do not last forever.[3] Many people have chosen to borrow against (or invest more) in home equity during recently favorable markets. A mortgage—whether you decide to refinance or not—can help you do just that.

The Decision to Refinance

Real estate authority and educator, Dr. Gary Eldred, writes that more than 10 million homeowners who should have refinanced in the past year did not take advantage of the opportunity. He speculates that it's because of the following reasons:

- They don't understand the refinancing choices available to them.

- They received bad advice from so-called "loan experts."

- They don't know how to shop for property financing.[4]

We will take a closer look at these barriers; however, if your home is financed with a balloon mortgage that is due soon—whether it is a first or second mortgage—you must refinance now unless you have an alternative way to pay off your loan when it is due. Not refinancing is playing a waiting game that can cost you your home in a changed general economy or if your personal financial circumstances change and your monthly payments are too high to carry. With that thought in mind, read the following sections with special care.

Understand Your Refinancing Choices

You can choose from literally hundreds of refinancing options. However, before you get overwhelmed or panicked, think of the advice and information available from real estate authorities and mortgage experts—real mortgage experts—available to you for the taking. Book stores, libraries, magazine racks, and the Internet are excellent resources connecting you to the "can-do" details about when and how to refinance. A lot of this information used to be unavailable to consumers, but it is freely available to you today. If you don't understand the refinancing choices, return to square one. Recall your experience in obtaining a mortgage to buy your home in the first place. Then retrace your steps, contact your present lender, and find out what terms the lender is prepared to offer if you decide to refinance.

Your present lender is not the last word, however. only a starting point. Check the lender's competition to ensure you get the deal you want and need. (Also check the "Recommended Resources" appendix at the end of this book to learn more about refinancing a mortgage.)

Receiving Good Advice from the Experts

Do not feel intimidated or fall victim to anyone who tries to hustle you into making a quick decision about any financial issue concerning your home. When thinking about refinancing, locate several prospective lenders and then interview them! Ask trusted friends and relatives for good leads to mortgage lending sources, but also consult books and Internet resources that are written for consumers by independent sources. This is an important distinction because if your "expert" works for a bank or mortgage company, he or she wants your mortgage business. This is fine, of course, as long as you research your options and understand what you are doing and why.

After you contact mortgage lenders or brokers, ask for references and learn how they earn fees. Study the terms of the mortgage loans they offer. Compare and contrast the details until you feel comfortable with the lender and the terms of your new mortgage loan.[5] You have seen what a disaster buying or selling a home can be when the big-picture decisions aren't carefully considered. Refinancing, especially when you plan to take cash away from the closing table, requires the same value-focused thinking as buying or selling your home. Your home is about every aspect of your life, so seek to be knowledgeable and to feel comfortable on all four deciding factors when you choose to refinance.

Here is the story of one family that failed to take time to learn more about what they were doing. This family paid the price financially and emotionally.

On the verge of retiring, Harriet and Ari consulted a home contractor about getting a new roof. The contractor also offered to paint the home and make other repairs and improvements, and he suggested that they refinance the small outstanding mortgage to pay for the needed repairs. The contractor told the couple to do this while Ari was still working. The couple consulted their son, Julius, to help them because they didn't know much about getting a mortgage loan. The three met with a lender, quickly decided on terms, closed the "cash-out" refinancing, and hired the contractor. Julius also joined the meeting with the contractor but had little to add because he had never dealt with a contractor himself.

Half way through the job, the couple learned that the construction costs would be more than the amount they initially budgeted. Payments to the contractor already exceeded what the couple had received from the refinancing, and their problems were far from over. They failed to check the credentials of the contractor who, it turned out, had overcharged them for work he was unqualified to do. Although Julius had been apprised of all the details of his parents' financing and construction plans, he later admitted he did not read the documents they had signed. In fact, he said, "He did not really understand them."

The consequences of Harriet and Ari's decisions were devastating to this couple who relied on Julius's ill-founded advice. When financial difficulties loomed in the wake of the contractor's high charges and poor construction performance, Julius then advised his parents to sell their unfinished home. Because of its condition, the couple received less than market value and had no funds left to buy another home. They ended up moving into an apartment. Julius helped them file a lawsuit against the contractor in hopes of recouping some of their money, but the contractor was nowhere to be found and the court papers were never served.

Shop Carefully for Your Mortgage Loan

A decision to refinance and to make home improvements involves serious study. You must take the steps needed to understand both the big picture and the little details. Do not make hasty decisions and be sure that unlike Ari and Harriett, you consult with competent people.

Before you begin to fill out mortgage application forms, review your overall financial situation. Just as when you bought your home initially, you need to know your personal financial status—your income, expenses, assets, current and long-term liabilities, credit account balances, terms, and names of creditors to report to your intended lender. If you are self-employed or own a business, you need to make similar information about your business available. With this knowledge, you can begin your search.

Eric Tyson and Ray Brown, authors of *Mortgages for Dummies*, aim their popular book not at dummies, but at those who are wise enough to know they need such a resource. The biggest dummy thing to do is impulse shop when looking for something as serious as a mortgage. Fight your instincts to take the first deal offered. Instead, check it out carefully to see if it is competitive with other deals.

Although refinancing doesn't have to go hand in hand with making home improvements, it often does. In fact, estimates suggest that as many as half of those who refinance take out cash and 42 percent of those spend part of the money on home improvements.

Home Construction Projects that Are a Pleasure

Polish up your Social Factor when you decide to enter into a home construction project.

Barn raisings fascinate us for good reason. The sight of a whole community lifting the side or roof up onto a building is the ultimate in human cooperation and the result is satisfying for everyone. Although you might not actually see all the members of the community involved in your remodeling or building project, they're there nevertheless. Be aware of your community members, understand who they are and what they do. You need to communicate clearly and calmly with representatives of your bankers and contractors even when you feel on the brink of losing control of a situation. This cooperative network can help you design, finance, and build your project no matter how large or small it might be. In the process, many people will be available to help you make hundreds of choices—materials, color, textures, fixtures, embellishments, and so on.

You also want to keep a cool head at home, especially when interacting with loved ones. A home construction project can be your worst nightmare or a creative experience that is exciting and fun. Even a construction project that proceeds smoothly, however, can generate stressful interactions. And, as homebuilders and architects know all too well, many a shaky relationship has collapsed in the middle of or following a home construction project. No one is exempt from the disequilibrium that can occur.

Donna, an architect, designed the home addition she and her husband Todd had been planning for several years. They used their home equity to finance the extensive remodeling, and they were ecstatic when, with permits in hand, their contractor finally broke ground. "You would think," she told me later, "that a person who had anticipated this project with great excitement, who knows design and building, who knows where all the pipes and ducts will run, and who can see beforehand what it actually will look like, would be immune from the emotional upheaval of living with home construction. I can report that this is not the case!"

Donna calls the process "a benign form of home invasion." "When piles of plywood block my view as I sit by the window to have early morning coffee, I feel off balance. The normal routine and privacy of our home is disrupted, nerves are exposed, small details seem immense, and tempers can fly. We have to be especially careful to note our own feelings and be aware of the feelings of others."

Despite the inconvenience and frayed nerves, home improvement has become the "great national pastime," according to the Joint Center for Housing Studies of Harvard University.[6] Although they trended upward in the late 1990s, repairs, maintenance, and home improvement projects (like refinancings) really took off in the last few years.

If you decide to start a building project, the following are some of the things you'll want to consider during the planning and construction phases to avoid mistakes:

- Don't go overboard and do more rebuilding than necessary even if money is no object. Remember, your home is not just your "castle." It is your best investment too.

- Don't plan an extensive remodeling project in a low-end neighborhood. If other homes in the area badly need work, but are not given the attention they need, the location will hold down the value of the property. This rule also applies to home building—it is never a good idea to build a home that is significantly bigger and better than those that surround it.

- Don't begin a project in an area where homes are decreasing in value—you might end up losing money in the process. It is best to plan a huge remodeling or building project in an area in which the neighborhood home values are stable or rebounding. Watch out for neighborhoods with falling market values.

- Avoid under-budgeting. Spend a lot of time researching the different items that you wish to incorporate into your home and take note of the costs, so that you know the ballpark estimate when bids come in. It is always a good idea to add about 15–20 percent to your budget to accommodate the virtually inevitable extras or higher costs. It is a nightmare to be in a situation in which you are halfway through a renovation and you run out of money for fixtures.

- Lock in extra time for the work schedule. A good baselineis 15 percent more time. Many unexpected problems can arise, such as delayed delivery of materials to the home site, workers not showing up on time, and bad weather to name just a few.

- If you are thinking about redoing more than one room over the next few years, it might be wise and cost effective to remodel all at once. Contractors are able to save money when placing larger orders and can replace flooring in two rooms at the same time for less than it would cost to replace it in one room at a time.

- Dot every "i" and cross every "t" throughout the life of a construction project. Ensure that required zoning and building permits are obtained and that the contractor is reputable, licensed, insured, and well known in the local community for excellent and reliable performance.

Customizing a New Home, Major Additions, and Building from Scratch

When you change the character of your home or build a new home altogether, in essence you have a blank canvas to create whatever you value. You can examine architectural drawings, builder's plans, and model homes to your heart's desire to get an idea for the particular layout you want. You can pour over details such as siding, flooring, roofing, or the quality of kitchen cabinets and countertops that you have always dreamed of. Even if you are engaged only in customizing the details of a new home already planned and under construction by a home builder, at least you can enjoy some of the creativity involved in designing "your home, your way."

Sam and his wife Margaret have always lived in custom built homes. Even their first home, a condo, was carefully outfitted to their exact specifications. "Designing our own space is the best way to get exactly what we want, especially because we both have home offices." When absorbed in designing the interior of their present home, they failed to notice the dirt bikes and all terrain vehicles (ATVs) speeding around their neighbors' properties on afternoons and weekends. Soon enough they became aware of the neighbors' shared hobby. "The noise is deafening at times," Sam told me, "We can hardly wait to leave." Sam and Margaret are hard at work on the design details of their next house, which is now under construction in a better location.

Margaret and Sam's story illustrates that even the best-laid building plans can go awry; however, they are old hands at it by now. (This is the third home they have built from scratch.) They work well together, know what they want, and know what to expect during the building process. They enjoy watching a new home come together from the idea stage right up until moving day. As for their present home—which they are selling—the market in their area is brisk and seller-friendly. They are confident they can to sell quickly and realize a profit on their investment.

Controlling the Building Process

Remember the barn raising? Home building is a cooperative effort, and unless you are a home builder by profession and experience, you probably don't want to undertake it alone. It makes little difference whether you are motivated to save money, to control the process, or a little of both. You can run into trouble if you aren't able to do the job correctly, arrange timely inspections, coordinate your construction loan advances, and a hundred and one other details that enter into the home-building process. You can end up calling in the professionals to fix the messes you create, now or when you decide to sell. This can result in twice the cost for labor and materials, so in the end, you do not save money.

Even Donna, the architect, who designed her own addition and is perfectly capable of acting as her own general contractor, decided not to take on this additional responsibility. Like a surgeon who does not operate on his or her relative, you will find that it is usually worth the cost to hire objective building professionals. In fact, these are tangible factor processes that can be eclipsed by social factors in actual practice. Even the building projects themselves are more about the intimate and social relationships in your life than they are about the remodeling, building, or decorating you plan to accomplish. Here's why:

- Home construction decisions are not simply challenging, frustrating, unsettling, or annoying at times. The results can have an impact on the quality of your daily life. If you fail to select the right builder, sub-contractor, mortgage loan, or location, you might get stuck in a quagmire from which escape can be impractical for several years.

- All of your customizing, remodeling, or construction goals must be shared if you have a partner, and you must be able to communicate about them daily until they're achieved. If you and your partner cannot discuss such details without emotional turmoil, you might risk your relationship itself. Home construction projects don't solve relationship problems. They can easily create them.

- The financial and other details of these decisions must be openly discussed with your builder, sub-contractors, and other community, real estate, and mortgage experts and officials. They are part of the system, which you must learn your way around or risk becoming trapped in a state of quiet desperation as you watch your home take shape without your leadership participation.

- Unless you are used to communicating openly about finances, chances are your home construction project will not proceed smoothly. Each detail you add to a home design comes with a price tag. Compromising, trading off, and looking for less expensive alternatives are the order of business—a fact that most people who enter into a major home construction project learn more than once during the design and building process.

- Plan to spend a great deal of time at your construction site. Questions inevitably arise about the building plans and other details, which you need to be available to answer on the spot. As you see the plans actually take shape, you might also want to change something before it's too late to do so. Being available helps improve and smooth the construction process for the owners, builders, and sub-contractors alike. Everyone likes to get feedback on the job as it progresses.

Working with Your Contractor or Builder

Ask anyone who has enjoyed undertaking a home construction project, and they will tell you that much of the pleasure with the building process is due to compatible and competent professionals on the job. Likewise, people who regret or dislike the home-building experience typically complain bitterly about the performance or incompatibility of the builder or contractor. Although it is crucial to shop around for the best construction quotes, it is even more important to find a contractor who works with you as a full partner in the building endeavor.

Find a reputable builder or contractor. Interview contractors until you find one who comes highly recommended and someone with whom you can communicate well and often. You want your contractor to lay out the building plan and explain each aspect of the contract. When you look over bids, make sure they are true cost estimates, especially if you plan to do some of the work yourself. Builders and contractors who are strictly interested in a specific profit for each project use only the square footage and a predetermined price per foot to arrive at an estimate for work. As you go over plans with your contractor or builder, make sure you ask a lot of questions and closely observe what the contractor inspects as he takes notes for the estimate. The estimate should contain a breakdown of the cost of labor and materials plus a calculation of profit for the builder. This way you can determine how much you can save by doing some of the tasks yourself.

Make sure that you oversee all phases of the building or remodeling project and know what is going on at all times. Remember to ask questions! An experienced contractor or builder can give you a good idea of how the finished product will look so that there are no surprises. See that the work-in-progress is in line with the signed contract and plans. The drawings, contracts, and specifications should be clear and comprehensive; but even so, as work progresses, you might think of something you forgot to consider initially. You should be allowed to make changes along the way if you are unhappy with something (within reason), although this might be costly, especially if materials for the initial plans have already been ordered.

There are a few things you should know when negotiating a contract. Make sure that your contract is specific! Clarify what is and what is not included in the contract to ensure that your expectations are met. Because homeowners don't know a lot of the language, standards, and specifications that are presented in these types of contracts, it is important to hire a reputable contractor, even if it means spending a little extra money. It may end up saving you a substantial amount in the long run.

Be sure to include a clause in the contract that allows you to make ongoing inspections during the construction period and also after the home is built. It is recommended that you do an inspection just as the foundation is laid and also just before the insulation and drywall are put in. Without the insulation and drywall, you will be able to inspect the plumbing and electrical systems, most of which should be in place.

If you are building from a model, include a clause in your contract that guarantees your house meets the quality standards of the model home. Many developers write clauses into the contracts that let them use cheaper materials if the housing market changes. Make sure that the contract specifies what model and standards should be used during each phase of the development. Also crucial for the new homeowner is an extended warranty, which ensures a new home against structural defects over the entire course of the warranty. In addition, in the first year, the home is protected against specified electrical flaws and problems with plumbing, cooling, heating, and mechanical systems. It also covers defects in workmanship and materials used in the building. As each year of the warranty passes, however, the house has less coverage.

If you think you have what it takes to undertake a home construction project, proceed with due diligence and determination. Little else, except maybe a barn raising, can be so creatively challenging and exciting, and feel so deeply satisfying and worthwhile when you are finished and ready to move in.

Points to Ponder

The secret to building success—no matter how small or large the project—is planning, then finding the right professionals to help you refine your plan and bring it to life.

Here are the seven steps I recommend you take before you make a decision to take on a home construction project. Unless you feel comfortable with each of these preliminary steps, you would do well to postpone your decision at the present time.

1. Using your Housing Profile, carefully think through the results you expect and value about the building process you are considering.

2. Compare your values and needs with those of your partner, so that your choice to take on a home construction project is a shared and mutually supported decision.

3. Run through as many scenarios as possible about what can go wrong during a home construction project and see if you can come up with solutions. This can help you feel prepared.

4. Set a preliminary budget and check your financial resources to see if they are sufficient. Remember to add at least 15–20 percent in case your costs exceed your expectations.

5. Seek out friends and acquaintances to learn about their experiences with home construction projects.

6. Have a consultation with a local architect or home builder who knows the area well and is acquainted with zoning regulations and building codes.

7. Consult one or several books and other resources to learn the steps involved in a home construction project.

End Notes

1 Joint Center for Housing Studies of Harvard University. The State of the Nation's Housing. Cambridge, MA: Joint Center for Housing Studies of Harvard University. www.jch.harvard.edu.

2 Ibid. Housing wealth is also more broadly based than stock wealth. Home-ownership is the cornerstone of household wealth in the United States.

3 Morgenson, Gretchen. "Housing Bust: It Won't Be Pretty," *The New York Times, Sunday Business,* 25 July 2004. This article predicts that the run-up in housing prices might be losing steam and also asserts that homes are currently over valued. Viewed historically, prices have climbed twice as much than during the bullish real estate markets of the mid-1970s and 1980s. Whether prices plummet at once or level out, the period of low interest rates and rising home prices enjoyed during the past decade or so is not likely to last.

4 Eldred, Gary W. *106 Mortgage Secrets all Homebuyers Must Learn—But Lenders Don't Tell.* Hoboken, NJ: John Wiley & Sons, Inc., 2003.

5 Tyson, Eric and Ray Brown. *Mortgages for Dummies.* New York: Wiley Publishing, Inc., 2000. *Mortgages for Dummies* is not just for the novice or uninformed. It is full of good ideas, and it has a checklist with forms you can use to compare terms and conditions of available loans.

6 Joint Center for Housing Studies. "Improving America's Housing: Measuring the Benefits of Home Remodeling." Cambridge, MA: Joint Center for Housing Studies, 2003. www.jchs.harvard.edu.

14

INVESTING IN OTHER HOMES

No investment philosophy, unless it is just a carbon copy of someone else's approach, develops in its complete form in any one day or year.

—Philip Fisher

Anyone who knows how to pick stocks can tell you that successful investment starts with understanding the business of the companies chosen. The same is true of investing in real estate. If you are thinking of buying a second home for vacation or for your future retirement, or if you want to try investing in a rental home, this chapter is for you. It is also helpful for readers who must relocate and want to find tenants to rent the home they have to leave rather than sell it.

If you have ideas about becoming a real estate investor in more than one or two additional homes, good for you, but take your time. Study your options, run and re-run the numbers, gather experience—and then lots of good luck to you. "Real estate gets in your blood," say the old-timers.

A Way of Life

Becoming an owner of rental homes has made millionaires of many who chose to take this investment path. If housing investment is your next move, chances are good that, like the family you are about to meet, you already own your own home, have savings and investments, a predictable income, and the confidence to recognize and take advantage of income potential and appreciation opportunity.

The story of Lucia and Manuel is testimony to the hard work and tenacious investment savvy of generations of Americans who arrived during the first half of the twentieth century. The story has been repeated many times over by individuals and families from every corner of the globe. It is important to note that it still happens for industrious and hope-filled "new" Americans today, and like millions of other unheralded success stories across the nation, it can also inspire you.

Manuel emigrated with his brother from Spain in the 1930s and met, courted, and married Lucia who was also from Spain. They soon after settled in Washington, D.C., and they lived in a four-room flat over the neighborhood grocery store they ran together. Manuel and Lucia scrimped and saved and soon were able to buy the building where they lived and worked. To pay the mortgage, they remodeled and rented out the top floor to another immigrant family. They had three children all of whom were brought up to work in the family business. With the growing success of the grocery store, Manuel slowly began buying and renting out other houses in the neighborhood.

Lucia was leery of her husband's housing purchases and, according to their daughter, Maria, who carries on his penchant for real estate investment, "Mom often screamed at Dad, 'How will we pay for this?'" But Maria carefully watched her Dad's investment activities, and two generations later, the extended family enjoys Manuel's legacy and the financial security of his example. Maria and her husband John still practice and teach their own children that prudent real estate investing, and the benefits of good timing and shrewd management, are a winning combination that can bring many rewards over time.

Contrast this family's real estate successes with the story about Lourdes's ill-fated entry into rental real estate. We met Lourdes in Chapter 11, "To Own or Not to Own, That's a Good Question," when she and her husband Andy became homeowners during a period of unreliable employment and instability in their relationship. Soon after moving into their home, Andy was offered and accepted a job in Phoenix, Arizona. Lourdes lost her job, and before following her husband to Arizona was left to find a tenant to cover the couple's house payments.

"What was I supposed to do?" Lourdes asked me. "What did I know about handling a rental?" Lourdes found the tenant by placing an ad in a local newspaper. He ended up "not paying the rent, and he trashed the place before he was finally evicted." Lourdes divorced Andy and after much hard work, she climbed out of debt and began a new life. Today she has a management position in a prestigious firm, and she is saving to become a homeowner once again. As for investing in rental housing—"Never again," she says, "I don't have the temperament or the desire."

It's a good idea to enjoy stability in both your employment and in your family or partnership relationships when you take on any type of real estate ownership. Owning and keeping a primary residence running smoothly and in tip-top shape requires "business" judgment. Owning a second home requires even more: good timing, financing savvy, patience, maintenance and management skills, and an eye for spotting value.

What Is a Second Home?

Researchers have trouble pigeonholing the reasons behind people's purchase of second homes.[1] Since 1999, the American Housing Survey (AHS) has included a question to learn people's reason for buying a second home. Owners report mixed motives. When asked, many answer that their second home is for "recreational purposes" and "investment purposes." The 2002 National Association of Realtors® Profile of Second Home Owners indicates that owners of second homes report purchasing their properties for vacation, investment, or some combination of the two. Broken down, about 78 percent of owners say their property is a vacation home; the remaining 22 percent indicate that they purchased it as an investment. The majority of both types of owners consider their second homes to be good financial investments. Among those surveyed, roughly 57 percent said they were seeking a family retreat and 18 percent were planning for retirement.[2]

In 2003, about four percent of homebuyers purchased a second home.[3] Buyers of second homes report spending less for second homes than on primary homes. They were three times more likely to buy a condo or apartment than were buyers of primary homes, and the location of the second home was less predictable than the location of primary homes.

There are many reasons to buy a second home, both personal and financial. If you want to become a second-home buyer, your reason(s) might be one or more of the following:

- You'd like to have a home where you can return periodically to vacation in a familiar place. It is strictly for vacations, but you want a home that appreciates in value over the years that you own it.

- You want to retire one day in an area where there are vacation facilities and you want to find a prospective property that you can rent out until then.

- You want a second home strictly for investment, either in a vacation area or somewhere else. It doesn't matter where it is located as long as there is the potential for a good return on your invested capital.

- You want a smaller home that you can buy and rent out. You might decide to remodel it and retire there when your primary home becomes too large or burdensome for you to handle.

- You plan to invest systematically in more than one additional home when the opportunities arise.

There are other ways to become a second-home owner. You might inherit the family home or a family member's vacation home. You can decide to relocate, rent out your present home, and buy another at your new location. Or, you might end up re-owning a home that you once sold and financed for a buyer who couldn't make the payments.

There are also many ways to hold title[4] to property: as a partner, timeshare owner, condominium owner, or owner in fee simple. Each of these is a complex subject that requires thorough understanding before you sign on the dotted line for any property. In addition, whatever your reasons are for buying a second home, its location is as important as it is for your primary residence. When a home is located in a desirable community, it is more likely to increase in future value, and it is easier both to rent and to sell. This is especially true for vacation or resort communities.

When purchasing a second home near water, golf courses, or ski slopes that are popular tourist areas, the value of your property is directly impacted by the quality of the resort or vacation area. Become thoroughly familiar with the area before you invest by visiting it many times as a vacationer. Study the market, visit several real estate and management firms, and talk to year-round residents and shop keepers. Understand local zoning, development and commercial growth potential, and check sales and rental data for the past few seasons.[5]

It takes study, analysis, and good timing to learn your way around the housing investment arena. The reasons given for second-home ownership are valid and meaningful to the people who invest in them. Although each circumstance is unique, there are certain principles that apply to second-home investment, depending of course upon what you hope to accomplish through your purchase strategy.

The Psychology of Home Investing

In addition to the principles of deciding to buy your primary home contained in Part 1, "Your Housing Psychology," all of which also apply to your decision to purchase a second home, there is another principle to keep in mind when considering whether to become an investor in a second home—that of risk tolerance. The answer to questions of risk tolerance for second-home investors derive in part from factual information: age, income, experience, savings, future need for cash, and investing time horizon. They are also answered by the realities of market timing: factors such as interest rates, inflation, credit availability, rental and selling markets, over which an aspiring investor has no direct control. However, like buying stocks "on sale" in a down market, a savvy real estate investor can also decide that a fluctuating marketplace offers investment opportunities that are simply unavailable in a marketplace that is roaring upward.

If we listen to the experts in real estate investing, emotion should be locked down for investors in second homes. "Gee that is a gorgeous home— just look at that view," is not appropriate, they might say, until after you've run the numbers and made an informed investment decision. In other words, don't "fall in love" with your investment real estate until it has earned its way into your affections. Love of place, however, does indeed hold sway for many second-home purchasers. And why not?

The same excitement, anticipation, and anxiety are often present when buying a second home, especially if its purpose in our lives is to bring relaxation, recreation, and social enjoyment. Still, the cautions that exist in our primary home purchases must also be present when considering a second home. In addition, lessons from the psychology of investing in the capital markets also apply to investing in real estate:[6]

- People in general are over-confident when it comes to their estimates of the earnings potential of their investments. Of course there are always nice surprises, but chances are that you will be overoptimistic about the investment potential of your second home.

- In real estate, like the stock market, people forget. Not only are homeowners overoptimistic about the prospective price appreciation of their homes, but so are analysts and other experts who are overoptimistic about general market trends as well.

- The evaluation of risk, by definition, contains important subjective elements and considerations. It is not purely rational, nor can it be if we are to be helped in our investment evaluations and decisions by our "emotional intelligence."[7]

Fear and greed are the psychological concepts that drive the markets it is often said, but psychologist Lola Lopes insists that most investors react less to greed and more to hope.[8] Nowhere is that more visible than in both primary- and second-home investment.

"Fear induces an investor to focus on events that are especially unfavorable, whereas hope induces her to focus on events that are favorable," writes Hersh Shefrin in discussing the theories of Dr. Lopes. The fact that a homeowner insists that her home is still worth its full value, despite a decline in neighborhood prices or even the overall economy, isn't based in greed, but in hope, as Dr. Lopes knows well. Only if and when it becomes absolutely necessary to sell a home in a down market will a homeowner finally and reluctantly accept the fact that the value of his or her home is less than it was before.

Second Homes as Rentals

Homes held strictly for rental and not for personal use are diverse and defy categorization. A rental home can be a cooperative in a big city, a duplex in an aging neighborhood, a bungalow in a suburb, farmland in a rural area, or a unit in a seashore resort. The owners of these properties can live anywhere. Although many investors prefer to own property they can easily access, many people who relocate choose to rent the home they are leaving rather than sell it. With enough cash flow, price appreciation, and skillful property management, this can be a good investment decision.

Valerie was 42-years-old when she moved 6,000 miles to the Big Island in Hawaii "just because she always wanted to live there." And no, she hadn't been there before. With a mixture of growing fear and excitement, she spent four months planning carefully to make it happen. Her savings would last for several months after she arrived. She could store valuables with a relative, sell some furniture she didn't need, and drive her car across the country to be shipped to Hawaii from California. The way was clear, but she needed to decide what to do about her house. Rent or sell? Sell or rent? She went back and forth when trying to make this decision. The indecisiveness "drove me crazy," she told me. If she sold, there would be extra cash that she could rely on, and it was a seller's market. There was only one problem with this, however. Valerie loved her home and did not want to part with it.

So Valerie decided to run an advertisement and find a compatible renter. She knew she would remain eligible for a tax-free sale if she lived in the home for at least two of five years at the time of a sale. So Valerie decided to try to trade a longer-term lease for a rental rate that would cover her housing expenses. Even as house sales were popping all around her, Valerie found the ideal tenants. The tenants were looking for a home to rent for 2 ¹/₂ years and they were willing to cover Valerie's costs, except for major repairs. Through good communication via the Internet and cell phones, all has run smoothly. Valerie visited the tenants only once in the first two years and both parties were pleased by the arrangement. Although Valerie had no cash flow to speak of from the rental, the property has increased in value by over $100,000 during the two-year period. Her new life in Hawaii is working out well, and she will take the equity as soon as the lease expires to buy her own home on the Big Island.

Rental property investing is a small business that can help owners gain financial independence. If you choose to hold or purchase one or more investment homes to rent, you are your own boss. You can set your own goals, make your own decisions, and work at your own pace. The return from a rented home can be in cash flow or in price appreciation or both. As long as the home is cared for and the carrying and maintenance costs are covered, you have little to worry about, except a steep decline in the housing market just when you want to sell. The trick, as Valerie knew, was to maximize her rental income, minimize her out-of-pocket expenses, and meet the needs of her reliable tenants.

The Business of Investing in Rental Housing

Reasons for owning one rental home include the opportunity to gain from price appreciation, to cover mortgage and other carrying costs, and to earn current income if that is possible. It is also a way to take advantage of tax incentives. So why not make the decision to buy more than one home—perhaps two, or three, or even more?

If you have what it takes to invest in and manage rental homes, you can reap many potential rewards. However, do not enter the rental housing market precipitously or expect to get rich quickly or believe you will have an easy time of it. Expect equity to build over time. Owning and overseeing rental housing takes the same effort and involves all of the ups and downs of any well-run small business.

Here are some suggestions from the experts:[9]

- When beginning your search for rental housing, check classified ads and interview Realtors® and other agents. Spend time looking at many different properties to find the locations and price ranges that you can comfortably handle. Drive through and scout neighborhoods that interest you and keep your eyes open for sale signs.

- Engage a buyer broker to scout properties for you. Ask what rental properties they have listed or which ones they know about that are not listed yet. Learn the values of comparable properties in every neighborhood that interests you.

- Take your time to research what you can and cannot afford. Estimate operational costs for each property including mortgage and interest payments, taxes, insurance, maintenance and repair costs, and the prices of water, garbage, and other utilities. Learn what the local customs are about paying for utilities. In some areas, landlords pay for certain utilities; in other areas, they do not.

- When estimating value, learn the tax assessment, lot size, zoning, subdivision requirements, special assessments, homeowner associations, easements, and any other information you can about the property that interests you.

- Verify that the market rental for the particular property you are investigating covers your expenses and financing costs. Also think about how you will finance, fix up, maintain, and manage the housing. Set up a cash reserve in case of emergency or have another plan in place for those times when you might have less income to depend on.

- If you end up with vacancies, how long is enough time to pay for expenses until new tenants move in?

- When you visit properties, bring a notebook to take notes and bring a camera to take pictures of the inside, outside of the property, yard, and surrounding neighborhood. The pictures and information should refresh your memory later—remember, you might end up looking at dozens of properties.

- What condition is the property in? Does it need to be repainted? What is the remaining life of the roof, the heating plant, and the appliances? How long ago were major improvements made?

- Pay attention to the size of the yard and to any landscaping you see in order to get an estimate of its maintenance costs.

- What neighborhood factors can add or detract from the future value of the property and impact the amount of rent you will receive? What is the proximity to shopping, nature areas, industrial areas, or major roadways?

Your goal should be to own a low- to mid-cost rental property in a mid- to high-cost neighborhood so that your property appreciates in value. As with the purchase of your primary home, you want to avoid property that declines in value. The causes of a major downturn usually stem from neglected properties that can spread to whole neighborhoods and contribute to the decrease in market values.

A Partnership or Family Enterprise

When Maria married Tom and began to carry on the real estate investment legacy of Maria's father, something wonderful happened in addition to the financial rewards the couple enjoyed during the ensuing years. They also enjoyed being partners in the enterprises in which they invested. There are important relationship principles and other life principles at work here that make their real estate partnership successful. These include the following:

- Satisfying, thriving marriages are models for outstanding business partnerships.

- Partners who know how to resolve conflicts, have complimentary skills, and give each other space to excel at what they do best, make the best investment partners.

- "Vision is greater than baggage," writes Stephen R. Covey in *The 7 Habits of Highly Effective Families*.[10] Covey talks about a couple or family that works together on a shared vision of where they want to go and how they want to get there. The reason is simple, according to Covey. "Have you ever done a jigsaw puzzle? How important is it that all who are working on it have the same final scene in mind?"

Working with a sense of shared vision in the real estate investment arena should not be understated for a couple or a family. It is a source of pleasure and it is potential profit for all involved.

"I'm very attached to this house," Wren said about a rental home she and her husband own in a resort community. "It was a sad looking house in need of many, many repairs, but now, it's a happy, colorful house…We were offered four times what we paid for it, but we are much too attached to it to sell it." Wren and her husband loved working together on the house and both share the same feelings for it. "We tend to be on the same page when it comes to home investing, renovations…we are very lucky and grateful."

The couple recently purchased another rental home because they have a waiting list for several dates on the first one. Rentals are in huge demand for big weekends at a nearby academic institution, and during the summer, they typically book almost every week/weekend. "It has been a lot of fun working on the house." They say they aren't doing it for profit from the rentals, but more for long-term investment. Property values are rising in the area and are looking good for the future. "We also love that people are creating vacation memories in a home we created for that purpose."

Wren and Joe have clearly profited by the shared experience of investing in this rental home, but their number one benefit might very well be the companionship and pleasure they take from the experience of working together in investment real estate.

Points to Ponder

- Don't be overoptimistic about the investment potential of your second home, especially if it will double as a vacation home. Check rental returns in the area carefully if you plan to buy in a resort community.

- Enjoy your second home rental property, but don't expect to become rich overnight. This is a small business that requires patience, management skills, and good market timing.

- When you've learned what it's all about and feel comfortable that you know what you are doing, you can buy your next property, but do not buy before you are educated and comfortable.

End Notes

1 "U.S. Housing Market Conditions," First Quarter, 2004. Office of Policy Development and Research, U.S. Department of Housing and Urban Development, Washington, D.C.

2 The National Association of Realtors® Profile of Second-Home Owners, 2002. The Research Division of the National Association of Realtors®, 430 N. Michigan Avenue, Chicago, IL 60611-4087. www.REALTOR.org.

3 Bishop, Paul, Thomas Beers, Shonda Hightower, and Kate Anderson. *The 2003 National Association of Realtors® Profile of Home Buyers and Sellers.* Washington, D.C.: The National Association of Realtors Research Division, National Association of Realtors®, 2004.

4 Holding title to an asset—in this case, a home—is the means by which the owner of the property has the just possession of the property under the law. The *title* is the evidence of ownership of the property. There are a number of different ways to hold title to property. Furthermore, the law is not the same in every jurisdiction. It is imperative that readers check with an attorney in their own jurisdiction to determine precisely what their rights are as owners. See Kuhn, Janet L. "Titling Assets" in Lois A. Vitt (ed.) *Encyclopedia of Retirement and Finance*. Westport, CT: Greenwood Press.

5 *Kiplinger's Buying & Selling a Home* by the editors of *Kiplinger's Personal Finance Magazine*. Washington, D.C.: Kiplinger Books, 2002.

6 This section borrows from the work of David Dreman, author of "Investor Overreaction," and Richard A. Geist, author of "The Emotions of Risk." Both articles can be found in Lifson, Lawrence E., and Richard A. Geist (eds). *The Psychology of Investing*. New York: John Wiley & Sons, Inc., 1999.

7 Goleman, Daniel. *Emotional Intelligence*. New York: Bantam Books, 1995.

8 Shefrin, Hersh. "Beyond Greed & Fear: Emotions and Risk." Working Knowledge, Harvard Business School Working Knowledge Newsletter, October 12, 1999. http://hbswk.hbs.edu/item.jhtml?id=841&t=finance.

9 This should be regarded as a quick checklist of items and issues gleaned from many sources as well as the experience of the author. If you are seriously interested in entering the real estate rental business, it is important that you check out the references on the Internet and at the end of this book in the "Recommended Resources" appendix. Interview others in the business and investigate some of the courses in real estate investment that are available in your local area.

10 Covey, Stephen R. *The 7 Habits of Highly Effective Families*. New York: St. Martin's Griffin, 1997.

Secret 9

Pack up your courage or your fears will move with you.

15

SELLING AND SAYING GOODBYE TO A HOME

Life is a series of hellos and goodbyes. I'm afraid it's time for goodbye again.

—*Billy Joel*

So you've made the decision to sell your home and to take that other emotional roller coaster ride that competes with buying a home. It's no secret that deciding to sell is a courageous choice for many people, and it is just one of many decisions that must be made throughout a nerve-wracking process that can last many months.

When will your home go on the market? Who will help you? Where will you find needed information? How will you work out the financial details? Addressing these questions and many other questions up front will help you maintain a sense of balance throughout the stressful process, which can bring with it feelings of frustration, resignation, determination, hope, anxiety, exhilaration, and finally, relief.

Studies attest to the fact that selling your home can be one of life's more difficult experiences, especially if it is combined with other upheaval, which it often is.[1] In addition, the commitment, formalities, language, and procedures of the transaction can be intimidating. Like many sellers, you might also have to wrestle with the myriad of "goodbyes" that can accompany the sale of your home. Few take on the process without hoping that the sooner it is over, the better!

Everyone at one time or another knows the sadness of losing someone or something near and dear. Selling a home can fall into this category. However, even if it doesn't, you aren't devoid of feeling when you leave the place you have called "home." Your feelings can range from eagerness to be unburdened and get on with your life to anger and regret because you must move from a home you love. Whatever you feel or try not to feel, if you are a prospective seller, this chapter is for you. The goal of this chapter is to help you avoid making the selling experience worse by:

- Second-guessing your reasons for selling.

- Having unreasonable expectations about the value of your home.

- Failing to do the same amount of homework as you did when you bought your home or being defensive about taking the steps necessary so it will "show well" to prospective buyers.

- Keeping ideas, feelings, thoughts, and anxieties inside instead of talking about them with competent and understanding people.

- Trying to sell your home on your own without understanding the amount of money, time, patience, and detached business acumen you need to handle it well.

Let's examine these possible complications one at a time to help smooth the way for you to move through and beyond them.

Clarifying Your Selling Priorities to Avoid Second-Guessing

Hints and tips on how to ready your home for sale and how to approach the selling process are plentiful.[2] Only you can know where your priorities lie, however. If you already have your eye on another home, then a clean, quick sale might be the answer to your prayers. If speed and urgency are not at the top of your list, holding out for the best offer might be the way to go. Whatever your reasons for selling, it's likely there will be several times as you market and sell your home that you'll want to remind yourself of your selling motivators.

Following are some reasons for deciding to sell:

- The upkeep of this home is too much work.

- You want to be in an urban (rural, recreational, or retirement) area.

- The cost of carrying this home is too high.

- This home is too far away from the people and, or places you desire to be.

- You need the cash from the home equity.

- You are moving across the country (or to another city) to take or find a new job.

- You want to find a smaller or bigger home.

- You are planning to move to a retirement community.

Before proceeding with your selling strategy, take some time to think through all of the reasons you want to sell your home by fully addressing the following deciding factors:

Your Personal Checklist of Selling Deciding Factors

I am/we are selling our home because of

Personal Factor reasons and feelings: _____

_____

_____

Social Factor reasons and feelings: _____

_____

_____

Tangible Factor reasons and feelings: _____

_____

_____

Money Factor reasons and feelings: _____

_____

_____

Take plenty of time to think through your reasons for selling, and then elaborate on each one. If you are selling your home, it is likely that you are also somewhere in the process of buying another home. This can be the cause of additional stress, especially if there is a time lag between selling your old home and moving into your new one. It's to your benefit to be specific and honest about the factors involved in selling your home and your accompanying feelings.

After your thoughts and feelings begin to flow freely (they will if you give them time), rank them in order of importance to you. Clearly stating your reasons for selling—to yourself now and to others later—will become the foundation of your selling strategy, the basis for your relationship with your buyer, agent, and, or lawyer, and for your own emotional steadiness and self-confidence. If you are selling with a partner, both of you need to complete this exercise and then discuss the thoughts that surface—even if you think you've heard it all before! Making sure your thoughts and reasons are shared is guaranteed to spare both of you significant emotional turmoil.

Now put your worksheets in a drawer where you can easily retrieve them whenever you need to review your thinking. In a few weeks, or even months, you might need to bolster your resolve or change your selling strategy. Going back to the source of your decision to sell your home becomes essential for clear headedness. It keeps you focused on your original reasons and helps you not to second-guess yourself. If you find that circumstances have changed significantly, you can adjust your decision making accordingly.

Valuing Your Home for Sale

Shelve your P Factor defensiveness when it comes to pricing your home for sale. Judgments about the value of your home are not about you. They are about the look, bricks and sticks, atmosphere, environment, and location of the home you are preparing to sell. You need to stay calm and objective. Face the financial facts and the reality of the marketplace. Keep in mind that pricing your home for sale is an M Factor decision, and no amount of wishing can make it anything else.

Price your home too high, and potential buyers will pass it by. If it is at the top or outside of their price range, buyers won't show up to look at the "special qualities" you believe add to the value of your home, especially if comparable properties are selling for less. Pricing your property too high also carries potential financial consequences. It might end up costing you more money because of the time spent waiting for a sale and missed market opportunities. If it stays on the market too long, buyers assume something is wrong with it besides price.[3]

You need to walk a fine line to arrive at the right asking price. Figure out what you would like to realize from the sale and also become knowledgeable about your local market. Look at other area homes for sale, read advertisements, and interview real estate agents, but realize that your ideas about value and your financial needs ultimately have no affect on what your home is actually worth. In the end, an offer to buy your home is strictly determined by the marketplace. Because most buyers place offers that are less than the asking price, allow some room for negotiation, but not so much as to discourage them altogether.[4]

Doing Your Homework

The "System" helps you sell your home, so be prepared to learn your way around this important segment of the real estate arena. Your home sale can net you proceeds that are higher than what you might ever experience from another investment, or like any marketplace, it can let you down. You can maximize your financial gain and minimize your losses by doing your homework before putting your home up for sale.

What's going on in your local market? Is this a good time to sell? What are buyers looking for? In what price range are other homes selling? What kind of financing is available? Are interest rates rising or declining? Many real estate agents will do a market analysis for you, and they are free because they want your business. Take advantage of this help and get to know your local agents. You might want to pick one to represent you.

But wait!

Do you feel like an ostrich hearing this? Do you want to bury your head and ignore this advice, hoping it will go away? Just when you most need to do your homework, you might feel frustration, even anger or impatience about the suggestion that you need to seek more knowledge. If this is even close to the way you feel, you might be identifying with the place you live. With so much of your time, sweat, energy, money, and creativity invested in your home, why must you have to work at selling it? It is possible that you also feel uncomfortable or anxious about the people who will traipse through your home, and examine, assess, judge, or perhaps criticize it unfairly? Acknowledging any such feelings is a good beginning. Then packing up your courage to head for your computer, real estate company, or nearest bookstore is the step that's most likely to help you supplant those feelings with positive "can-do" resolve.

Compare your home to similar homes in your neighborhood—this means going to see them whenever you can. You cannot meaningfully compare prices of similar properties from other neighborhoods because location—as almost everyone knows—determines price variation. By comparing your home to similar homes that are now on the market or have recently sold, you can collect your own market data—the actual value placed on homes like yours in the current climate. If a quick sale is what you are after, then you might want to consider offering buyer incentives, such as paying some of the closing costs, giving the buyer a repair or redecorating allowance, or a home warranty. This is particularly beneficial when selling an older home that might need repairs. A friend of mine offered to escrow an amount for repaving when buyers became concerned about the unsightliness of a rutted driveway. It was enough to close the sale and calm the concerns of the buyers.

Although you might follow the guidance of advisors, including an agent or appraiser, it is still your responsibility to stay on top of changes in the local market and to be aware of comparable properties. When you do, you have more confidence in the selling process, you better understand the market-place, and you know what your home is truly worth. You need to be flexible and creative, do your homework, and be an active partner with your selling agent. Use your knowledge to make informed judgments—not emotion-laden reactions—throughout all of your selling negotiations.

Showing Off Your Home to Buyers

Make it as easy as possible for your buyer to imagine living a happy, healthy, and successful life in your home and do not expect them to put any effort into summoning up the results. Some people are not visionaries and cannot look past what is actually there. What this means is that you must remove clues to the manner in which you live your life, including your personal effects to the extent possible, and any signs of disorganization and clutter. If this is inconvenient and stressful for you, then scream into a pillow and afterwards do it anyway.

Some people even hire *stagers* to set the rooms up, help them declutter, and emphasize the most attractive features of your home. Your buyers want to imagine how *they* will live in your home, not how you do. It is definitely worth the inconvenience and cost to rearrange your home so that it shows in the best way possible. Try to consider your home through your prospective buyers' senses—their sights, sounds, smell, touch, and feelings.

The outside appearance of the house is the first impression buyers form as they pull up to your home. If it is not attractive, you might lose a buyer even if the inside of the home is in great condition. Ensure that the gutters are intact, the roof is in good condition, doors and windows are clean, the paint is in good condition, and the lawn and flowerbeds are healthy and appealing. Buyers remember how good your property looked when they first approached it long after they have left the site. If these simple steps can make your house more appealing than other properties, then you might get the sale.

Make your house as clean and bright as possible. Deal with the most obvious problems first: fix cracks, peeling paint, masonry or carpentry in bad condition. Be wary, though, of spending large amounts of money on renovations or additions hoping to obtain a higher price for your home. Spend only the amount needed to make your home appealing. Often the least expensive way to do basic improvements is to do them yourself—minor repairs and a coat of paint might be all that's required. Touch up any paint that looks tired, scratched, or stained with neutral colors, such as white or off-white. Replace carpeting if it is worn or an unusual color. Although this is a little more expensive, it can greatly improve the overall look of your home. Remove curtains to let in the maximum amount of light. If you need electrical or plumbing work done, have the professionals fix the problem, but take care of it before it is found by a house inspector. If you do not, you will have to take care of it anyway.[5]

I know a Realtor® who advises people to get an official inspection done before putting their home on the market. Then, you can fix minor repairs that a potential buyer might insist you hire a professional to do later. This can get your home ready to sell and it avoids waiting to learn about problems after you have found a buyer and an inspection has to be done.

Polish your windows and clean the kitchen and bathrooms until they sparkle. Ensure that all surfaces are free of clutter. Few things put off buyers as much as a dirty bathroom or kitchen. If these two important rooms are not clean, they give the impression that the whole house is dirty and unhygienic. Invest in air fresheners to rid the home of any smells, such as smoking, pets, or food that you have been unable to remove completely through cleaning. Remove ashtrays, pet food bowls and beds, and litter trays prior to an open house or prior to showing the house by appointment. This helps reduce unpleasant odors, and it should remove the need for concerns on the part of the buyer about stains, scratches, or burns caused by pets or cigarettes. Finally, buy some flowers or potted plants. Extra touches often clinch the deal![6]

Rooms look more spacious when as many of your belongings as possible are cleared away. Store items at a friend or family member's house or put them into storage until you move. You might be surprised at how much you can actually throw away, and this has the added bonus of reducing the amount of sorting, packing, and moving to be done later! If you ensure that your house looks (and smells!) its best, you can greatly reduce the inconvenience and frustration of a drawn-out selling process. Another bonus: You enjoy your home more during the final weeks and months that you live there.

You are not alone. In 2003, more than 6 million existing homes were sold across the nation. In 2002, over 5.5 million existing homes were sold, according to the National Association of Realtors®.[7] Although these have been exceptionally good years for home sales, sellers are also more knowledgeable about taking the steps necessary to ensure that their home shows in its best light. Okay, we said that selling your home is a stressful experience, but you are in good company. Almost everyone selling a home follows the hints and tips contained in this chapter and set out in much more detail in other books, articles, and on the Internet, which you need to obtain and explore. You will get much more of what you want if you follow the trends.

Sharing Feelings, Ideas, and Anxieties

It isn't weakness to share your ideas, plans, hopes, and anxieties. It is strength with a capital "S." The strongest person and smoothest sale I know occurred in a small, semi-rural community near a major metropolitan area, a place where everyone knows everyone else.

Sally's dad was widowed and not in good health. Although she frequently traveled the 200-mile distance to see him, her concern for him increased after each trip. So Sally began to think about selling her home and leaving the community she had lived in for 25 years to be closer to her ailing father. After a few months, Sally made the decision to move. It wasn't an easy decision to pick up her life and move to a place where she knew no one. In addition, she had to leave her work as an interior designer and try to find new clients—tough going in uncharted waters.

Sally first bought a beautiful home site in a village a few miles from her father's home. Then she returned home to strategize about how to sell her present house. She studied the market carefully, priced comparable homes, added a little to her price for the gorgeous pastoral views and gardens, subtracted a little because it was on a heavily traveled road, and then she checked her price with knowledgeable friends and professionals in the area. She decided to sell it herself and systematically began networking until a local real estate broker brought her serious buyers. She came down a little on her asking price for the buyers, sweated inspections and closing, paid the broker a 3% commission, and moved, all within approximately 60 days.

"I came out of the move stronger and wiser," Sally wrote to me recently. "The process of buying land alone, selling my house alone, moving alone, and building a new home alone has given me mileage and confidence. I'm even working on a new business with some local people I met since I moved."

Bottom-Line Lessons

Sally sold her home for more than double what she had originally paid for it, partly because it was located in a "high-end" community and partly because she was a talented decorator and gardener and it showed well. She built her new home in an area where property costs were a lot less.

- Through careful planning, Sally was able to move into her new home free and clear of any mortgage indebtedness.
- Sally was also greatly rewarded for her courageous planning and selling strategies.

Although Sally made all the decisions on her own, she was not shy about asking for help from friends, relatives, and area professionals. She asked questions, admitted her lack of knowledge, and sought reassurance from friends when she felt uncertain or regretful about leaving the home she had known and loved.

You expect to feel sadness when you lose a friend or loved one. It is equally important to realistically assess the loss of familiar surroundings when relocating to another home, or another city or region. As we have seen through many examples, a home has an impact on the quality of your life, whether you know it consciously or not. The kind of upsetting experiences that follow any loss or separation can also apply to the sale of a home. Take the case of Kevin who, unlike Sally, pushed down all his anxieties and regrets about selling his home instead of facing them squarely.

After a bitter divorce, Kevin was forced to sell a stately home that he had gutted and completely rebuilt. For nearly two of the five years they lived there, Kevin and Judy had rearranged walls and rooms, changed the location of stairs and doors, installed skylights and sunken bathtubs, selected materials and paints, and stretched to keep their contractors paid. They'd recorded it all in photo journals along with the history of the house since the first owner built it during the mid-nineteenth century. Now, five years later, Judy was gone and the numbers said it all.

The house was being sold to affluent new owners at a favorable price, thanks in large part to Kevin's renovation and remodeling skills. With cool determination, Kevin signed the contract, endured the housing inspection process, moved into his new home on the other side of town, and prepared to close. A few days before closing, a small leak in the garage roof was detected and the new owners asked that the roof be repaired. Although the money involved to repair the roof was small and the request reasonable, Kevin exploded and refused to settle. For several days it was touch and go until Kevin reluctantly agreed to fix the roof and close the sale. His sadness lingers and he often drives blocks out of his way just to avoid the neighborhood.

Kevin never addressed his feelings about the loss of his home, which also "housed" his marriage and his creative interests. These and other pressures lay just below the surface when the buyers made the request that caused Kevin to erupt in anger and frustration and refuse to settle. He risked a lawsuit and a myriad of circumstances that added to his already strained emotional state. To this day, he has not healed from the experience. He lives in a small condo, dreams and sometimes talks about escaping to the country, but without some serious reflection, I doubt he ever will move. It seems clear, for now at least, that Kevin doesn't want to lose his heart or his wallet to another old house.

Should You Work with A Real Estate Broker?

When asked, most people who use a real estate agent to sell their home say they would choose to do it again. Whether this option is most suitable for your needs is a question that requires some research and careful introspection. Although selling your home on your own might appear to benefit you financially, you must be ready and willing to assume the personal costs in research, networking, stress, time and effort. Here are some of the questions, according to Susan T. Shay in *The Consumer's Guide to Experts*, you need to answer as you consider representing yourself when you sell:[8]

- If a prospective buyer shows up at your door at the crack of dawn on a Saturday, are you ready to show your home?

- If the right buyer doesn't show up before you have to move, what do you do?

- If you must be out of town on occasion and there is no one to "man the phones" or, for that matter, the property itself, how can you be responsive to prospective buyers?

- If a buyer does appear, are you knowledgeable about the negotiations, customs, inspections, and paperwork that are required for you to close the deal?

- How do you know that your price is right if no buyer seems interested?

- Are you savvy about gaining access to computer networks so you can showcase your home?

Although the task is difficult, 20 percent of homeowners who decide to sell their homes will do so themselves.[9] Some are prepared to go it totally alone. Others will work with companies that specialize in helping do-it-your-selfers with advertising and paperwork for a flat or sliding fee arrangement. Still others, like Sally, will work diligently at local networking and be lucky enough to attract a real estate broker with a willing buyer.

The other 80 percent of sellers work with real estate agents who traditionally earn between 5 percent and 7 percent of the purchase price of the home at closing. This percentage varies from place to place, and it is entirely negotiable—do not believe that it is a "fixed fee." It is not, especially when you try to sell an expensive property.

My own preference is to work with another broker or agent when I am a homebuyer or seller. I'd rather not worry about the fine points of the real estate transaction, and find that I think more clearly and objectively when I am represented. I have been paid back in many ways by choosing to work in this manner with someone I can rely on to oversee these details for me. It is simply that S Factor at work in my financial life, and the knowledge that two heads are almost always better than one!

Who Is a Realtor®?

Only members of the National Association of Realtors (NAR) can call themselves Realtors®. NAR members must uphold the association's code of ethics, and the NAR is a valuable source of information for consumers. Check out this association when you search for a broker or agent to learn more about the NAR and its members.

Realtors® and other agents help you achieve a fast and fair sale because they have access to a large group of potential buyers. There are several tips to follow if you decide to use the services of an agent. Look at the advertisements for evidence that their photographs and property descriptions are about homes similar to your own. When you interview agents, don't be timid about asking for an explanation of each step in the listing and selling process.

Never leave an agent interview or sign a listing agreement if you do not completely understand the terms and conditions of this employment contract. You pay for a service, and you are fully entitled to understand the transaction in which you participate. If ease of transaction is a priority, choosing a reliable, conscientious, and amicable real estate agent can remove much hassle from the selling process. If you have already purchased another home, it makes sense to use competent help so you can sell your home more quickly and avoid double housing costs.[10]

Understanding exactly what you want to accomplish, however, is your most important task, and clearly and directly communicating to your broker or to a buyer must be your first priority. Good communication is essential to choosing the selling strategy for the most satisfactory outcome with the least disruption to your life.

Choosing an Agent

Choose agents who are specialists in your local area and who specialize in selling homes like your home. Ask for references and talk to former clients about the level of their knowledge, service, and communication skills. How quickly were phone calls returned? Did the closing go smoothly? Would they work with the agent again? How close was the asking price to the selling price?

The two types of brokers most important to sellers are the seller-broker (brokers who solely represent the seller) and the dual-broker (usually a company in which one agent represents the buyer and another agent represents the seller). Keep in mind that whoever pays the brokerage fee is where a broker's obligations lie. Licensed brokers are bound by law to disclose all relevant information about agency representation. Ask for an explanation of the documentation that you are given. Don't leave a broker's office until you fully understand his or her obligations to you. All dual brokerage arrangements have obvious complexities: Whether a company or individual broker represents both sides, the obligation is to you, the seller. Avoid them if you can. If not, understand them completely.

There are many good references for choosing the right real estate agent. Check out the "Recommended Resources" appendix of this book to learn how to find them.

It should go without saying that until you are totally committed to selling your home, you should not place your home on the market. The penalties can be costly and unpleasant if you change your mind or become uncertain once an eager and capable buyer is found. These can range from destroying relationships with agents, which can cause problems if you choose to sell your home in the future, to lawsuits if you change your mind during a later stage of the selling process.

Points to Ponder

Selling and saying goodbye to your home can be a difficult experience. Use these tips to guide you through the process.

- Clarify your reasons for selling, then prioritize them.

- Don't let your P Factor influence what you price your home— it is an M Factor decision.

- Find out what is going on in the market, and then show off your home.

- Share your feelings and use a realtor if you need someone to help you manage the selling process.

End Notes

1   Anosike, B. *How to Buy/Sell Your Own Home Without a Broker or Lawyer.* Newark, NJ: Do-It-Yourself Legal Publishers, 2000.

2   See the "Recommended Resources" appendix at the end of this book for several references books, organizations, and other sources available to help you sell your home.

3   O'Hara, S. and Lewis N. *The Complete Idiots Guide to Online Buying and Selling a Home,* Fourth Edition. Indianapolis, IN: Alpha Books, 2003.

4   Ibid.

5   Kloian, M. *Sell it By Owner and Save.* Howard City, MI: How To LLC, 2001. See also Roberts, Ralph. *Sell it Yourself.* Holbrook, MA: Adams Media Corporation, 1999.

6   All three of these books by Robert Irwin are worth examination:

—*Power Tips for Selling a House for More.* New York: McGraw-Hill, 2001.

—*The Home Buying and Selling Juggling Act.* Chicago, IL: Dearborn Trade, 1999. This is an especially valuable reference when you are buying and selling a home at the same time

—*Tips and Traps When Selling a Home,* Second Edition, New York: McGraw-Hill, 1997.

7   National Association of REALTORS®, "Existing Home Sales End 2003 on Strong Note, Set Annual Record." http://www.realtor.org/publicaffairsweb.nsf/Pages/ DecEHA04? OpenDocument. National Association of REALTORS®, 430 North Michigan Avenue, Chicago, IL 60611. 1-800-874-6500.

8   Shay, Susan T. *The Consumer's Guide to Experts.* Washington, D.C.: Kiplinger Books, 2001.

9   Bly, Amy Sprecher and Robert W. Bly. *How to Sell Your House, Condo, or Co-Op.* New York: Consumers Union of the United States, Inc., 1993.

16

NATURAL, RELATIONSHIP, AND OTHER DISASTERS

What keeps some people going strong, while others seem to have given up on life?...I am convinced the difference lies in having a purpose.

—Jim Donovan

Disasters are a part of life, and home plays a central role in most of them. Some disasters, such as death and divorce, wreak havoc in human terms. Others occur in nature and can strip away our homes and security. Still others are caused by crime or other acts of aggression. For those who experience such devastation, life can be forever altered.

This chapter is for you whether you have actually experienced a disaster or fear that one could happen to you. The reality is that disasters of varying types and intensity occur more frequently than we acknowledge. Children often endure the traumatic loss of a parent and a home. Older adults must give up cherished family homes, and broken relationships between partners separate one or both from the home they had together. As for natural disasters, we regularly see images of grieving individuals and families on television after a fire, raging storm, or chaotic weather pattern. Most people shown have seen their homes destroyed and possessions lost in the devastation.

Just a few years ago, fear of being harmed or losing one's home as the result of a terrorist attack on U.S. soil was nearly unheard of. Increasingly in the aftermath of September 11, 2001, whether talked about openly or not, the possibility of harm and loss will cross the minds of many Americans as they reflect upon where and how they want to live. Yet potential harm and loss is present already in the paths of yet-to-happen fires (the number one cause of home loss), earthquakes, hurricanes, tornados, and floods. The pain and consequences of separation and loss are felt each time a couple or family gives up on a relationship. And imminent danger already affects the security of too many inner-city neighborhoods.

Since ancient times, disrupting and destroying people's homes has been a weapon of conflict and war. Those who survived rebuilt their homes, migrated, or were taken into other homes. If you must rebuild your home and life in the wake of a disaster, finding the way that works best for you may take some time. It is well worth the effort, however, when you can finally see the benefits that rebuilding brings. You can face the world more open-mindedly and understand your life priorities more clearly. You can decide to let go of fear more readily, and when you do, you are no longer pushing away experiences that you were meant to know.[1]

Here are the five keys to rebuilding your home and your life in the wake of a serious loss:

1. Define your actual loss and, or fears of future loss in detail.

2. Explore the why, how, and when of your experiences as well as your thoughts and feelings about them.

3. Share them with competent, understanding, and empathic friends, relatives, counselors, or therapists.

4. Accept that they exist for you.

5. Face your experiences and fears and learn to take control of them so that they will not control you.

Like Lilly, a Japanese-American who was interred with her family as a young girl, the effects of fear rooted in trauma and involving a home—especially in childhood—might never be entirely eliminated.

Lily's father was a successful landscape gardener when World War II began. The family also ran a rooming house and small hotel in California. When the authorities came to remove Lily and her family from their home, she remembers thinking that "something terrible was happening." She told me, "Everyone around me was crying. I thought that somebody must be dying." The family was moved into barracks, and Lily remembers helping to fill sacks with straw for their beds. The crying continued around her for the whole time she lived in the barracks. Lily continued to believe that people must be dying, even though her parents protected her and told her she would be safe. After a year in the camps, Lily and her family were freed to become sponsored farm workers, and they went to live in Wyoming and Colorado. After the war, the family moved on, but no one was ever able to return to their former home.

As an adult, Lily became an educator and school principal for the Department of Defense and throughout her career lived in housing provided by the U.S. military. Before she retired, Lily finally bought her first home— a one-bedroom condo in an urban setting. Although she loves owning her home, she regrets having chosen a one-bedroom condo. "My reason for buying such a small place," Lily explained, "was so I could afford to live there during all my retirement years." I wondered out loud whether her housing history, and the loss of her home as a child, might have had something to do with her decision. As her eyes filled with tears of remembrance, we both knew the answer. Lily wanted to be certain that no one would ever take her home away from her again.

Lily was surprised by how her fears of losing her home affected her retirement housing decision after so many years. She lives a rich and full life, enjoys a network of many loving friends and relatives, travels, and works part-time in retirement. Perhaps she can feel more secure now after sharing her poignant childhood story with dear friends. She might even decide one of these days to trade up to a two-bedroom condo.

With time, effort, and the help of healing social connections, most of us can learn to take charge of our fears and decide not to allow them to interfere with the quality of our lives. Millions of people all over the world have done this in the face of pain, adversity, even terror, and so can we.

When a Couple or Family Relationship Ends

According to the U.S. Census Bureau, National Center for Health Statistics, the last-reported provisional divorce rate for 2002 stands at 40 percent. To many going through a divorce, the forced relinquishment of the family home can be traumatizing. For divorcing couples, home often represents comfort and stability at a difficult time. They face changing identities and roles, and they can be fearful and resistant about making the additional change of giving up their home. According to New Jersey divorce mediator Anju D. Jessani, "The house, as well as the furnishings in the house, may also represent a happier and more hopeful time in the marriage. However, sooner or later in the divorce process, at least one of the partners, and sometimes both, will move, and decisions have to be made about what happens to the house."[2]

These decisions are especially difficult, given the emotional turmoil that accompanies most divorces. Do you keep the house for one of the parents and children? Do you sell the house and split the proceeds? Do you keep the house and rent it so you can sell it for a better price later? Justin Pankey, a Realtor® in Almont, Michigan, tells divorcing clients that they have four options:[3]

- Sell the house now and divide up the proceeds.

- Buy out your spouse.

- Have your spouse buy you out.

- Retain ownership.

Professionals in the divorce arena concede that "the house" can loom large as a point of contention. Partners often have a strong emotional attachment to the family residence. "One of the largest decisions you will face in getting divorced is whether or not to stay in the matrimonial home," counsels Angela Gougeon in *Divorce Magazine*. If either partner has limited earning potential, particularly women, the reality is that if the existing family residence is sold, the capacity to acquire another home can be greatly diminished.[4] The stress of meeting a monthly mortgage payment when financially strapped sometimes outweighs the benefits of staying put. Although your home is a refuge in a sea of uncertainty during divorce, and you may long to stay there after the divorce, the big question is whether keeping the home makes financial sense. Remaining in the comfort of familiar surroundings is tempting, but consider how you will pay the mortgage by yourself or how you will be able to buy out your partner.

In her seminal work on divorce, *Crazy Time*, author and journalist Abigail Trafford says that separating couples go through stages: First there is the mourning of the loss of the marriage; second, the emergence or reconstruction of the self over the two-year period that it takes most people to get divorced. Usually one person is initiator and the other noninitiator—what Trafford terms "Divorce Seeker" and "Divorce Opposer." Divorce Seekers are usually about a year ahead of Opposers in the stage they are experiencing; they might be almost through the mourning and grief periods, looking to what lies ahead. Opposers, on first hearing that their partner wants to separate, often experience disbelief, a response that can act as a stalling action. Their instinct is to maintain the status quo: keep the house, keep the income, keep the kids in school, and do not change anything, least of all the marriage.[5]

Initially, Trafford notes, even Seekers are not often prepared for the slap of permanent parting, eager as they are to be relieved from the misery of their marriages. In one study, only 37 percent of the husbands and 30 percent of the wives reported having been prepared for the divorce, in spite of the fact that 53 percent of the men and 47 percent of the women had undergone at least one trial separation.

During the average two-year divorce period, Trafford writes, a great deal of anger and guilt is played out in the details of the property settlement and custody agreements. Often lawyers are called in to manage the conflict. The home often ends up as a major stake in these battles for supremacy and revenge, and legal fees accumulate as the courts decide or force the issue of selling the home.

Whoever keeps the house must usually give up something in exchange. In many cases, the house is the major and sometimes the only marital asset, so there is nothing to trade off. If investments, savings, pension, or 401 (k) plan balances are substantial, however, one partner might opt to keep the home and the other will take other available assets. The home often represents stability, comfort, and something to cling to as a marriage falls apart. Despite its frequency, divorce is a financial and emotional trauma that few ever plan or save for. When funds must be supplied to divorcing partners, sale of the family home is the most practical and sometimes the only solution.

Even those who are seemingly financially secure can find themselves in strained circumstances. A woman whose husband generated a sizeable income as the sole breadwinner might assume she will be awarded the home, especially if the divorce was caused by a cheating partner. That, however, might not be the case. Jocelyn is a case in point.[6]

When her husband, a highly paid vice president of a film company, asked for a divorce, Jocelyn figured she would be entitled to their home in Beverly Hills. While Jocelyn was at home "living like a nun with the children," David was off in London living and traveling with someone who referred to herself as his "wife." When the marriage ended, David's business manager came to see Jocelyn and they negotiated a settlement. The business manager calculated how she could manage her share of the home expenses, and how David could cover the costs of insurance and taxes.

"I thought it was all settled, but the next day David screamed at me over the telephone, 'I'm not going to pay for this, I'm not going to pay for that.' That started three years of financial hell for me," she said. Jocelyn's car was repossessed. Her bank account was emptied, and David's business manager stopped putting in his $3,000 to $4,000 a month. Untrained for a professional career, she felt abandoned and scared. "Your house is your refuge; the walls are your walls of protection, whatever the difficulties. That includes protection of your secrets, even your lies to the world, which bind you together as much as the truths," she said. In the end, expensive lawyers worked out a settlement, and Jocelyn and the children moved to another, much more modest home. "The first thing I did was to get rid of all my attachments to luxury, living in the grand house with the beautiful things. I had to give all that up, bit by bit, item by item." Jocelyn might have lost the marital home, but, she says, "I gained a life. I finally did it, I finally did it!"

Nature's Fury and the Loss of Home

A month after tornadoes roared through his community in Tennessee, Frank is working to strip the rain-soaked interior of the basement of his devastated home. He has had his day of crying, giving vent to his feelings of loss, anger, and grief. He plans to manage the reconstruction of his family's home and lay the bricks himself. Although insured, Anthony discovered his insurance will fall short of the cost of rebuilding by $37,000, so he sought help from the Federal Emergency Management Agency (FEMA) to compensate for the shortfall. Meanwhile, like hundreds of other families who lose their homes to natural disasters, his family is living in a rented home. They rely on friends and rented cars to get to work and transport children to school and activities. While cleaning up the debris that was once their possessions, they are reminded of how hard they worked to get to where they were and how much the disaster has taken from them.

After devastating wildfires in Los Alamos, New Mexico, the Woodward family home, like many others, was a total loss. With nothing left, the family of five stayed in an American Red Cross shelter while making some hard choices, including the decision to temporarily relocate to another state to live with relatives. After a fire, everything—all those things that define your personal history, your past, and the memories you treasure—is gone. The emotional trauma from a fire can be more severe than that of hurricanes, tornadoes, or floods when some contents of a home are salvageable, according to Jill Hoffman, a mental health counselor with the American Red Cross. In addition to the loss of personal history is the loss of control, the sense of vulnerability, and the violation of all that you value in your home.

Some people who have experienced the loss of a home in a natural disaster will often refer to "life before the flood" or "before the earthquake" or "after the tornado" or "hurricane Charley." For them, life has been forever marked by their experience. A colleague, Marjorie, once described for me in detail the fire that destroyed the home she shared with her husband and children in Southern California. Halfway through the story, Marjorie's eyes filled with tears as she recalled for me the devastation that had robbed the family of all their belongings. Marjorie's feelings were so deep and her memories so vivid that I was surprised to learn the fire had occurred nearly 25 years earlier. She dated most of the events of her adult life as "before the fire" or "after the fire."

In May, 2004, the Institute for Business & Home Safety (IBHS) and the Tampa Museum of Science & Industry launched a partnership to create the country's first interactive learning center for understanding and surviving natural disasters. The National Center for Disaster Safety is the newest attempt at providing the public with information for preparing for and surviving the many types of disasters that can threaten the safety of our homes and loved ones. FEMA offers excellent printed and online information about disaster preparedness and practical advice about coping in the wake of a disaster. Their publication, "Are You Ready? A Guide to Citizen Preparedness," is an excellent, detailed, and comprehensive guide to preparedness, survival, and recovery. The American Red Cross also offers much useful information, including a guide to the financial issues involved in disaster recovery. "Disaster Recovery: A Guide to Financial Issues" was written and produced through a partnership between the National Endowment for Financial Education (NEFE), the American Red Cross, and the American Institute of Certified Public Accountants (AICPA) Foundation. This useful book covers financial recovery from disaster step by step and week by week.[7]

From the Start

Your homeownership decision should include, from the very start, a realistic awareness of potential disaster scenarios and an informed plan to mitigate their possible effects. Before buying or building a home, check with the local planning authority and the local emergency management office to determine which disasters can strike your community. They will know the risks, such as histories of severe weather, location of annual flood areas, frequency of wildfire outbreaks, and local storage or production of hazardous materials. Knowledge about potential threats in your area can help you to fortify your home against damage, prepare realistic emergency plans, and lower the risk of serious loss. If you live in or near a designated flood plain, in an area that experiences frequent wildfires, or in an earthquake zone, you might face certain additional building requirements for home construction as well as find that you can heed further suggested protective measures.

Insurance is the first line of protection for any homeowner. Most generic homeowner policies guard against hurricanes, fire, and other typical damage. Depending on the area in which your home is located, however, you might need specialized protection against earthquakes or flooding. In addition to having insurance that covers as many types of disasters as possible, it is equally important to keep your insurance up-to-date. Every year, thousands of homeowners discover they were underinsured and will not be able to afford a comparable replacement for their lost home.

When hurricane Isabel hit Dare County, North Carolina, 2,730 residents filed insurance claims. Nearly one third received nothing. Many more found that their insurance payments were far lower than their repair and replacement costs. The problem? Claims adjusters estimate losses based on the cost of new construction under average building conditions, whereas reconstruction in the wake of a natural disaster can cost up to one and a half times more because of limited access, the need for demolition, scarcity of materials, scarcity of qualified builders, new disaster-related building requirements, and other problems. Federal aid, too, is limited. As the head of the FEMA's Outreach Team explained to members of the coastal community, "Uncle Sam is in the flood insurance business because no one else wants to be." The National Flood Insurance program does not give the same level of coverage as a homeowner's policy.

Have a Plan and Be Prepared

The key to your best chance of surviving and recovering from a disaster is having a contingency plan. Two national polls conducted in 2000 to assess the knowledge and level of preparedness of homeowners in hurricane-vulnerable states revealed the following:

- Homeowners' level of perceived risk of hurricanes in their areas was low given the actual threat.

- A disconnect existed between the homeowners' perceived level of preparedness and their actual level of preparedness.

- Homeowners' mistaken belief that preventive actions recommended to reduce the impact of a hurricane to their homes were too expensive.

- When actual costs of prevention were known, most said it was lower than expected and that they would spend the money.

Our perceptions of risk and the cost of being prepared for a disaster are often underestimated and can lead to unnecessary losses. The message is clear: Good preparation is essential to surviving a disaster. It will minimize the potential emotional, physical, and financial hardships you face in a possibile disaster or catastrophic event.

Have a Plan for All Types of Emergencies

Although 84 percent of Americans say that it is important to have disaster plans, fewer than half actually have created plans against the eventuality of an emergency or disaster situation. To be prepared, most guides suggest that your household disaster plan include the following:

- Decide how each member of your household will respond to a variety of emergency situations. Assign tasks to members as appropriate. In an emergency, each will carry out his or her task and defuse the potential panic and anxiety that can cost time and cause unnecessary loss.

- Make sure all family members are aware of emergency exit procedures for your home. All should know the location of emergency supplies, such as flashlights, escape ladders, ropes, and fire extinguishers.

- Discuss what you will do in an evacuation. Agree on two meeting places: one close to home and the second away from your neighborhood in case you cannot return home. Update these locations as needed to accommodate changes in work, school, and availability of transportation.

- Have a plan for how you will communicate with one another. Cell phones, although useful, may not work in all areas. As a backup, designate a relative or friend who lives out of the area to be the point of contact, and have all family members check in with that person.

- Determine where and how important papers and contact numbers will be stored. This will make all the difference during the time it will take you to recover. Deeds; insurance policies; wills; banking information; and important family, medical, and business contact numbers should be available to gather up or put in a well-protected (fire- and water-safe) place if you are unable to take them with you. Ideally, a safety deposit box should hold copies of all important information.

- All household members should know how and when to shut off water, gas, and electricity at main switches. (Gas should not be turned off unless local officials advise it. It might be needed for heating or cooking and can be turned on only by a professional.)

- Consider taking first aid and CPR training. In the event of a disaster situation, the usual emergency services and personnel might not be available.

- Create an emergency savings account that can be used in a crisis and keep some cash or traveler's checks in a safe and accessible place. Emergency cash assistance might be available from federal, state, or local government following the declaration of a disaster by the president or the governor, but it will take time to access such resources. Be aware, too, that although a credit card cash advance might seem like a good idea, most cards charge their highest interest rates on this type of transaction, if allowed at all.

- Make arrangements for pets. This is an often-overlooked aspect of disaster planning. You should be aware that pets are usually not allowed in public shelters. Check the locations of hotel, motel, and boarding facilities where pets are allowed, including some outside of your immediate area. Make sure your pets have implanted microchips for pet identification as well as securely fastened identification tags. Include supplies for your pets in your disaster kit. If large animals or livestock are part of your home or farm, your plan should include arrangements for emergency shelter, food, and care for these animals.

- Special needs of family members on medication or disabled family members should be included in all disaster planning.

- Check on the emergency plans of your children's schools. You need to know whether they will keep children at the school, to whom the children can be released, or whether children will be sent home. Make certain schools and recreation program facilities have your most recent contact information and expect that the schools' phones will be overwhelmed during times of emergency.

- Assemble two disaster supply kits, one for your home and the other for your car. The kits should contain water, up-to-date, ready-to-eat foods (canned or dried), first aid supplies including at least a three-day supply of any necessary prescription drugs (check expiration dates frequently), tools, and emergency supplies (including a battery-powered radio).

Practical guides for planning are available through most of the national disaster relief agencies, local emergency response agencies, and the FEMA Web site. Check the "Recommended Resources" appendix for more information about this most important subject.

The Aftermath of a Disaster

It is often said, "The disaster was bad...but the recovery was worse." The health and safety of your family and neighbors are usually the first matter of concern after disaster strikes. Putting your home, your community, and your life back to normal can take weeks, months, and, sometimes years after a devastating event. The emotional toll of disasters can be more devastating than the financial strains. Traumatic loss of life, home, and personal property can have deep and long-lasting effects.

Children are often more severely affected by the trauma of a disaster. It is therefore not recommended that children be exposed to news reports showing potentially disturbing images of these events. Looking for signs of distress and getting timely and proper treatment are important for everyone's recovery. Older children should be allowed to help in the recovery effort; keeping busy and helping others will help them to cope with their own fears and losses.

The recovery period is a time for grieving losses, even as you and your family begin the process of rebuilding and moving on. During this time, rumors fly, tempers flare, and fears, frustrations, and anxieties abound. These are all natural characteristics of the grieving process. Trying to move ahead during recovery can feel overwhelming. After you have returned to your home or settled into temporary housing, reach out and get the aid you need to begin to rebuild your home and your life.

Being prepared, well informed, and having access to your personal documentation is key to surviving the recovery period. This is especially helpful for homeowners, who even in the face of total loss, are determined to reclaim their homes. As one victim said after the Los Alamos fire totally destroyed her family's home and contents, "But what can you do? We can go on, we can start over...Everybody is safe, and we're all together. That's the important thing. We can build from there."

Points to Ponder

- Most of us identify with our current or past home, or both. When we fear loss of home—whether our fears are real or imagined—they are real in their consequences and we must heal them.

- Healing fears, or actual experiences of loss, requires identifying them, sharing them, getting help with them if necessary, accepting that they exist for us, and summoning courage to live our lives fully by letting them go.

- You are not alone. Everyone has fears that must be managed.

- Get practical and do something about your fears. "Let's roll."

End Notes

1 Deits, Bob. *Life After Loss: A Practical Guide to Renewing Your Life After Experiencing Major Loss*. Cambridge, MA: Lifelong Books, 2004. This is a seminal work on loss and can be helpful to anyone who is grieving or who wants to be of assistance to someone who is experiencing the aftermath of serious loss.

2 Jessani, Anju D. Undated article. *The House—What Happens in Divorce—Do Not Ignore the Tax Consequences*. This article should be required reading for anyone with a house who is in the midst of a divorce. There are tax consequences, oddly more often in amicable divorce settlements, that might not be anticipated by the parties. Visit http://www.divorcesource.com/NJ/ARTICLES/Jessani1.html.

3 The following information is taken from a pamphlet titled *Divorce: What You Need to Know About Your House, Your Mortgage, and Taxes*. It was sent by Justin Pankey, Statewide Real Estate, Main Street, 844 Van Dyke, PO Box 325, Almost, MI 48003. Tel. 810-798-8591.

4 Canadian residential mortgage manager Angela Gougeon is quoted in *Divorce Magazine* (http://www.DivorceMagazine.com/ON/pro/tdct/shtml).

5 Trafford, Abigail. *Crazy Time: Surviving Divorce and Building a New Life*. New York: HarperCollins Publishers, 1992.

6 Jocelyn's story is from *Divorce, An Oral Portrait,* by George Feifer, New York: New Press, 1995. Feifer conducted interviews with 40 people about their divorce experiences.

7 See the list of organizations with Web site addresses and other resources listed under Natural and Other Disasters in the " Recommended Resources" appendix.

17

OVERCOMING MOVING
STRESSES

It can be exciting to think about moving…But grown-ups and children can feel sad about saying goodbye to the people and places they've come to know and love.

— *Fred Rogers*

Borrow from the Boy Scout motto as you plan to move—"Be prepared!" Like parenting, few of us are taught to move. We are just expected to know how.

Moving is a huge job and an emotional chore. It is a factor on any test or chart that measures personal stress, and it is often accompanied by the added stress of divorce, death of a family member, change of job or career, retirement, or any number of other anxiety-provoking life changes or events. Courage, diligence, planning, organizing, and a positive attitude are guaranteed to reduce your moving stresses. Along the way, your experience, the new information you acquire, and the new skills you develop will help you become more competent, not just in moving, but in life transitions in general.

Learning How to Move

Fortunately, the relocation of corporate executives and managers over many years prompted companies to begin taking note of how moving affects employees and their families. As a result, you can now benefit enormously from the plentiful resources available to help you, your partners, and family members get through—and way beyond—the pressures and upheaval of a move. Detailed advice about how to plan a successful move is readily available in books and on the Internet. Almost everything you could possibly need to know can be found in excellent resources that guide you both through the practical tasks before you and the emotional work of separating from the old and settling into the new.[1] Implicit in any resource you consult are three essential requirements for a low-stress move:

- Time

- Assistance

- Self-care

Time: Give yourself (selves) as much time as possible.

Giving yourself time does not mean procrastinating. As soon as you know where and when you are moving, make a written plan with assigned tasks with timelines. What needs to be done, who is going to do it, and by what date must it be done? The sooner you begin planning, the more time you will have to complete the identified tasks, and you will perceive less stress. For those of you who proceed through life in an organized fashion, this step is a no-brainer. For those of you who fly through life by the seat of your pants, it will be a stretch. Do it. Include in your plan specific dates to take stock and monitor your progress.

Assistance: Enlist help.

Moving advisors generally agree that it is not wise to scrimp on help. If you have the financial resources, pay to be moved. Price shop with movers, but do not get hung up on nickels and dimes. Good service is what you need and knowledge about the ins and outs of selecting and interacting with a moving company.[2] Through the *American Moving and Storage Association* (AMSA) Web site, www.amconf.org, you can make your first cut by identifying companies that are AMSA certified. By participating in this certification program, these companies commit to providing a professional level of service and prompt complaint handling and dispute resolution (arbitration). Local carriers representing these national companies vary in the quality of their services, so you must check them out as well. The bottom line: Obtain local references and check complaint records with the Better Business Bureau.

If you possibly can, pay the movers to pack for you. Not only will you cut down on your workload, you will also reduce your levels of stress. The meaning embedded in your belongings can make packing an emotional process. As Cathy Goodwin points out, if you are packing yourself, you are already undergoing some stress just trying to find enough boxes and the time you need to fill them up. The temptation you face to "ponder the significance" of your belongings will slow you down and tax your emotional and physical stamina.[3] You need to be past the emotional work of processing your housing history by the time you are actually ready to move. It is time to be industrious, calm, and forward thinking instead.

If you must pack yourself, start early. Internet sources offering tips for packing are plentiful. Your moving company will give you booklets on packing and will sell you all the packing supplies you need. Most moving company Web sites are loaded with practical information as well. If you cannot afford to buy packing supplies, reach out to local merchants and ask them not to break down boxes but to keep them for you. Reach out to your friends and family and ask them to save their newspapers. Collect the supplies they are saving for you frequently so that they are not inconvenienced and find a place to store them at home so that you will not be too inconvenienced either. Enlist the support of your friends and relatives in making your transition a smooth one. Let them know ahead of time the type of help they can give you. Do not be shy about asking for assistance—it can benefit you in ways you might not anticipate.

Self-care: Nurture your mind, body, and spirit throughout the process.

It is tempting to allow the pressures of moving to transform a healthy lifestyle into a fast track to a heart attack. To the greatest extent possible, maintain healthful eating habits, continue to exercise, and take time out to appreciate life and survey the beauty of creation. If you are feeling stressed, acknowledge your feelings and take some action. Go for a walk. Book a massage (or ask a friend or partner to give you one). Go to a movie. Meditate. Take an hour and finish that novel. Call your best friend. If your usual habit is to grab dinner at a fast-food restaurant or your idea of exercise and relaxation involves watching TV and drinking beer, you probably are not going to change to healthier habits during the process of your move.

And you should not. Do whatever works to feel cared for and relaxed. Then help your partner and family members find their highest comfort levels, too.

An important part of self-care involves knowing the stages of a well-managed move and taking the necessary planning steps well in advance. Invest time into doing the research required to understand the nuts and bolts of your moving tasks and their financial consequences. Share this knowledge and divide up the tasks with those who will be moving with you.

Bruce and Linda, both working professionals with no children, found the home of their dreams after a long search, and they were very excited. Located about 10 miles away, they reasoned the move into their new home should be a snap. Except for calling a moving company to reserve a date for their move, they made few other arrangements. Just a few days before the big move, Bruce told Linda he needed to be out of town on moving day. In a flash, Linda saw the consequences of their unwise procrastination and the multiple burdens that were fast falling upon her shoulders. Confronting Bruce brought her small comfort. "A critical out-of-town meeting had already been scheduled," he told her. "There was nothing he could do."

Linda could do little about her last-minute predicament either. Another family was scheduled to arrive with a truck within hours after their move, so it could not be postponed. She had asked no one for help with moving-day chores, and sure enough no one was available now. Linda called the moving company to arrange for the packing supplies she now had to buy because she had waited until the last minute.

While she packed, cleaned, and otherwise turned the impossible into a one-woman heroic set of accomplishments, Linda arrived at her new home exhausted, alone, angry, and resentful. When Bruce came home the next day, all smiles and excited to join Linda at their wonderful new home, he was greeted instead with withdrawn silence. The mutual blaming continued for several days. They finally called a truce, but the glow of moving into their dream home had dimmed considerably by the time they did.

What otherwise could have been a pleasant, constructive, and companionable project turned into a grim illustration of the need for advance joint planning. If Linda and Bruce had organized their move in advance, Bruce would have told his employer in time to avoid having been sent out of town on moving day. The actual move would still have entailed plenty of work, but it would not have been so taxing physically for Linda and, as it turned out, so emotionally draining for them both. Clearly they missed a great opportunity to enjoy the challenges involved in their move and to experience the pleasure of claiming the new home they had anticipated so eagerly.

The Emotional and Practical Considerations of Moving with Children

Your children are the most precious of all that will be moving into your new home. Although the chances of "breaking" them are slim-to-none, you must handle them with care nonetheless. Moving can be a time of great insecurity for children; but just as for adults, it is also a time filled with many opportunities for expanded understanding. A move is a family event. Going through it can strengthen family bonds or weaken them. Informed and intentional parenting during a move will increase your chances of seeing its long-term effects turn out to be positive and personally rewarding.

Relocating children complicates both moving and parenting, so it is no wonder that much has been written on the topic. Take advantage of the many available resources and consider upgrading your parenting knowledge and skills throughout all the stages of your move—from thinking about it, negotiating the changes, deciding, planning the move itself, and helping everyone to settle in. Experts agree that moving affects different age groups differently. It is important for you to understand how to address the concerns relevant to your children's age group as well as those unique to each child. Here is some general advice that applies to moves with children of all ages and temperaments:

- Tell your children about the move as soon as you have made the decision. If kids sense that something is up, but are left in the dark, they will feel insecure. If there is tension in the air, they might act out in negative ways, reinforcing their underlying fear that they are the ones to blame for a negative family atmosphere. In addition, kids of all ages need time to adjust to a move. The more time, the better.

- Be respectful of their reactions to the move. Give them space to ask questions and let them freely express their feelings. They need to feel understood and supported. Reassure them that you will do your best to honor and meet their needs.

- Involve your children in planning and executing the move. It will boost their sense of competence and control and enhance their self-esteem.

- Let them help pack and unpack their own things and make their rooms the last to be packed, and the first to be unpacked.

- Give them as many choices as possible in deciding how to re-create their personal space in their new home.

- Let them bring all of their stuff. Moving advice books differ on whether you should use your move as an opportunity to hold a garage sale or otherwise get rid of excess household baggage. If you are packing yourself, you will be tempted to "toss it," but unless it is a financial necessity, err on the side of excess when it comes to the children's belongings. They need no extra grief at such a time.

- Help them say goodbye to the old and hello to the new. Provide them with the time and opportunity to say goodbye to their important people, places, and things. Walk around the old house, yard, and neighborhood together; take photographs; and share memories and feelings of loss. Take time out together to smell the roses in your garden. Dig out a few of their favorite bulbs or bushes to transplant at their new home. Make the transplanting a family activity. Brainstorm other ways to "claim" your new abode, and do it upon arrival. Plan frequent family outings during the first few days to help children get a feel for their new neighborhood. Walk around your new neighborhood, wave to neighbors, picnic in the parks, and eat at local restaurants.

- Help your children grieve their losses. Do not dismiss their feelings of sadness or rush them to "get over" those feelings.

- Keep routines as close to normal as possible. Healthful family meals and early bedtimes with their usual rituals are important.

- Take care of yourself. Children react to the emotions of the significant adults around them. If you are positive about the move and set about your moving tasks with good humor, your children will feel secure. If the stress of the move is overwhelming you, you will not be able to care for the emotional well-being of your children.

On Moving Day

- Have a plan to keep pets and young children safe and out of the way, and older ones occupied.
- Have a plan to feed everyone before and after the move.
- Have a place for everyone to sleep, which might or might not be the new home.
- Pack a survival kit of clothes, toys, and personal necessities for each child (and each adult) and keep them out of the moving van.

Like adults, children differ in their degree of attachment to place. Some children have intense reactions to leaving a home or a neighborhood, whereas others take it in stride. School-aged children and teens will be most disturbed by moves that involve a change in community or school district. The current thinking on the timing of moves for school-aged children is that mid-year moves are preferable to summer moves. A mid-year move gives children an immediate opportunity for social interaction, as well as opportunities for achievement. The following are some important rules of thumb:

- Enroll children in the new school before you move.

- Visit new schools with your children before the move if possible, or before the student's first day, and arrange for tours and meetings with key personnel.

- Investigate differences in academic standards that might impact your child's adjustment and performance.

- Get involved. Your immediate involvement in school activities will go a long way towards facilitating the community's acceptance of your children.

Adolescents are particularly vulnerable to the effects of moving because they are already in the midst of a major life transition. It is difficult enough for teens and parents in the most stable of environments to negotiate the "inner turbulence" that is characteristic of this developmental stage.[4] Moving can be an especially upsetting event.

A Tale of a Successful Family Move

One of my favorite moving memories happened when my children were preadolescent and adolescent—the oldest of 6 children was just 13-years-old. We were moving from a rented farmhouse to a wonderful, old, historic home I was able to buy with my parents' help. We had been able to see the original building agreement in the county records. "A cow, a pig, food, and lodging for a year" is what the builder had charged the owner for his labor in 1840. My young children and I were very happy and excited about the move to our own space. Our landlord, a retired military officer, was stern and disapproving of our relaxed and fun-loving lifestyle. He had made us all feel uncomfortable more than once when he visited unannounced, and we looked forward to leaving his home and his visits behind.

We had little money to spare. But my oldest son had an idea, and it turned the drudgery of our move into a family endeavor that made it memorable. "Why not ask our neighbor to borrow his pickup?" If we had transportation, the reasoning went, we could all help to load and unload the truck. I could make the several trips back and forth needed for the entire move. I had my doubts, but the children had none. "Please, Mom," they begged, "We can do it, you'll see."

Moving day was hard work, but it was fun and everyone helped. Nine, ten, eleven, and then twelve loads and many hours into the evening later, we gratefully returned the small pickup to our generous neighbor. My parents had been generous, too. They cleaned our rented house until it was spotless to ensure the return of our security deposit. And as we left that farmhouse for the last time, we were very tired but happy, too. "Pack Up Your Troubles in Your Old Kit Bag and Smile, Smile, Smile…" was the song we sang together on our way to the old house that awaited occupancy by its newest family.

As this story illustrates, children want to be included, and they are surprisingly competent when we give them a chance to show their competence. They also like demonstrating that they are dependable. Praise them for their dependability when they deserve it, even when it turns into an unanticipated crisis.

In *Guide to a Stress Free Move*, the authors recount a story that happened to the Alexander family when they moved from the Midwest to a city in the Northwest. 12-year-old Brendon had straightened up the cab of their rented moving truck just prior to departure. He had done a great job, too. "He cleaned out one side of the truck, then locked the door and went around to the other side. He cleaned that side, locked the door, and returned to the house"—you guessed it—without the only key. Of course, this happened on a Sunday.

After advice from neighbors and friends and several phone calls, a towing service arrived and popped the door open quickly. Soon after, the Alexanders were on their way. It is a pretty sure bet that Brendon felt awful that he had inconvenienced everyone. He had done a good job of cleaning out the truck as Dad had asked, and anyone could have left that key on the dashboard in the midst of the very same task.

"Stay calm. Keep in control," advises Judy Ramsey. This is always good advice when dealing with your children. It is essential on moving day.

Children's Personal Factors

Feelings of being in control and social identity are central issues for children and adolescents just as they are for adults. These needs are felt more urgently when we are young, and geographic relocation presents major challenges to both. Being in control depends on having a sense of being competent and of mastery over one's life. The ideal context for the development of competence is one that is consistent, reliable, and familiar. Moving upsets that apple cart in a big way. It represents a major loss of control, because a young child or adolescent has little if any influence over the decision to move. At the same time, moving creates an unknown, an expansion of the world that the adolescent must master. The future looks uncertain. The development of social identity in adolescence hinges on recognition and validation from a peer group. "Belonging" is a major concern. Moving your child away from a peer group in which she or he is recognized and valued is undoing the natural (unconscious) work of adolescence. In the new location, she or he will be an "outsider" for a time, a very painful role at best. Expect reactions.

The following suggestions may help ease the transition. They can also help your adolescents enhance their sense of competence and belonging:

- Assign lots of responsibility for moving-related tasks. Show your appreciation for a job well done.

- Validate their feelings about the move.

- Find out as much as you can about the new school and its culture before the first day of class. Help them obtain clothing that "fits in."

- Make sure your children are placed in classes appropriate to their skill level.

- Make sure they are oriented to transportation in the community and know how to get around.

- Make sure they know how to reach you in an emergency.

- Let them express themselves. Listen. Expect and tolerate new expressions of style.

- Help them connect with clubs and organizations that support their interests and talents.

- Support them in maintaining old friendships and in establishing new ones.

Nida and Heller's *The Teenagers Survival Guide to Moving*, written for adolescents, would be a thoughtful gift for your teenaged son or daughter while you are preparing for your family move.[5]

Moving Your Pets with Love and Care

People are not the only ones to find moving stressful, or to cause you added stress during a move. Your pets can be afraid, confused, or even become ill during a move. Worse, they can run away. That is what happened on moving day to Jean and her young daughter, Emily.

Jean discovered their cat was missing just before driving away. They had to meet the loaded van at their new home five hours away, so they were forced to entrust neighbors with finding the cat. 4-year-old Emily, already grieving over the loss of her home and friends, was now hysterical over the loss of her pet. Several tense days later, Jean received a call that the cat was safe. She and Emily made the ten-hour round-trip to fetch him, but on the return trip, the car broke down.

Jean, Emily, and the cat rode in the tow truck to a repair shop, where the car had to stay overnight. Fortunately, they had relatives in the area who rescued them, but Jean still shudders when she recalls the unlit road where they waited for their rescuers, who were unfamiliar with the area at night. "It was a lesson well learned," Jean told me. "In the future, I will plan more carefully and pay handsomely if necessary to prevent such stress."

Here are some ways to minimize the stress of moving pets:

- If you are moving out of driving range of your current veterinarian, make sure you have your pet's medical records.

- If you are crossing state lines, determine the state's pet-entry laws by contacting the state's department of agriculture.

- If you are moving to a new community, check with the municipal offices to learn about applicable pet ordinances.

- Make sure your pet's name and your new address is securely attached to the collar.

- Keep food, bowls for food and water, and litter boxes with you when you transport your pet.

- Give your pet time to adjust. Keep an eye on eating habits and elimination behavior.

In addition to people, pets, and belongings—including the special methods for handling plants—you must also plan for cleanups, overnights, possible delays, and priority needs at the end of your move. Let the experts guide you through your relocation process. You will find hundreds of suggestions and tips designed to make moving easier, less costly, and even pleasurable. And nowhere else in the housing literature are authors more knowledgeable about the psychology of housing than these relocation experts.

Points to Ponder

- After the decision to move is made, give yourself and those who move with you the gift of kindness.

- Take time to plan the details of your move in advance.

- Ask for assistance from family and friends or hire people to help you. Moving is not the time to save nickels and dimes—go for the help instead!

- Take especially good care of yourself during the move. Ease your stresses with self-nurturing, and then help your partner and family members find their best comfort levels too.

End Notes

1 See especially Steiner, Clyde and Shari Steiner. Steiner's *Complete How to Move Handbook,* Second Edition. San Francisco, CA: Independent Information Publica-tions Consumer Series, 1999; Goodwin, Cathy. *Making the Big Move: How to Transform Relocation into a Creative Life Transition.* Oakland, CA: New Harbinger Publi-cations, 1999; Levine, Leslie. *Will this Place Ever Feel Like Home? Simple Advice for Settling In After You Move.* Chicago, IL: Real Estate Education Company, 1998.

2 Kozak, Donna and Tara Maras, 2004. "Twenty-Nine Days to a Smooth Move: Your Complete Moving Manual." Amazon.com (PDF downloadable).

3 Goodwin, Cathy. *Making the Big Move: How to Transform Relocation into a Creative Life Transition.* Oakland, CA: New Harbinger Publications, 1999.

4 McCollum, Audrey, Nadia Jensen, and Stuart Copans. *Smart Moves: Your Guide Through the Emotional Maze of Relocation.* Lyme, NH: Smith and Kraus Publishers, Inc., 1996.

5 Nida, Patricia Cooney and Wendy M. Heller. *The Teenagers Survival Guide to Moving.* New York: Simon & Schuster, 1985.

Chapter 18

Secret 10

**Your housing value system will
live as long as you do.**

18

EMPTY NESTS AND
RETIREMENT YEARS

*Moving is like climbing a mountain…Someday you may be ready to try
again, or you may decide you've had enough adventure for a lifetime.*

—*Cathy Goodwin*

Be careful whom you call "elderly" these days. Typically, retirement and
other benefit programs define adults aged 65 as "the elderly." But this artifi-
cial group identification flies in the face of reality. I once observed focus
groups being conducted in several cities across the nation from California to
New York. Participants in each group, all ages 55 to 75+, were questioned
about their perceptions of growing old. "At what age do you believe people
become elderly?" the interviewer asked each group. Their response was
unanimous, "When they become unable to get around on their own."[1]

If you are a caregiver, a baby boomer, or about to enter or are now enjoying your golden years, this chapter is especially for you. If you are helping
to choose housing for an older relative, try putting yourself in that person's
place as you read through this chapter. As for who is elderly, you will have
to ask your parents or grandparents. Or yourself.[2]

Ginny failed to ask her parents anything. She assumed they were elderly because they had both reached 65. In a gesture born of concern and gen-
erosity, Ginny gave her parents the keys to an apartment she owned in an

upscale urban neighborhood and helped them settle into what she believed would be their home "in retirement." Ginny returned to her condo in another city feeling relieved and pleased that she had been able to be helpful. Before the year was out, however, her parents moved themselves into a rented apartment in the suburbs and returned to full-time jobs. They told their daughter, "Thank you, but we were bored with our lives in the city."

Ginny was flabbergasted. As a successful corporate manager, she was used to planning for others and to having things go according to plan. In this case, however, she and her parents had not communicated their needs and values to one another. Ginny thought they should be ready for retirement, and her need was to settle them into an "appropriate" living space so she could stop worrying about them from afar. She believed she was helping her parents by moving them where she knew they would be safe and financially secure. She erroneously believed they would also be *content*. Her parents found it impossible to say "no" to Ginny and thought they should allow Ginny to help them out. They knew city living was not their cup of tea, and they did not think they were ready for retirement living. But Ginny had been so generous and so persuasive.

For a time afterward, Ginny nurtured feelings of rejection—a counter to her need for approval and appreciation. Her parents felt the guilt that often occurs when we fail to live up to someone else's expectations of what we should be doing. None of these feelings were ever shared among them, and the experience was soon buried and "forgotten." By the time her parents were ready to accept Ginny's help, they had lived busy, independent, and self-sufficient lives well into another decade.

Misunderstandings like this occur all too frequently among family members who barely understand their own needs and values, much less those of their loved ones. Instead of being guided by one another's needs and values, their concerns may be dominated instead by self-centered wants or well-intentioned shoulds. When we are persuaded to follow the wants and shoulds of others—even when we know they have our best interests at heart—resentment can fester and lead to outright rebellion. When we take the time to engage instead in value-focused thinking, we can end up getting most of what really matters to us all.[3]

Being Free of "Shoulds" in Retirement

The most important—and potentially difficult—housing decisions of your life involve where and how you will live as an older adult. But making choices about your home as you age is bound up with your retirement preparedness. If Ginny's parents had made definitive plans for their later years, she might not have worried or tried to engineer their later lives for them. And even if she had, her parents may have responded more easily to her concerns by telling her, "Thanks, but we've made other plans."

Are you planning, or have you planned, for your golden years? Or are you letting aging, and the money and housing issues of aging, just happen to you? If the latter is the case, your Money and Tangible Factors will take front and center stage—by default—as you grow older, and your shoulds will be made crystal clear to you by others. You might reach a point where decisions are beyond your financial or physical ability to consider, and as a result your sense of control will be severely eroded. In short, people who plan to move and do it are happier than people who do not plan to move but end up having to move anyway. Unless you prepare in advance to control your own housing destiny, you might have no choice but to swallow your autonomy and march to other people's solutions for your problems. Worse, you might be forced to sacrifice the deep satisfactions that reside within your Personal and Social Factors at a time when you are likely to value those most.

As you grow older, you must choose your living environment wisely. Your home or homes must span the transition from your active early-retirement years to a more restricted, support-dependent lifestyle. Your physical and personal needs will change and cause a shift in your requirements. When considering rent-or-buy decisions in Chapter 11, "To Own or Not to Own, That's a Good Question," we organized the order of your deciding factors so that your Money Factor was your first priority. In retirement planning, the emphasis changes to (1)Tangible Factors, (2) Social and Personal Factors, and (3) Money Factors. In other words, you want your finances—and financial planning decisions—to support the housing goals you have for yourself as long as you live. Here are some of the issues you need to consider as you examine your retirement options:

- **Tangible Factors**—You need to address questions about the "family home." What will you do over the long term about home maintenance, safety, home modifications, home equity conversion, moving to a smaller home? How will you live when your mobility and strength are diminished? What will you do if your physical condition becomes such that you are homebound? Will you stay in your home and make the necessary physical modifications, move in with an adult child, or choose from among the assisted-living options in your community or another community?

- **Personal Factors**—You want to deeply consider what you will really value most about your new identity in retirement. If you have children, how will you want to live when the children are grown? Do you want to maintain a home that suddenly is too big for you, or do you relish the thought of spreading out into space you can finally claim as your own? Will you want to maintain some type of employment after you retire, or will you want to travel for all or part of the year? After you retire, will you want to move to a warmer climate or take advantage of communities that are "service-rich" for seniors?[4] Does such a lifestyle match your idea of who you really are?

- **Social Factors**—If your partner passes away or you get a divorce, will you stay in your home or even want to stay? What is your vision of someday living as a single person? Will you enjoy the solitude, or do you have needs for companionship that would be better served by living in a shared or communal arrangement? Is there an appropriate support network in your community to meet your physical and social needs as you age? What services are available? Do you have sufficient family, friends, and neighbors who will be your companions and helpers?

- **Money Factors**—How have your planned to cover your costs of life in retirement? Will there be enough money? How long will your resources last?

Accumulating sufficient financial assets to care for yourself in later life has become much more important in recent years as employers, health insurers, and government policies have shifted dramatically. Many retirees today—77 percent of all older homeowners in fact—live in homes that are free of mortgage debt. But having a home that is free and clear of a mortgage is the result of intentional planning, and trends among midlife homeowners today is to spend their home equity—not to save it for retirement.

My friend, Craig MacBean, coauthor of *Thriving after Fifty-Five*,[5] asks readers to answer two questions:

- How will you live in later life?

- How will you pay for it?

In seminars, he asks participants to recognize and accept that they are aging, that aging is a fact of life, and that we are all living in an aging society in which costs are escalating. He is utterly devoted to getting out this all-too-true message, and he is not alone. Almost all personal finance authors, financial planners and advisors, and financial educators from diverse government and privately sponsored organizations are trying to impress people with these same facts of contemporary life. But who is listening?

Resisting Retirement Planning and Housing Choices

Before long, baby boomers will start joining their parents as the nation's "older adults." Nearly all will face the need for making housing decisions that will impact their later-life quality. Life expectancy is at an all-time high: The average for women is 80-years-old, and for men it is 74. That means a longer later life for which everyone should be celebrating. And planning, planning, planning.

Planning is the key to financial preparedness in later life. Chapter 17, "Overcoming Moving Stresses," shows that planning leads to a successful and stress–free move. It is also essential for less-stressful aging. Like the housing decisions you make to accommodate your current lifestyle, the ones you make for your later years must be based on your housing value system. However, your ideal living arrangement might be out of reach financially if you do not begin planning for it now.

Elaine Wethington, Cornell professor, sociologist, and co-editor of *Residential Choices and Experiences of Older Adult: Pathways to Life Quality*, writes that "Senior citizens who plan ahead report a high degree of control over their moves and a greater sense of mastery than those who don't plan ahead…and this sense of control is linked to feeling physically and psychologically healthy over time."[6] Knowing the decisions that you must make and thoughtfully considering your options in light of your personal and social values, physical needs, and financial resources can go a long way toward preparing you for living comfortably throughout your retirement years.

But if Simmons and MacBean are right, too many of us deny our impending aging and are failing utterly to prepare for the decisions we must eventually face about how and where we will live.

Magical Thinking Versus Optimistic Determination

Baby boomers are particularly good at denial and notoriously bad at thinking about and planning for retirement, ill health, or frailty, according to Sarah Zapolsky in "Baby Boomers and Retirement."[7] "The lack of readiness for retirement is overwhelming, says AARP Policy and Strategy Director, John Rother."[8] Two-thirds of today's retirees live almost entirely on Social Security. The same is going to be true for the baby boom generation unless they begin to take action now," cautions Dallas Salisbury, Chairman of the American Savings Education Council.[9]

According to the results of the 14th annual Retirement Confidence Survey,[10] more than half of working adults are close to clueless about the need to save and plan for retirement. In their sample, about three in five workers and, or their spouses (57 percent) have not even attempted to figure out how much money they will need to have saved by the time they retire. Four in ten workers (42 percent) are not currently saving for retirement, and those who have saved report low levels of savings. In fact, 45 percent of workers with savings report total household assets, not including home equity value, of less than $25,000.

Yet most individuals who expect to retire within 15 years say they hope to travel, pursue a broad range of interests, visit children, and give presents to grandchildren after retirement. Why are these workers not making the financial arrangements required to achieve their stated goals? Various surveys by the research firm Mathew Greenwald & Associates provide the following insights into people's lack of retirement savvy or diligence (or both):[11]

1. They underestimate how much living in retirement actually costs.

2. They do not have a grip on how long they might live.

3. They overestimate their ability to earn money after they retire.

4. They believe Medicare pays higher healthcare benefits than it actually does.

5. They fail to face the probability that they might not be well or able to move around someday.

6. They underestimate the real costs of assisted-living and long-term care arrangements for older adults.

Is this lack of knowledge due to legitimate oversight and procrastination or to "denial" as often charged?

We are in denial if we believe that the average person will be ill enough at some point during later life to require nursing home care, but believe at the same time it will not happen to us. Yet that is precisely what the Greenwald surveys revealed. Nearly 70 percent of workers age 45 and older believe that it is at least somewhat likely the average older person will spend time in a nursing home, but only 43 percent think it could happen to them.

"Magical thinking" is a pattern of unrealistically approaching the future based more on hopes, dreams, and desires than on objective assessment of actual circumstances. When we project a rosy picture of life in retirement— frequent travel, golf, gifts to grandchildren, and the like—without saving a penny to prepare financially for retirement, we are engaging in magical thinking.

We can easily differentiate magical thinking from optimistic determination by examining the actual steps being taken toward retirement planning, or the degree of actual financial comfort being enjoyed by someone already in retirement. Take the case of Hubert, my colleague Laura's father.

Laura's parents were in their late 80s when her mom died after a long illness. Even as her father, Hubert, was mourning the death of his wife of more than 50 years, he announced to his daughter and son-in-law, George, his intention to buy a house he had seen in a close-by neighborhood. To Laura and George, a house purchase at his age and life stage seemed inappropriate. But Hubert would not listen to "reason," and over his adult children's objections he closed and moved in. Hubert had just turned 90, and he was thrilled to be in his "own home" at last.

Laura grew up in a northeastern city where she lived with her little brother and parents in a building they owned in a thriving working-class neighborhood. It had three flats on three floors. Laura's family lived in the middle flat and rented out the other two. For as long as she could remember, Hubert had wanted to move to a single-family detached house, which he considered more of a proper home. But Laura's mom refused to leave the financial security and familiarity of their flat and the immediate neighborhood. What Laura and George had underestimated was Hubert's single-minded determination to reach his American Dream at any age. Hubert died only a year later, but during that year he had finally managed to have a "proper" home. In a surprise ending to the story, Laura and George who only recently had taken early retirement themselves, decided not to sell Hubert's home but to move back to Laura's childhood hometown and into her father's cherished house.

A Home of One's Own in Later Life

If you are like most Americans, you will want to remain in a home you own as long as possible, even when your loved ones think your choice is illogical. Why do we tenaciously cling to our homes as we age? Because our connections with home do not ever magically disappear, as illustrated by Hubert's story.

Like everyone else, older adults tie their identities to their living space. When we begin to lose some of our long-standing social roles and the social status attached to them—our role as parents diminish as our children age, our roles as employees and professionals evaporate as we retire, and our roles as consumers erode as our earning potential declines—our identity and social status as a homeowner is elevated in importance.

In fact, the importance of home and homeownership intensify:

- As a material resource, homeownership is the number one key factor related to financial self-sufficiency in later life. When we are not owners, we are more vulnerable to possible poverty in later life, especially if we are women.[12]

- As a psychological resource, homeownership contributes to feelings of independence, identity, control, and security, all of which maintain and enhance self-concept.

Home remains an arena in which we can still express our personal sense of style. It is a witness to our personal history, and often holds memories of a lifetime. If we have lived in one place for a long time, our home and neighborhood might become so much a part of our identity that we cannot imagine who we would be without it. As we age, home increasingly is the center of our existence. For older homeowners, home is often the one surviving area over which they perceive they have control. Aging adults can take comfort in the belief that they may remain "forever" in the home they love—if they can afford it. If they cannot, they are at risk for a heightened sense of vulnerability.[13]

Whereas for many older Americans aging in their own home is a well-thought-through preference, for others it is the result of lack of planning rooted in anxiety about change and fear of the future. Successful aging at home takes as much, if not more, planning than relocation, and many unknowns must be anticipated.

When my father was older and infirm, he suddenly refused to shower or bathe. He was afraid of the bathtub for fear he might fall down, but he did not admit this; he just would not go into the tub, and I did not guess why at the time. I also was unaware of the home modifications designed to improve bathroom safety, so I hired a caregiver to help him to bathe instead. Did I strip my stepfather of his precious privacy and independence by hiring someone to help him take a bath? Looking back, I know he would have preferred a few bathroom modifications. Would you know what to do in a similar situation?

Here is a partial list of things for you to consider when you are caring for older loved ones or planning for your own future well-being:

- How will you modify your home to accommodate your possible diminished mobility or disability?

- When is it likely that major systems and appliances will break down?

- Will the neighborhood continue to be safe, or will it decline and pose a hazard for you and, or your loved ones?

- Will you still have friends and, or relatives in the community to fulfill your social and recreational needs?

- How long will it be physically possible to care for your lawn and garden?

- How long will you be able to drive, and how will you get to the places you must go when you are no longer able?

- Who will help you with activities of daily living when you are at the point of needing help?

- Can you pay for all of the help you may need?

Understanding the costs and benefits of available options is a major step in planning for your future housing. Although many sources of information are available, the Internet site www.seniorresource.com is a good place to begin. It discusses the issues to be considered in any plan to "age in place," and identifies and defines a multitude of possible alternatives to remaining in your own home. In addition, it provides links to many important resources.

Explore the senior housing options in the "Recommended Resources," appendix of this book. There are many excellent guides to help you through a thoughtful consideration of the pros and cons of each housing option. For a fearless, insightful, and upbeat review of senior housing options, including some of the more untraditional ones that could make aging truly an adventure; I recommend *Just Pencil Me In: Your Guide to Moving & Getting Settled After 60*, by Willma Willis Gore, who has moved 6 times since turning 70.[14] Gore's optimism ranks equally with her experience and practical wisdom, giving us inspirational guidance with which to consider alternative lifestyles that challenge limiting stereotypes of what it means to be "old."

Turning Home Equity into Income

Obviously, you have the option of selling your home and using the money to change your living environment. The quality of that environment will depend on the amount of money you have after the sale and on the other financial resources available to you. You might use the proceeds of your home to add an apartment onto the home of an adult child, buy a spot in a retirement community, or secure space in an assisted-living facility. Or, if you want to remain in your home, as most of us do, you might be eligible for and interested in a reverse mortgage.

A reverse mortgage allows homeowners who are 62 and older to borrow against the equity of their home. Unlike a conventional mortgage where the borrower makes periodic payments to the lender, a reverse mortgage lender provides payments to the borrower. Payment of the accrued debt and interest are payable upon the borrower's death or departure from the residence. Older homeowners may receive payments from reverse mortgages in one of the following ways:

- A lump sum received at the time of the loan

- Monthly payments for as long as the borrower resides in the house (tenure payments)

- Higher monthly payments for a fixed period of time (term payments), after which the borrowers may continue to live in the house and defer repayment

- A line of credit with which the borrowers may vary the amounts and timing of payments up to a maximum

- Some combination of all of the above

Two other alternatives to a reverse mortgage that can provide extended tenure for an older homeowner are as follows:

- **Sale and lease-back agreement**—The home is sold to an investor, family member, or friend; unlike an ordinary home sale, however, the older person remains in the home as a tenant and pays a monthly rent to the new owner, who assumes the role of a landlord. Typically, the new owner guarantees the older person the indefinite right to renew the lease.

- **Life estate agreement**—The ownership of the home is transferred to an investor, family member, or friend, but the older homeowner is guaranteed the right to stay in the home, typically at no cost, for the remainder of his or her life.

In addition to these possible alternatives, other home equity conversion programs might be available through the public sector to assist lower-income, older homeowners with the repair or improvements necessary to remain in one's home and, or the payment or deferment of property taxes. The structure and availability of these programs is community-specific and eligibility criteria vary. Check with your local agency on aging to find out about the resources available in your community.

If you own your own home, some or all of the these possibilities are available to you in the event that the cost of illness or unexpected home repairs or modifications are more than your assets and income can bear. Although these alternatives are not without their risks and consequences, you do have these options. Reverse mortgages have upfront costs and limit the home equity you may be able to leave heirs. Sale and leaseback agreements and life estate agreements can have implications for sibling relationships if one of two, or several, siblings is in a position to acquire and maintain the property, whereas the other(s) are not. There are tax implications and other legal issues to consider, and these require the advice of an attorney and housing counselors who are knowledgeable about real estate, elder law, and, in particular, the details of home equity conversions. And finally, extending your stay in your own home can lead to a false sense of security. Our common exclamation, "They'll have to carry me out of here in a box," flies in the face of the realty that many of us may actually face. Long-term care facilities that are filled to the brim, and have long waiting lists for admission, testify to the possibility that frailty or unexpected debilitation will force you out of your home, alive and kicking, at an advanced age.

Points to Ponder

- If you are helping to relocate older relatives, try to learn what they cherish and value. Then try to put yourself in their position if you can.

- Create a housing plan for your own golden years, so someone else won't have to do it for you.

- Have regular heart-to-heart conversations with family members. Share your housing plans for your golden years with loved ones. Help them get to know the "real you" long before these precious times are gone forever and it is too late.

End Notes

1 This research was conducted by the *Institute for Socio-Financial Studies* (ISFS) for the National Council on the Aging during 1999–2000. The Seniors Research Group of Livonia, Michigan, conducted the focus groups.

2 I recently had the pleasure of working with more than 180 authors, all experts in various topics about the finances of aging. Our project resulted in the *Encyclopedia of Retirement and Finance*, published in 2003 by Greenwood Press in two volumes. As editor-in-chief, I was often able to change text references from the old-fashioned "the elderly " to "older adults." I know this newer identification is appreciated by older adults themselves—even if they do not yet perceive themselves as "older."

3 Keeney, Ralph L. *Value-Focused Thinking: A Path to Creative Decision Making.* Cambridge, MA: Harvard University Press, 1992.

4 From the http//:AARP.org web site, you can download, *Livable Communities: An Evaluation Guide*, by Patricia Baron Pollak of Cornell University. It contains a survey instrument addressing eight areas of concern to seniors—public transportation; driving; walking; housing; shopping; and municipal features, services, and leisure facilities—that can be used to evaluate a given community. Also included in this guide is a comprehensive bibliography, a list of state offices on aging, and a list of other agencies relevant to the eight topic areas.

5 Simmons, Henry C. and E. Craig MacBean. *Thriving After 55: Your Guide to Fully Living the Rest of Your Life.* Richmond, VA: PrimeDynamics, 2000.

6 Wethington, Elaine. "Residential Differences in Life Stress and Perceived Health," in John A. Krout and Elaine Wethington. (eds.) *Residential Choices and Experiences of Older Adults: Pathways to Life Quality.* New York: Springer Publishing Company, Inc., 2003.

7 Zapolsky, Sarah. "Baby Boomers and Retirement," in Lois A. Vitt (ed.) *Encyclopedia of Retirement and Finance.* Westport, CT: Greenwood Press, 2003.

8 AARP-Rothberg.

9 Salisbury, Dallis. "Introduction," in the *Encyclopedia of Retirement and Finance.* Westport, CT: Greenwood Press, 2003.

10 Mathew Greenwald & Associates. *2003 Retirement Confidence Survey.* Employee Benefit Research Institute (EBRI) and the American Savings Education Council (ASEC). Washington, D.C.: EBRI, 2003.

11   Greenwald, Mathew. "Retirement Preparedness," in Lois A. Vitt (ed.) *Encyclopedia of Retirement and Finance*. Westport, CT: Greenwood Press, 2003. More striking results were found in the National Association for Variable Annuities 2002 national survey of people 45 years of age and older who had incomes of over $50,000 and did not own annuities. In this sample, only 23 percent of the respondents reportedly calculated the amount of money they needed to save in order for them to live comfortably in retirement.

12   Daley, Nancy. *When Baby Boom Women Retire*. Westport CT: Praeger, 2000.

13   Golant, Stephen. "Homeownership," in Lois A. Vitt (ed) *Encyclopedia of Retirement and Finance*. Westport, CT: Greenwood Press, 2003.

14   Gore, Wilma Willis. *Just Pencil Me In: Your Guide to Moving and Getting Settled After 60*. Sanger, CA: Quill Driver Books, 2002.

APPENDIX A

RECOMMENDED RESOURCES

Moving

Alpert, Arlene. *Moving without Madness: A Guide to Handling the Stress & Emotions of Moving*. Jupiter, FL: Gemini Press, 1997.

Eliot, Betsy Rossen. *The Moving Book: Everything You Should Know from Packing Up to Settling In*. Colorado Springs, CO: Shaw Books, 1998.

Gore, Willma Willis. *Just Pencil Me In: Your Guide to Moving & Getting Settled After 60*. Sanger, CA: Quill Driver Books, 2002.

Kozik, Donna, and Tara Maras. *29 Days to a Smooth Move*. San Diego, CA: Donna Kozik, 2003.

Poage, Martha. *The Moving Survival Guide: All You Need to Know to Make Your Move Go Smoothly*. Guilford, CT: Globe Pequot, 2004.

Steiner, Clyde and Shari Steiner. *Complete How to Move Handbook, Second Edition*. San Francisco, CA: Independent Information Publications Consumer Series, 1999.

Moving for Kids

Berenstein, Stan and Jan Berenstein. *The Berenstain Bear's Moving Day*. New York: Random House, 1981.

Davis, Gabriel. *The Moving Book: A Kid's Survival Guide*. New York: Little, Brown, and Company, 1996.

Helmer, Diana Star. *Let's Talk About Moving to a New Place*. New York: Rosen Publishing Group, 1999.

Relocating

Adams, Karen G. *Moving...A Complete Checklist and Guide for Relocation*. San Diego, CA: Silvercat Publications, 1994.

Carlisle, Ellen. *Smooth Moves: The Relocation Guide for Families on the Move*. Charlotte, NC: Teacup Press, 1999.

Goodwin, Cathy. *Making The Big Move: How to Transform Relocation into a Creative Life Transition*. Oakland, CA: New Harbinger Publications, 1999.

Hayes, Nan DeVincentis. *Move It! A Guide to Relocating Family, Pets, and Plants*. New York: Dembner Books, 1989.

Laycock, Angelina B. *Pulling Up Stakes: A Relocation Guide for Families*. Ann Arbor, MI: Roma Communications, 2002.

Levine, Leslie. *Will This Place Ever Feel Like Home? Simple Advice for Settling In After You Move*. Chicago, IL: Real Estate Education Company, 1998.

McCollum, Audrey, Nadia Jensen, and Stuart Copans. *Smart Moves: Your Guide Through the Emotional Maze of Relocation*. Lyme, NH: Smith and Kraus Publishers, Inc., 1996.

Roman, Beverly and John Howells. *Insider's Guide to Relocation*, Second Edition. Guilford, CT: Globe Pequot Press, 2004.

Web Sites

http://www.movinglady.com
http://www.monstermoving.com
http://www.RPSRelocation.com

Divorce

Colbert, Judy. *Divorce Common Sense Handbook: 180+ Things To Do and 8+ Things Not to Do Before Your Divorce.* Crofton, MD: Tuff Turtle Publishing, Inc., 1999.

Davis, Akeela. *Your Divorce, Your Dollars: Financial Planning Before, During, and After Divorce,* Self-Counsel Reference Series. Bellingham, WA: Self-Counsel Press, 2003.

Margulies, Sam. *Man's Guide to a Civilized Divorce: How to Divorce with Grace, a Little Class, and a Lot of Common Sense.* New York: Rodale Books, 2004.

—*Getting Divorced Without Ruining Your Life: A Reasoned, Practical Guide to the Legal, Emotional, and Financial Ins and Outs of Negotiating a Divorce Settlement.* New York: Fireside, 2001.

Mercer, Diana and Marsha Kline Pruett. *Your Divorce Advisor: A Lawyer and a Psychologist Guide You Through the Legal and Emotional Landscape of Divorce.* New York: Fireside, 2001.

Smith, Gayle Rosenwald. *Divorce and Money: Everything You Need to Know.* New York: Ace Books, 2004.

Stoner, Katherine E.. *Using Divorce Mediation: Save Your Money and Your Sanity.* Berkeley, CA: Nolo.com, 1999.

Trafford, Abigail. *Crazy Time: Surviving Divorce and Building a New Life.* New York: HarperCollins Publishers, 1992.

Walker, Dolores Deane and Carol A. Butler. *The Divorce Mediation Answer Book: Save Time, Money, and Emotional Energy with a Mediated Separation or Divorce.* New York: Kodansha America, 1999.

Woodhouse, Violet and Dale Fetherling. *Divorce and Money: How to Make the Best Financial Decisions During Divorce.* Berkeley, CA: Nolo.com, 2002.

Web Sites

http://www.divorcesource.com

http://www.divorcenet.com

http://www.divorcemag.com

Natural and Other Disasters

Organizations

Federal Emergency Management Agency (http://www.fema.gov)

The American Red Cross (http://www.redcross.org)

Small Business Administration (http://www.sba.gov)

The Salvation Army (http://www.salvationarmyusa.org)

U.S. Geological Survey (http://www.usgs.org)

Books

King, Douglas. *Emergency Disaster Survival Guidebook*. Sandy, UT: ABC Preparedness Co., 1999.

Spigarelli, Jack P. *Crisis Preparedness Handbook: A Complete Guide to Home Storage and Physical Survival*. Alpine, UT: Cross-Current Publishing, 2002.

Stahlberg, Ranier. *The Complete Book of Survival: How to Protect Yourself Against Revolution, Riots, Hurricaines, Famines, and Other Natural and Man-Made Disasters*. New York: Barricade Books, 1998.

Stuart, Catherine. *Simply Essential Disaster Preparation Kit*. Canada: International Self-Counsel Press, 2002.

Wright, Ted. *Wright's Complete Disaster Survival Manual*. Charlottesville, VA: Hampton Roads Publishing Co. Inc., 1993.

Zubenko, Wendy N. and Joseph Capozzoli. *Children and Disasters: A Practical Guide to Healing and Recovery*. New York: Oxford University Press, 2002.

Buying and Selling

Organizations

National Association of Realtors® (http://www.realtor.com)

U.S. Department of Housing and Urban Development (http://www.hud.gov)

American Land Title Association (http://www.alta.org)

The National Institute of Building Inspectors (http://www.nibi.com)

The National Lead Information Center (http://www.epa.gov)

The American Society of Home Inspectors (http://www.ashi.com)

Books

Albrecht, Donna G. *Buying a Home When You're Single,* Revised and Updated. Somerset, NJ: John Wiley & Sons, 2001.

Anosike, Benji O. *How To Buy/Sell Your Own Home Without a Broker or Lawyer.* Newark, NJ: Do-It-Yourself Legal Publishers, 2000.

Easter, Bob. *The Fourteen Home-Selling Secrets.* Austin, TX: Easter & Easter, Inc. 1994.

Effros, William G. *How to Sell Your Home in 5 Days.* New York: Workman Publishing, 1998.

Garton-Good, Julie. *The Frugal Homeowners Guide to Buying, Selling, and Improving Your Home.* Chicago, IL: Dearborn Trade, 1999.

Goodman, Jordan E. *Everyone's Money Book on Real Estate.* Chicago, IL: Dearborn Trade Publishing, 2002.

Irwin, Robert. *Tips and Traps When Mortgage Hunting,* Second Edition. New York: McGraw-Hill, 1998.

—*Home Buyer's Checklist: Everything You Need to Know—But Forget to Ask—Before You Buy a Home.* New York: McGraw-Hill Trade, 2001.

—*Tips and Traps When Selling a Home,* Second Edition. New York: McGraw-Hill, 1997.

—*Tips and Traps When Buying a Home.* New York: McGraw-Hill Professional, 2004.

—*The Home Buying and Selling Juggling Act.* Chicago, IL: Dearborn Trade, 1999.

—*Power Tips for Selling a House for More.* New York: McGraw-Hill, 2001.

Janik, Carolyn. *Kiplinger's Homeology.* Washington, D.C.: The Kiplinger Washington Editors, Inc., 1998.

Keating, David. *The Smart Home Buyers Handbook.* New York: Open Road Publishing, 1998.

Kiplinger's Personal Finance Magazine. Kiplinger's Buying and Selling a Home, Your All-In-One Guide for Success from America's Leading Personal Finance Authority. Washington, D.C.: The Kiplinger Books, Inc., 2002.

Kloian, Michael. *Sell it By Owner and Save.* Howard City, MI: How To LLC, 2001.

Lank, Edith and Dena Amoruso. *The Homebuyer's Kit,* Fifth Edition. Chicago, IL: Dearborn Trade, 2001.

Myers, David W. *If You're Clueless About Buying a Home and Want to Know More*. Chicago, IL: Dearborn Trade Publishing, 1999.

O'Brien, Matthew. *The Complete Idiots Guide to Online Buying and Selling a Home*. Indianapolis, IN: Alpha Books, 2000.

O'Hara, Shelly and Nancy D. Lewis. *The Complete Idiots Guide to Buying and Selling a Home*, Fourth Edition. New York: Alpha Books, 2003.

Roberts, Ralph. *Sell it Yourself*. Holbrook, MA: Adams Media Corporation, 1999.

Tyson, Eric and Ray Brown. *Homebuying for Dummies,* Second Edition. Somerset, NJ: John Wiley & Sons, 2001.

First-Time Homebuyers

Organizations

Fannie Mae Foundation (http://www.fanniemaefoundation.org)

Fannie Mae (http://www.fanniemae.com)

Freddie Mac (Federal Home Loan Mortgage Corporation) (http://www.freddiemac.com)

Ginnie Mae (Government National Mortgage Association) (http://www.ginniemae.gov)

Veteran's Administration (VA) (http://www.homeloans.va.gov)

The National Fair Housing Alliance (http://www.nationalfairhousing.org)

Books

Glink, Ilyce R. *10 Steps to Home Ownership: A Workbook for First-Time Buyers*. New York: Three Rivers Press, 1996.

—*100 Questions Every First-Time Home Buyer Should Ask: With Answers from Top Brokers from Around the Country*. New York: Three Rivers Press, 1999.

Irwin, Robert. *Buy Your First Home!* Second Edition. Chicago, IL: Dearborn Financial Publishing, Inc, 2000.

—*How to Buy a Home When You Can't Afford It.* New York: McGraw-Hill Trade, 2002.

Mungo, Ray and Robert H. Yamaguchi. *No Credit Required: How to Buy a House When You Don't Qualify for a Mortgage.* New York: Signet Book, 1993.

Kenyon, Flip and Heather Flip. *The Smart Money Guide to Buying a Home: Ten Steps to Owning a Great Home and a Great Investment.* Tampa, Florida: Palladian Publishing, 1996.

Kiplinger's Personal Finance Magazine. Kiplinger's Buying and Selling a Home. Washington D.C.: The Kiplinger Washington Editor's, Inc., 1999.

Myers, David W. *If You're Clueless About Buying a Home and Want to Know More.* Chicago, IL: Dearborn Trade Publishing, 1999.

O'Hara, Shelly and Nancy D. Warner. *The Complete Idiot's Guide to Buying and Selling a Home*, Fourth Edition. Indianapolis, Indiana: Alpha Books, 2003.

Web Sites

The Federal Citizen Information Center (http://www.pueblo.gsa.gov)

Buying

http://www.homeadvisor.com

http://www.homefair.com

http://www.homestore.com

http://www.inspectamerica.com

http://www.kaktus.com

http://www.realestate.com

Mortgage Information

http://www.amortgage.com

http://www.bankrate.com

http://www.citylinemortgage.com

http://www.homepath.com

http://www.mortgagebot.com

http://www.premierequity.com

Selling

http://www.domania.com

http://www.homebytes.com

Home Warranties

http://www.2-10hbw.com

Senior Decisions

Organizations

AARP (American Association of Retired Persons) (http://www.aarp.org)

American Seniors Housing Association (http://www.seniorshousing.org)

Senior Resource (http://www.seniorresource.com)

Books

Ballman, T.E. *The Reverse Mortgage Handbook.* Kissimmee, FL: Jawsbone Publishing Co., 2004.

Gore, Willma Willis. *Just Pencil Me In: Your Guide to Moving and Getting Settled After 60.* Sanger, CA: Quill Driver Books, 2002.

Jakesm P. David. *The Decision Is Yours: Help for Senior Adults and Their Families with Housing Options.* Nashville, TN: LifeWay, 1995.

Lanspery, Susan and Joan Hyde. *Staying Put: Adapting the Places Instead of the People (Society and Aging Series).* Amityville, NY: Baywood Publishing Company, Inc., 1996.

Scholen, Ken. *Reverse Mortgages for Beginners: A Consumer Guide to Every Homeowner's Retirement Nest Egg.* NCHE Press, 1998.

Staff, Phyllis. *How to Find Great Senior Housing: A Roadmap for Elders and Those Who Love Them,* Second Edition. Dallas, Texas: The Best Is Yet.Net Press, 2004.

Stuart, Lettice. *Making the Move: A Practical Guide to Senior Residential Communities.* Sanger, CA: Quill, 1997.

Telford, Gillian Eades. *Making the Right Move: Housing Options for Seniors,* Self-Counsel Reference Series. Bellingham, WA: Self-Counsel Press. 2004.

Vitt, Lois A. Editor. *Encyclopedia of Retirement and Finance*. Westport, CT: Greenwood Press, 2003.

Wasch, William K. *Home Planning for Your Later Years: New Designs, Living Options, Smart Decisions, How to Finance It*. Middletown, CT: William K. Wasch Associates, 1996.

Young, Heather M. and Rheba De Tornyay. *Choices: Making a Good Move to a Retirement Community*. Seattle, WA: ERA Care Communities, 2001.

Building or Remodeling

Organizations

National Association of Home Builders (http://www.w.nahb.org)

National Association of the Remodeling Industry (http://www.nari.org)

The National Trust for Historic Preservation (http://www.nationaltrust.org)

The American Institute of Architects (http://www.aia.org)

The Manufactured Housing Institute (http://www.manufacturedhousing.org)

American Construction Inspectors Association (http://www.acia.com)

Books

Beneke, Jeff. *Converting Garages, Attics, and Basements*. Menlo Park, CA: Sunset Publishing Corp., 2001.

Buchholz, Barbara Ballinger. *Successful Homebuilding and Remodeling: Real-life Advice for Getting the House You Want Without the Roof (or Sky) Falling In*. Chicago, IL: Dearborn Trade Publishing, 1999.

Connell, John. *Homing Instinct: Using Your Lifestyle to Design and Build Your Home*. New York: McGraw-Hill, 1998.

Fields, Alan and Denise Fields. *Your New House: The Alert Consumer's Guide to Buying and Building a Quality Home*. Boulder, CO: Windsor Peak Press, 1999.

Gonzales, Steve. *Before You Hire A Contractor: A Construction Guidebook For Consumers*. Fort Lauderdale, FL: Consumer Press, 1999.

Irwin, Robert. *Tips and Traps When Renovating Your Home*. New York: McGraw-Hill Professional, 2000.

—Home Renovation Checklist: Everything You Need to Know to Save Money, Time, and Your Sanity. New York: McGraw-Hill. 2003.

Kitchen, Judith. *Caring for Your Old House: A Guide for Owners and Residents.* Somerset, NJ: John Wiley & Sons, 1995.

Meany, Terry. *The Complete Idiot's Guide to Remodeling Your Home.* New York: Alpha Books, 1999.

Meyers, Kevin C. *Buy it, Fix it, Sell it: Profit!* Chicago, IL: Dearborn Trade Publishing, 2003.

Plesset, Diane. *THE Survival Guide: Home Remodeling.* Portland, OR: D. P. Design Publishing, 2003.

Scutella, Richard M. and David Heberle. *How to Plan, Contract, and Build Your Own Home.* New York: McGraw-Hill Professional, 1999.

Smith, Mark A. *The Owner-Builder Book: How You Can Save More than $100,000 in the Construction of Your Custom Home*, Third Edition. Provo, UT: The Consensus Group, 2002.

Web Sites

http://www.doityourself.com

Investing in Rental Housing

Books

Armstrong, Mabel. *How to Invest in Rental Properties Without Mortgaging Your Soul.* Marcola, OR: Stone Pine Press, 2003.

Benke, William. *All About Real Estate Investing: The Easy Way to Get Started.* New York: The McGraw-Hill Companies, Inc., 2001.

Edwards, Brian F., Casey Edwards, and Susannah Craig. *The Complete Idiot's Guide to Being a Smart Landlord.* Indianapolis, IN: Alpha Books, 2004.

Frank, Scott and Andy Heller. *Buy Low, Rent Smart, Sell High.* Chicago, IL: Dearborn Trade Publishing, 2003.

Mc Lean, Andrew James and Gary Eldred. *Investing in Real Estate*, Fourth Edition. Hoboken, NJ: John Wiley & Sons, 2003.

Gaddy, Wade E. *Real Estate Fundamentals*, Fifth Edition. Chicago, IL: Dearborn Financial Publishing, Inc., 2000.

Irwin, Robert. *The Landlord's Troubleshooter*, Second Edition. Chicago, IL: Dearborn Financial Publishing, Inc., 1999.

Jorgensen, Richard H. *The New No-Nonsense Landlord: Building Wealth and Rental Properties*. New York: The McGraw-Hill Companies, Inc., 2003.

Shemin, Robert. *Secrets of Buying and Selling Real Estate...Without Using Your Own Money*. Hoboken, NJ: John Wiley & Sons, 2003.

   —Successful Real Estate Investing: How to Avoid the 75 Most Costly Mistakes Every Investor Makes. Hoboken, NJ: John Wiley & Sons, 2003.

Summey, Mike and Roger Dawson. *The Weekend Millionaire's Secret to Investing in Real Estate: How to Become Wealthy in Your Spare Time*. New York: McGraw-Hill. 2003.

Taylor, Jeffrey. *The Landlord's Kit*. Chicago, IL: Dearborn Trade Publishing, 2002.

Thomas, Suzanne P. *Rental Houses for the Successful Small Investor*. Boulder, CO: Gemstone House Publishing, 1999.

INDEX

E

F

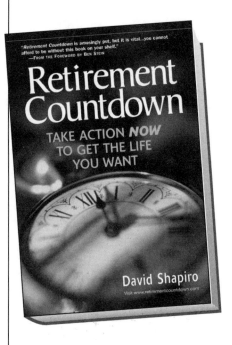

Retirement Countdown

This is a step-by-step action guide to making sure readers have the money they need to live a long and comfortable retirement—going beyond the platitudes and abstractions found in so many retirement books. Retirement planning expert David Shapiro introduces a proven process for setting goals (Goal Oriented Financial Planning)—and achieving them in small, manageable steps.

"You cannot afford to be without this book on your shelf."
—Ben Stein, economist, lawyer, writer, TV personality and Honorary Chair of the National Retirement Planning Coalition

ISBN 0131096710, © 2004, 400 pp., $19.95

Your Credit Score

In the past five years, a simple three-digit number has become critical to your financial life: your credit score. It not only dictates whether you get credit: it can dictate how much you'll pay for it. This book could save you tens of thousands of dollars in reduced credit costs, lower insurance rates... even better employment opportunities. Liz Pulliam Weston is one of the most-read columnists for MSN Money and author of the question-and-answer column "Money Talk," which appears in newspapers nationwide. She appears weekly on CNBC's Power Lunch and regularly on other television programs, including NBC's Early Today, to discuss credit and other personal finance issues.

ISBN 0131486039, © 2005, 192 pp., $17.95